Gay Relationships

Gay Relationships

John P. De Cecco
Editor

Harrington Park Press
New York • London

ISBN 0-918393-33-7

Published by

Harrington Park Press, Inc., 12 West 32 Street, New York, New York 10001
EUROSPAN/Harrington, 3 Henrietta Street, London WC2E 8LU England

Harrington Park Press, Inc., is a subsidiary of The Haworth Press, Inc., 12 West 32 Street, New York, New York 10001.

Articles in this book were published in *Journal of Homosexuality*, Volumes 1-12, 1976-1986.

Cover design by Marshall Andrews.

Library of Congress Cataloging-in-Publication Data

Gay relationships.

Includes bibliographies.
1. Homosexual couples, Male. 2. Lesbians. 3. Interpersonal relations. I. De Cecco, John.
HQ76.G35 1987b 306.7'66 87-11958
ISBN 0-918393-33-7 (pbk.)

CONTENTS

Gay Relationships

I. INTRODUCTION

Obligation versus Aspiration

John P. De Cecco, PhD

A gay relationship constitutes a commitment of usually two men to fulfill each other's needs, desires, and expectations. ("Communal" or "family" arrangements involving three or more gay men will be discussed later.) This commitment is based on several assumptions that are rarely spelled out by most partners. It assumes *self-awareness*, that each individual knows what he needs and wants and that this is communicated with some degree of clarity and persuasiveness to his partner. It assumes *reasonableness* of need and expectation, avoiding the wasteful pursuit of the extravagant fantasy that *every* desire will be fulfilled, so that the relationship does not consume its partners or leave them chronically dissatisfied. It assumes *compatibility*, that the fulfillment of one partner's needs does not interfere with the satisfaction of the other's. It assumes *congeniality*, and intermeshing of the partner's desires so that the relationship is motivated less by obligation than the joy in making and keeping each other happy. It assumes *reciprocity*, so that the fulfillment of one partner's needs is matched by the satisfaction of the other's, with neither partner's enjoying an absolute priority. It assumes *honesty* and *trust*, that each partner avoids deception, confides in to keep promises made to the other, modifying or breaking them only with prior notification that allows the other the freedom to protect his interests in the relationship. Finally, it assumes *charity*, that what you perceive as inbred weaknesses and failings of your partner are recognized and treated with some degree of tolerance and compassion (and that he reciprocates in your case).

The range of need, desire, and expectation is as wide and varied as the individuals involved in gay relationships. Categorically they include the physical, the erotic, the social, the moral, and even the political. In the *physical* realm the relationship is often expected to provide sexual release, orgasms and ejaculations, on a more or less regular and reliable basis or in response to the initiatory moves of the needy partner. Physical release is expected to occur in an *erotic* context, with a partner who is physically desirable and who can creatively provide the sensuous stimulation and responsiveness that each enjoys. The partner is expected to be emotionally desirable, someone you can love and even admire, so that the relationship satisfies the longing to be bonded to another human being, to be loved and cared for in a very personal way, to provide solace in difficult moments, to escape loneliness.

The relationship must satisfy several *social* requirements in its internal structure and in meeting demands of the external world. It must be a home base where one can indulge in and share particular lifestyles, such as tastes in decor, books, music, food, and play. If the partners live together (something that should no longer be taken for granted), it must provide for domestic maintenance, the day-to-day housekeeping as well as the money to keep the whole enterprise solvent. It must assign tasks and assess performance. It must accommodate and sometimes resist the occupational demands of the partners or decide that one partner will be the breadwinner, the other the homemaker.

Any gay relationship has *political* implications beyond its internal structure. In the gay community it has become a symbol of self-acceptance of one's homosexuality, an index of psychological health, of self-esteem. The gay relationship is almost the political cell of the gay liberation movement; it is viewed as the unification of the sexual and the emotional that comes from being gay and proud. It politically stands in defiance of the heterosexual marriage, as if to proclaim, "Anything you can do I can better." At the same time, in emphasizing durability as its essential feature, it is at least a partial endorsement of marriage as the model for intimate relationships. That two men who have sex together can also love each has come to symbolize the ultimate detoxification of homosexuality and justifies the addition of the gay relationship to the pantheon of human achievements.

The gay relationship also represents a *moral* commitment of two men to each other. Because it assumes reciprocity in the fulfilling of needs, desires, and expectations, it places both partners under shared obligations to treat each other with sensitivity and fairness so that the balance of gains and sacrifices does not tip radically in the direction of only one of them. Because it requires trust it must include confiding and the vulnerability that comes with the personal and material dependency of two people on each other. Because it deals with each partner's expectations for the future, it must allow breathing space for each, room for experimentation, for growth, for individual autonomy of thought and action, for a future that is not a mere duplication of the past.

A gay relationship consists of the intricate balancing of the *obligations of reciprocity* and the *aspirations for change*. If the balance tips too far in the direction of obligation, the relationship becomes stultifying and restrictive. If it too much favors aspiration, it becomes unglued, subject to the whims and fancies of the moment, a relationship without steady shape and substance.

There is no ideal balance; each couple must find its own. Some will favor the web of mutual obligation that models the traditional marriage, keeping the relationship comfortable and secure, especially in a world of male ambition, greed, and vanity, where coupledom is like a surf board tossed about by the waves. Others will favor riding the waves, the excitement of aspiration and change—relationships in which partners assume that their lives apart from each other would sail ahead, yet with possibly less contentment and more loneliness than they now experience. Since gay relationships contain elements of both obligation and aspiration in dynamic juxtaposition, this balance will change as the men involved in them change.

EARLIER BOOKS ON GAY RELATIONSHIPS

There have been a number of books on gay relationships that have come from the pens of psychotherapists, social scientists, and journalists. A constant theme of these works, particularly the earlier ones, is that the major difficulty faced by men in gay relationships was the lack of its endorsement by straight family members and relatives and sometimes by a gay community that is chiefly organized around the "single" lifestyle.

Mary Mendola's (1980) *The Mendola Report: A New Look at Gay Couples* is a report on both lesbian and gay relationships. Mendola concluded that both would prosper with social support, legal recognition, and established precedents for their management. The fact that partners of the same sex cannot be assigned the role of husband or wife on the traditional basis of biological sex can open the way for considerable innovation in dividing up responsibilities and result in immensely fulfilling relationships. Mendola believed that the key to the success of gay relationships lay in the ability of partners to remain free of the conventional entrapments of the feminine and masculine stereotypes.

In the following year, Charles Silverstein (1981), the distinguished founding editor of the *Journal of Homosexuality* and the coauthor of the *Joy of Gay Sex*, published *Man to Man: Gay Couples in America*. The book described a rich variety of gay relationships, often in the words of the men he interviewed, how they were affected by the partners' childhood relationships to their parents, particularly fathers, how religion shaped sexual attitudes, and the problems of maintaining relationships. Silverstein divided the men he interviewed into "excitement seekers," those who have an insatiable appetite for sexual adventure, and the "home builders," those whose joy lay in the comforts of the hearth. In the author's judgment, partners of both types can build enduring relationships if they can resolve issues of sexual exclusivity, jealousy, envy, and dependency.

The large-scale project by two sociologists, Phillip Blumstein and Pepper Schwartz (1983), *American Couples: Money, Work, Sex*, compared the "marriages" of heterosexual and homosexual couples. Their study describes how couples handled financial matters, how they balanced their commitments to work and to their relationships, and their sexual behavior. The authors' conclusions suggest that the most enduring gay relationships are like their heterosexual counterparts—those to which the partners are most committed financially, emotionally, and sexually—those in which the partners' sense of mutual obligation outweighs each one's independent aspirations for the future.

In the following year, David McWhirter and Andrew Mattison (1984) published *The Male Couple: How Relationships Develop*, based on interviews of gay couples and the authors' professional experience in couple counseling. The first part of the book lays out their six stage-theory of male relationships, which covers the first two decades. (This theory is adumbrated in Section IV, How to Maintain A Gay Relationship.) The second part describes the partners themselves and what they thought about their relationships. A difficulty faced by gay males who pursue coupledom, in the authors' opinion, is "connecting sex with love," although the authors concluded that extra-coupledom sex need hardly destroy and could possibly enhance a gay relationship.

Three other books that appeared in the seventies devoted considerable attention to gay relationships in the course of portraying broad pictures of homosexuals and homosexuality. A colleague of Alfred Kinsey, who had assisted him in his studies of female and male sexuality, Clarence Tripp, published *The Homosexual Matrix* in 1975. His theory of complementation, distancing, and resistance was used to explain the dynamics of straight and gay relationships. *Complementation* referred to a process of "tension-reduction" that presumably occurs in heterosexual relationships when the biologically-endowed masculine characteristics of the male are amalgamated with the biologically-endowed feminine characteristics of the female to produce two united and quiescent partners. But without tension, Tripp theorized, relationships lose their interest. Therefore, partners had to find ways alternatively to increase and relieve it. To increase tension, partners could resort to *distancing*, avoiding too much closeness (e.g., a night out with the "boys" or "girls") and to *resistance*, avoiding too much complementation. In Tripp's judgment, the bane of gay relationships was that both partners were of the same sex. This eliminated not only the need for complementation but also the tension that sparked any relationship. Gay partners, therefore, had to resort to artificial (i.e., non-biological) distancing and resistance in order to keep their relationships tense and challenging.

Two large-scale empirical inquiries into homosexuality also dealt with gay relationships. In 1978 Alan Bell and Martin Weinberg, in their *Homosexualities: A Study of Diversity Among Men and Women*, an investigation of homosexual men and women in San Francisco in the late sixties, developed a typology of couples. There were the Close-Coupleds, which referred to relationships in which partners looked chiefly to each other for companionship and sexual gratification. In the Open-Coupleds relationships, partners were each other's chief companions but not exclusive sex partner. The men in either type of relationship were happier than the Dysfunctionals, who were having sex with anyone and had no relationship, and the Asexuals, who had neither a relationship nor sex. The Close-Coupled partners were reported to be happier than the Open-Coupled partners, presumably because the former were faithfully living up to marital canons.

In a book entitled *The Social Organization of Gay Males*, Joseph Harry and William De Vall (1978) included a study of "gay marriages." The authors reached three notable conclusions: (1) that these partnerships are patterned after the best-friend rather than husband-wife model; (2) that the partners come to accept the fact that they have "impersonal sex" outside their relationship; and (3) that the inherent egalitarianism of the best-friend model precludes the issue of male dominance from arising in their relationships.

THE ORGANIZATION OF THIS BOOK

The topic of gay relationships has been a continuing theme in articles published in the *Journal of Homosexuality*, almost from its inception in 1974. Those I have chosen for this book probably represent the most diverse theoretical and empirical body of knowledge on the topic yet to appear. As the *Contents* reveals, I have organized the articles under five major headings that reflect either their major thrust or recurrent issues in the research on gay relationships.

The beginning of this introductory section, as you have seen, provides a general framework for the consideration of obligations or aspirations that may shape gay relationships. The reader can use this as a list of questions or issues that the ensuing articles try to address. In addition to referring to the major studies of gay relationships that have appeared in book form, this section also includes two articles that provide an overview of gay relationships, John Alan Lee's typology of gay love styles, and Letitia Anne Peplau's summary of the empirical research.

The second section addresses the question of where to look for lovers. The answer, you will discover, is almost anywhere, but with the blossoming of the gay lifestyle there has been a corresponding growth in places and occasions for male social contact. With these alternatives available and with the fear and prospect of catching AIDS looming over gay life, there is probably less reliance on classified ads in gay newspapers and magazines, but these continue to flourish possibly because they meet the needs of the busy and timid, those remote from gay urban centers, those with voracious sexual fantasies and appetites, and the financial needs and aspirations of advertisers and publishers.

The answer to the question of where to find lovers, as you will see, imperceptibly transforms into the question of whom to choose as a lover, the subject of the second section of this book. It is hard for any of us to know exactly which characteristics we prefer in lovers. The classified ads at least offer a crude menu of options that provides a beginning, useful at least until personal taste and trial and error develop more refined knowledge and until we muster the resolve not to make the same mistake twice. Unfortunately, knowing the characteristics you desire in lovers, is not alone going to solve the problem of whom to choose since what attracts us to men compared with what makes it possible for us to live with them, as the authors in this section imply, are not characteristics that always harmoniously blend into idyllic relationships.

The question of how to maintain a relationship, the third section of this volume is therefore inevitable, since it is unlikely that most of us will be lucky enough to enter one that happily perpetuates itself. The authors who have thought about and studied gay relationships have some very instructive things to say about what lies ahead and how you might avoid some pitfalls and extricate yourself from others. You will find that the female authors have extraordinary insight into how to avoid the trap of rigidly assigning roles based on sex-role stereotypes and the male authors into how the joys of physical sex (inside and outside the relationship) can figure in to the affection partners have for each other.

The emergence of gay relationships as a way for two men to live their personal lives and perhaps to immensely enrich them is so recent that less attention has been given to how to resolve their possibly unique problems. The articles in the last section of this book at least provide some benchmarks for knowing whether or not the relationship is working, when it is doomed, and the recognition that the problems that do arise will change as the relationship changes. The need to learn how to negotiate resolutions of conflicts is particularly important in gay relationships since neither partner usually enjoys a priority of need and since power is shared.

TYPES OF RELATIONSHIPS AND AN OVERVIEW OF THE RESEARCH

The first two articles in the introductory section provide overviews of gay relationships. John Alan Lee has developed a typology of gay relationships, which he calls "styles of love." He defines a gay relationship as any positive, intimate, adult affection related to partner selection. Lee also gives us a brief history of love in western civilization. Before the medieval period there was mostly *agape*, self-sacrificing, altruistic love, and *pragma*, in which social and personal compatibility were the chief ingredients, as in family arranged marriages. Romantic love was the invention of the 12th century.

For our own era, in addition to agape and pragma, Lee has conceived four types of relationships: *eros*, the search for the ideal, physically beautiful lover (not unfamiliar to the ancient Greeks); *ludus*, the joyful, ephemeral affair; *storge*, companionship that arises out of long acquaintance; and *mania*, jealous possessiveness, the insane love of the movies. Lee's article is particularly important because it describes modifications that the Gay Liberation movement introduced into the traditional marriage model and into gay relationships that once imitated it: the overcoming of a form of the "incest taboo," that is, having sex with friends; the group "marriage" or gay commune, which combines the companionship of storge with the playfulness of ludus; the criss-crossing of the twosomes in the commune and sexual relationships with possibly any or all its members; and resisting the temptation to be exclusive and to make binding promises about the distant future. Lee suggests that much can be learned by heterosexuals from such innovations in gay relationships.

Letitia Anne Peplau and her associates at the University of California at Los Angeles, particularly Susan Cochran, have pursued the empirical study of lesbian and gay relationships at least since 1977. In the article that follows, Peplau summarizes that research up to 1982, which she points out represents a dramatic change in focus in the study of homosexuality—from a concern with "pathology" and "deviance" to its depiction as an "alternative lifestyle." Peplau has been interested in what makes gay relationships last. Her review suggests several factors: the resemblance to the "best-friend" rather than the marriage model; the avoidance of feminine and masculine role-playing; the combination of sexuality, affection, and companionship; the pyschological health of the partners; and the ability of partners to accommodate sexual openness.

CONCLUSIONS

As you can see from even this brief introduction to the literature on gay relationships, there are recurrent themes and conclusions (and some disagreements) that could be of considerable practical help to gay people involved in them. Although you will discover that the research and reflections on gay relationships are better in identifying than in solving problems, knowing what the problems are, and even anticipating them, may be the crucial ingredient in learning how to make relationships work and last for you and your partners.

REFERENCES

Bell, A. P. & Weinberg, M. S. (1978). *Homosexualities: A study of diversity among men and women.*

Blumstein, P. & Schwartz, P. *American couples: Money, work, sex.* New York: Simon & Schuster.

Clark, D. (1977). *Loving someone gay.* Millbrae, CA: Celestial Arts.

Harry, J. & DeVall, W. B. (1978). *The social organization of gay males.* New York: Praeger.

McWhirter, D. P. & Mattison, A. M. (1984). *The male couple: How relationships develop.* Englewood Cliffs, NJ: Prentice-Hall.

Mendola, M. (1980). *The Mendola report: A new look at gay couples.* New York: Crown.

Silverstein, C. (1981). *Man to man: Gay couples in America.* New York: Morrow.

Forbidden Colors of Love: Patterns of Gay Love and Gay Liberation

John Alan Lee, PhD
University of Toronto

My title combines two other titles—*Forbidden Colors*, a novel about Japanese gay life by Yukio Mishima, and *Colors of Love* (Lee, 1973), a typology of love styles. Mishima's (1970, p. 90) hero, Yuichi, sits in a Tokyo gay bar: "Whenever a man entered, all the guests would look up. The man coming in would be instantly bathed in glances. Who could guarantee that the ideal sought for so long, would not suddenly take shape and appear through that glass door?"

Similar scenes are familiar in gay bars from Toronto to Stockholm, San Francisco to Munich. After interviewing over 200 heterosexuals and homosexuals for my typology of love styles, I am convinced that gay and straight alike face the sad truth of Erich Fromm's (1963, p. 4) remark: "There is hardly any activity, any enterprise, which is started with such tremendous hopes and expectations, and yet which fails so regularly, as love."

The parallel problem of "single" men and women, gay or straight, encountering suitable partners for intimacy and possible mate selection is emphasized by the convergence of life-styles of single people in the large city. Judith Rossner's (1975) *Looking for Mr. Goodbar* might have as easily and credibly been written about gay men or women.

Morton Hunt (1966, pp. 96-98) describes the search for love, but to which sexual orientation does the following refer? "A loosely integrated, semi-secret society within a society . . . seeking out places where they can receive a given service . . . mingling with potential mates . . . on the lookout . . . at the local pickup bar." The description is that of divorced people in America's *World of the Formerly Married*, not homosexual males. But the fear that "you're nobody till somebody loves you" motivates gay and straight alike to exclaim, "I want a lover!" (Belkin, 1975).

In this paper I will outline very briefly some of the major styles of loving relevant to male homosexuals, and relate the changing fashions in gay love styles to gay liberation and the gay subculture. The method by which the types or styles of loving were developed is rather complicated and can only be summarized here (cf. Lee, 1973, Appendix, for detailed explanation). A quota sample of men and women of various ages and social classes, in England and Canada, were interviewed on their experiences of intimate adult affiliation ("love" or "being in love."). The interview instrument was an original one devised by the author, consisting of an omnibus love story, which combines into one set of card selections, all the possible varieties of basic intimate events of every conceivable love story. This "Love Story Card Sort" was developed out of an exhaustive review of the fictional and nonfictional literature of love. Using its 1500 cards, each respondent could compose and reconstruct his or her own experience of love with another person. The Sort was produced in appropriate variations for sex, multiple relationships, and special situations such as illicit affairs. In the occasional event for which no card was supplied, the respondent provided the details by using an "other" card. Since all the anticipated events were already precoded, further coding required only the classification of "other" unanticipated events.

Several methods of data processing, including cluster analysis and Guttman scaling, were used to sort the variety of relationships described by the respondents into certain basic sequences of events. There was clearly no single, universal pattern, and thus no one "true" style of loving. However, the varieties in styles of loving are surprisingly small, just as are the number of primary colors necessary to an artist, from which all other hues and shades may be constructed. Thus a small taxonomy of types of loving was developed, each type characterized by its most salient features. As will be seen below, it is as easy to recognize each lovestyle, and distinguish it from the others, as to recognize red, blue or yellow. There are six primary styles of loving, but one of them, altruistic, self-sacrificing *agape* (commonly called "Christian love") is not very relevant to this study, and is not described below. As in colors, it is possible to mix primary lovestyles to produce secondaries – for example, eros and ludus to produce ludic-erotic love.

A TYPOLOGICAL APPROACH TO LOVE

How long should a relationship last before it qualifies for the name of love rather than infatuation? How exclusive is the experience of "real love"? How jealous should "true love" be? Capellanus (1941, p. 53), the codifier of 12th-century courtly love, argued that the lover who is not jealous is not a true lover. Margaret Mead, however, believes that "jealousy is not a barometer by which depth of love can be read, but merely records the degree of the lover's insecurity" (Krich, 1960, p. 94).

Various observers of love have argued its "true" nature for 2,000 years, and littered our fictional and nonfictional literature with various definitions of love. Indeed, the idea of love is considered the most complex in Western ideologies (Hazo, 1967, p. xi). My approach is that of constructive typology (McKinney, 1966). Rather than attempt a definition of love, I have accepted any consistently definable pattern of positive, intimate adult affiliation related to mate selection as a "style" of loving, and endeavored to produce a typology that distinguishes each love style by its most salient characteristics (Lee, 1974).

A taxonomical approach to love has important advantages. It ends the frustrating debate about whether "you *really* love me," or "love me *as much as* I love you," and directs attention instead to the ways in which each of us loves "after our fashion." We may then determine to what extent our love styles are compatible or congruent. The search for a suitable mate becomes that for a partner with an appropriate love style. The derogatory definition of discordant love styles, by such labels as "puppy love," infatuation, mere sexual attraction, or "only an affair" is discouraged. The temptation to rewrite our own biographies through alternation (Berger, 1963, p. 54) is reduced; instead we can learn from each love experience, and more clearly define our preferences in love styles, just as a variety of experiences enables us to choose more aptly a satisfying lifestyle.

One cautionary note is always necessary when introducing a theory of love styles. The typology is one of relationships, not of lovers. An individual may move through a love career in which one preferred love style gives way to another; and a relationship itself, over time, may be altered in predominant love style. When I refer, for example, to a "manic lover" I mean simply a lover who, in the relationship in question at the time in question, was enacting a manic love style. Some lovers, of course, remain within the same love style for a lifetime.

EROS

This love style is the search for a partner whose physical presentation of self—visually, orally, tactilely, and so forth—conforms with an ideal image held in the mind of the lover. The definition of this image varies with individuals, and almost any would-be lover has some notion of what attracts him, but in the erotic love style first priority is given to this image. The lover is not interested in becoming acquainted with candidates who do not hold out the promise of conformity with the image.

The erotic lover is usually aware of the rarity of individuals conforming to his ideal, among the persons he encounters daily. When a hopeful encounter occurs, there is a surge of anticipation and excitement. Stendhal (1957, p. 53) called it a "sudden sensation of recognition and hope."

Any statistician could tell an erotic lover how poor his chances are for even a short list of desired qualities that must all occur in the same person. The odds must be awesome indeed for an erotic lover who advertised in a gay paper: "White male seeks lover. You should be 19 to a youthful 30, good-looking, no beard or mustache, blond hair and brown eyes, slender, under six feet, well endowed, well shaped very hairy legs, masculine, straight-looking. Write with photo to ______."

A gay male who consistently pursues a narrowly defined ideal image becomes known among his friends for "his type." The type, or ideal image, becomes a screening mechanism. He walks into a bar, looks over scores of men, and grumbles, "There's no one here tonight."

When he does meet a possible incarnation of the ideal image, there is an urgency that may spoil his management of front and presentation of self. He is in danger of "rushing" the prospective partner to bed, because usually intimate tactile contact and full revelation of the body are necessary to assure the lover that the ideal image is fully actualized. The discovery, for example, that the candidate has a very hairy back, when the ideal image demands smoothness of skin, would promptly disqualify an otherwise suitable partner.

LUDUS

The ludic lover (the term comes from Ovid, *amor ludens*) has a playful style. While aware of the differences between bodies, he considers it foolish to restrict one's chances by specializing in only one type. As in *Finian's Rainbow*, when he doesn't find a face he fancies, he fancies the face he finds. Love is expected to be pleasant and noncommittal, lasting as long as the two parties enjoy the relationship, and no longer. Ludus is not merely one-night stands or casual sex; on the contrary, it may become an elaborate ritual of behavior, as in the courtly love style of 17th century France.

At some periods in history, ludus has been depreciated as exploitation, manipulation, even seduction, but a playful style of love like that proposed by Ovid 20 centuries ago is again gaining widespread currency. An example of a gay advertisement for a playful partner reads: "Adventuresome 27-year-old, not sick of the bar and bath scene, charming and attractive, likes fun, travel and love and affection. Seeks man with lots of money who is fun to be with. Age not important. We can bring much warmth into our lives if you are ready."

Sometimes a gay couple who have established a more committed love style for their own relationship will seek playful relationships with others outside the pair. An ad titled "Three is no crowd" sought "fun-loving companions" for such a couple. This emphasizes the point that a lover may enact different love styles in different, concurrent relationships.

STORGE

This ancient Greek term (rhymes with "more gay") for affectionate companionship arising out of gradual acquaintance, as between cousins or childhood friends growing up together, is appropriate for the style of loving in which an individual "grows accustomed to" the partner, rather than "falling in love."

Storge is not the sort of love in which one can advertise for a partner, obviously, so I will refer to interview reports instead.

> Andy and Alan have been together for 15 years. They first met and became friends while at college.
>
> It was more than 2 years before each discovered the other was gay. Indeed, it was in relation to the other that each realized his own gayness. Andy and Alan are not so much homosexuals as they are homosexual in relation to each other. Neither has had a gay relationship with any other man.

A love relationship does not require two individuals with identical love styles, though in most cases that would assure the greatest agreement.

> Barry is a balding professor of 40 years, whose charm and sophistication compensates for homely appearance. His preference in love styles is eros, and his ideal image is the tall, blond Scandinavian youth. This is a type generally in great

demand in North American gay places, and considering Barry's looks, his chances of mating with such an ideal seemed slim.

But Barry was lucky. He met Alan, a handsome Scandinavian new in town and looking for friends. Alan grew up in a small town and had the typical rural manner—shy, dependent, and reserved. He was turned off by the "pretty boys" who fell all over him, but was drawn to Barry's self-assured, steady, and gentle style. Alan has no ideal image of a sought-for partner; his style of loving is storge. Barry nicely fulfills Alan's prescription, and Alan, Barry's.

The typical storgic lover prefers a gradual process of self-disclosure, especially of the physical body in sex. Thus Barry could easily have ruined his chances by rushing Alan to bed. Fortunately, his long years of searching had taught him to respect the potential partner's love style. Even luckier, he met Alan in the shower room of a swimming pool, so he knew that Alan's body fully conformed to the desired ideal.

MANIA

A lover who feels lonely and discontent with life anxiously seeks a partner—almost anyone will do—to fill the void left by his own lack of self-esteem. He will likely act out a manic style of loving. The symptoms are all too familiar: intense mental preoccupation with the beloved, who is often an unlikely and even unwilling choice, jealous possessiveness, repeated demands for assurances of love by the partner, dramatic scenes, even violent expressions of love.

The manic lover has no ideal image but becomes obsessed with whoever is chosen as the object of fixation. A gay ad reads: "Wanted desperately, a friend for long-lasting companionship. Size/looks unimportant. Am new to gay scene."

A common theme among those whose style of loving is mania is the fatigue and despair resultant from repeated rejection in the bar scene. The playful, noncommittal style of ludus works well in the bar, especially for those who are self-assured, even vain. If one has good looks to be vain about, so much the better. The typical manic lover, by contrast, "has had it with bar people" and is "tired of tricks and insincere people."

The sociopsychological factors that predispose some heterosexuals to mania, especially discontent with life and low self-esteem (Reik, 1949, p. 96), are even more likely to occur in homosexuals coping poorly with homophobic social environments, disapproving parents, the anxieties of living "in the closet," and similar factors. If the lover has internalized society's disapproval as a form of self-oppression (Hodges & Hutter, 1974), then he may also despise any partner, who becomes an unconscious accomplice in the lover's homosexuality. This condition facilitates the familiar love-hate ambivalence so typical of mania.

PRAGMA

The Greek root for pragmatic or practical refers to an approach to love in which considerations of social and personal compatibility are paramount. The education, race, social class, vocation, religion, politics, or similar characteristics of candidates are of first concern to the pragmatic lover. If the lover's social norms of mate selection include certain prescriptions of physical appearance (such as a stigma on excess weight), these will form part of the pragmatic lover's shopping list, but he will be otherwise relatively indifferent to considerations of physical attractiveness.

Pragma is a style of loving easily converted to utilitarian manipulation, whether through "arrangements" by a marriage broker or by computer dating and similar facilities. The object is a compatible union; if compatibility goes out of the relationship through change of one or both parties, this style of loving defines disengagement as perfectly reasonable – in contrast to mania, for example, where a threat of separation may even lead to counterthreats of suicide.

Social stigmatizations of homosexuality has made pragmatic mate selection difficult. While an increasing number of heterosexual computer dating agencies flourish in large cities such as Toronto, using the most sophisticated technology such as closed-circuit television, several attempts to establish a gay introduction service have failed. In the United States, such services seem rapidly to degenerate into sources of sexual assignation and one-night stands.

An alternative pragmatic method is the use of newspaper advertising. Even the use of photographs does not provide much assurance for the erotic lover, but a lengthy, detailed description of one's own social and personal characteristics, together with a list of those desired in the partner, can perform much the same function as a computer dating service. If there is a hazard for the pragmatic advertiser, it is in the exploitation of the same medium by playful, ludic lovers who do not share the pragmatic lover's earnest desire for a long-term, committed relationship (assuming a compatible partner is located).

A probable pragmatic advertisement reads: "Looking for mature male, who is easygoing, sincere, faithful, to share my interest in theater, books, art, quiet evenings at home, music; for friendship which hopefully can lead to a permanent relationship. I am 38, quiet, reserved, professional. If you are seriously looking for a lover, looks are not important."

A determination of which personal advertisements in a gay newspaper originated from lovers preferring a pragmatic love style, in contrast to those preferring eros, ludus, or mania, would be somewhat arbitrary. While an element of desperation, loneliness, and indifference to type of partner would indicate mania, and a playful, permissive (or pluralistic), nonjealous attitude would indicate ludus, with eros suggested when there is a great emphasis on physical appearance, together with the insistence on a photograph, there are many ads that lack the necessary clues. The tendency to almost unintelligible ads encouraged by line rates (rather than word rates) is a factor: "W/m, 36, stable, educ., Fr. act. sks. W/M 18-30, sinc. affect. for lstg. frdship. Box 201."

When one comes to consider sadomasochist advertisements, with their special requirements and unique argot, the problem of classification is magnified. By excluding these, together with the obvious sexual-service offerings ("Horny tonite? Call Bob"), we may nevertheless develop some approximation of the practical considerations that gay males have in mind when advertising for a partner.

The *Advocate*, a biweekly gay newspaper with a circulation of 60,000, originating in California but circulated widely throughout the United States and Canada, provides a suitable source of gay male advertisers. About half of the personal ads originate from West Coast addresses or telephone area codes.

In three randomly selected issues of the *Advocate*, the total number of personal ads was 876. After exclusion of sadomasochist ads (with no moral disapproval implied, but merely for heuristic convenience) and sexual-service ads, some 248 ads remained that dealt with sought-for partners. Since the pattern of advertising varies (for example, there seem to be more playful ads in the summer, more serious partnerships sought in the winter), the following statistics should be regarded as indicative rather than conclusive.

CHARACTERISTICS OF ADVERTISERS

Five characteristics occur in the ads with regularity: sex (exclusively male), age, race, preferred sex role, and socioeconomic status. About 87% (218) of the advertisers state their age (Table 1). Whether they are truthful or not, the pattern of distribution of ages at least indicates what the advertisers regard as acceptable self-disclosure.

In 63% of the ads, the race of the advertiser is indicated. Of these, 92% are white, 5% Oriental, and the remainder black. Thirty percent of the advertisers include their preferred sex role. Greek passive leads slightly, but Greek active and passive and French active and passive account for more than three-quarters of the prefer-

TABLE 1
Age of Advertisers

Stated Age	Proportion of Advertisers Who State Age
Up to 25 years	24%
26 to 34 years	47%
35 to 44 years	20%
45 and over	9%

ences. Other alternatives, such as j/o (masturbation) are less common. Some advertisers are "versatile."

Probably the least reliable data are those on socioeconomic status. One would expect even greater distortion toward socially expected status than with age. About 23% of the advertisers indicate status, with "professional" and "businessman" the leading categories, and "student" a poor third.

DESIRED PARTNERS

There are 20 categories of desired characteristics of partners specified in at least 10% of the advertisements. These are listed in rank order in Table 2, ranging from acceptable age of partner, specified in 73% of the ads, to nonfrequenting of bars, mentioned in 10% of the ads.

Preference for a limited age range may relate to any of several styles of loving—playful, pragmatic, or erotic—but the second most mentioned requirement, a faithful, lasting relationship, clearly excludes ludus and would be most likely to occur in pragma. Only when we reach the fourth priority, a specified physique, are erotic elements clearly identified, and the next clearly erotic prescription does not occur until Rank 10. Overall, the top 10 prescriptions are more relevant to a pragmatic search for a "marriage" partner than to any other style of loving.

Indeed, the majority of the 20 most commonly prescribed characteristics desired by *Advocate* advertisers are remarkably similar to those one would encounter among heterosexuals looking for a marriage partner: age, race, education, various aspects of character, recreational interests, and general physical attractiveness. The most significant item ranked low on the gay list but high in the heterosexual search for partnership is socioeconomic status or occupation and income. The most distinctively gay requirements not commonly paralleled in heterosexual mate selection are preferred sex role—which gender itself defines in heterosexual marriage—and "straight appearance." The latter may be a reflection both of the stigma attached to homosexual unions in American society (thus Rank 15,

TABLE 2

Desired Characteristics of Partners Specified in 248 Advocate *Advertisements*

Rank Order	Quality Desired in Partner	Percentage Seeking Desired Quality
1	Age within a specified range	73%
2	Partner must want a faithful, lasting relationship	53%
3	Straight or masculine appearance	45%
4	Specific kind of physique (height, weight, build, musculature, etc.)	42%
5	Sincerity, honesty, seriousness	40%
6	Interest in specified social activities, hobbies, sports, arts, etc.	33%
7	Warm and/or affectionate	31%
8	Specified race	23%
9	Preferred sex role (e.g., butch, top man)	22%
10	Handsome, good-looking	20%
11	Qualities of character (sensitivity, stability, etc.) that are not listed above	19%
12	Not a drug user	18%
12	Not into sadomasochism (S & M)	18%
13	Intelligent and/or educated	16%
13	Not fat	16%
14	Size of penis or type of penis (e.g., "uncut")	15%
15	Discretion	14%
16	Smooth or hairy	12%
16	Socioeconomic status	12%
17	Not frequently at the bars	10%

noting a desire for discretion) and of the increasing "virilization" of the homosexual male subculture, examined by Laud Humphreys (1972).

The apparently "democratic" attitude of *Advocate* advertisers implied in their unconcern with socioeconomic status might seem to support Paul Goodman's (1973, p. 23) argument that homosexuality "throws together every class and group more than heterosexuality does." However, sociological studies of satisfying, long-term heterosexual marriages indicate that the illusion that "romantic love" may safely ignore considerations of socioeconomic background is merely that—an illusion contradicted by statistics (Burgess, 1953, p. 436). There is a tendency, reflected in Goodman's writings, for many gay men to believe that they have "something in common" with each other, merely because they share the same sexual orientation. Not only may homosexuality be insufficient as a social bond, in the absence of other affiliative qualities, but it may even be divisive, if preferred sex roles do not interlock.

The *Advocate* sample shows all the "ageism" generally characteristic of North American society since the "discovery" of the generation gap, and its implicit conviction that individuals on two sides of an arbitrary chronological point live in two different worlds. In the case of *Advocate* advertisers, the magic watersheds that seem to divide the acceptable from unacceptable candidates are 30 years, in the case of advertisers under 30, and 40 years for the remainder. Not only are there few advertisers who admit to more than 40 years, there are few who will consider partners over that age. Most of the "older" advertisers (keeping in mind that a 45-year-old in American society is barely halfway through his expected adult life span) try to play down their age, with phrases such as "42 years young" and "47, but I pass for 35."

The author, who passes for 30 without difficulty, though over 40 years of age, has discovered that age considerations are so important in advertisements that it is preferable to advertise according to one's apparent age, then slowly reveal one's true age in personal encounter. For the older gay male who is seeking a "discreet" union, there is the problem of a double denial of self. He cannot acknowledge to his social community that he is gay, and he cannot be his own age within the gay community (Lee, 1975).

Greg Lehne has pointed to a third bind that the would-be gay lover may have to cope with: the fantasy for a partner who is remote in age and thus unlikely to share the same life experiences and world view. After noting that the fantasized partnerships of his 50 gay male respondents "support the supposition of fairly widespread ageism," Lehne (1974, pp. 15-25) notes that ageism is especially pronounced among older men, 80% of whom are seeking partners younger—and often more than 10 years younger—than themselves.

In this respect my *Advocate* sample is less disheartening. Of the advertisers who state their own age (87% of the sample), about 77% also state the preferred age range of the partner. In all but 17% of these ads, the age of the advertiser falls within the preferred age range of the partner. Of course, this could be an artifact of the advertising medium, compared to the probably greater honesty of respondents in Lehne's anonymous survey. Advertisers may recognize the bind they are in, and deliberately specify the desired age of partners so as to include their own age. However, when the letters come in, they may tend to ignore most of those in the upper end of the specified range.

GAY LOVE AND GAY LIBERATION

The problems of gay men in finding a satisfactory mate are similar to those of other marginal and stigmatized categories in North American society, as a comparison of the difficulties of divorced heterosexuals readily demonstrates (Hunt, 1966). At least the gay male has the advantage of a supporting subculture with relatively diversified facilities for various styles of loving and various patterns of encounter. The lesbian has much less adequate subcultural support (Abbott & Love, 1972, p. 69; Martin & Lyon, 1972, p. 91). Indeed, the opportunities for social encounter with other lesbians have actually *decreased* in Toronto over the past 5 years, with the closing of some clubs and their nonreplacement, while the clubs catering to males have increased. Bisexuals are another minority without a supportive subculture to facilitate encounter and interaction.

Albert Cohen (1966, p. 86) defines certain subcultures as "systems of interaction occurring when a number of social actors come together with similar problems of adjustment." In the process of solving their mutual problems, such subcultures may develop social patterns which, while initially deviant, are predictive of social change in the larger culture. The subculture is truly "innovative" in Merton's (1949, p. 141) sense of deviant behavior.

Much social change begins at the margins of society, and this is also true of styles of loving. For example, until the 12th century in western Europe, the prevailing definitions of a legitimate love relationship were *agape* (Christian altruistic love) and *pragma*, in the form of feudal arranged marriage. As Herbert Moller (1959) first noted, status anxiety and rivalry for scarce resources led the landless knights, who had been recruited among the peasantry in order to man the castle defenses, to adopt a new definition of love: *Amour courtois*, or courtly love, provided a legitimation for courtship of the daughters of the nobility who would otherwise have been beyond the knight's reach.

The new notion of courtly or romantic love replaced considerations of title, lands, and inheritances in the negotiation of marital unions. Slowly this concept that people who marry must be "in love" rather than pragmatically "suited to each other" (or more realistically, suitable to the parents involved) spread to other marginal and emerging groups in society, particularly in the newly flourishing free towns. The landed gentry vigorously opposed the new notions (cf. Ashley, 1963; Chaytor, 1923), and the rights of the parents gave way to those of the lovers only slowly and with the sort of conflict immortalized in *Romeo and Juliet.*

Not all patterns initiated by marginal groups are adopted in a wider social scale, obviously. The dalliant style of loving favored by the "affluent itinerants" of aristocratic society in the 17th century—the Jacques Casanovas and Don Juans—did not become adopted by society in general. Though this playful style had some support among the aristocracy (as immortalized in Laclos' *Liaisons dangereuses*) it was crushed by the bourgeois revolution that ended feudalism.

Thus it cannot be assumed that recent developments in styles of loving in the gay subculture are necessarily predictive of future social trends. However, since some of these developments have arisen in response to subcultural problems that have a parallel in the main heterosexual culture (as I noted in opening this paper), it is reasonable to extrapolate from present gay love styles to future heterosexual styles. Two patterns in particular are worthy of note.

GAY COMMUNES AND GROUP MARRIAGE

Heterosexual speculation on the future of marriage has recently been turning toward various extensions of the married pair/nuclear family formation (Constantine, 1973; Kammeyer, 1975; Libby,

1973; Rimmer, 1973). As James Ramey (1972) notes, the communal or group marriage, which combines commitment to the group with multiple pair-bonding among members, is the most complex form of marriage.

In terms of the typology of love styles, a group marriage would probably function with the least friction arising from jealousy if there were an appropriately balanced mixture of two love styles: storge and ludus. Storge would supply the communal loyalty and companionship between pairs, while ludus would provide a sufficient degree of playful detachment from excessively intense or passionate involvement within any dyad. In the traditional romantic union, the necessary social limitations on libidinal withdrawal into the dyad are provided by a system of family and community obligations centered on kinship and procreation (Slater, 1963). These are often lacking in the new forms of group marriage, such as the "corporate marriage" (Rimmer, 1968, 1973).

Since the same traditional controls described by Slater are also lacking in the gay commune, it provides a useful model for resolution of some of the problems likely to face heterosexual group marriages. Westley and Leznoff (1956) reported that gay friendship groups commonly functioned with social controls on intimacy akin to an "incest taboo." Such friendship groups continue to exist. For example, in Toronto a group of business and professional gay males living in the affluent suburb of Forest Hill enforce a strict requirement to "be married" in order to participate in the group's parties and dinners. Each gay couple in the group is expected to maintain what George and Nena O'Neill (1972) have called a "closed couple front."

However, one of the important products of the gay liberation movement has been the breakdown of the "incest taboo" on having sex with friends. On the contrary, there is now a positive emphasis on sex (one or several encounters) as a legitimate and desirable part of the process of becoming better acquainted.

A sociology student under my supervision has completed a participant-observer study of a circle of 14 gay males who define themselves as a friendship group. If this were a group of the type described in Forest Hill, there could be only seven acceptable sexual relationships, in pairs (Figure 1).

Other relationships among the 14 members would be expected to be nonsexual friendships. If any of the 14 felt the need for sexual variety, he would be expected to seek it outside the group, in a covert and nonaffective manner—for example, at the gay baths (Westley & Leznoff, 1956).

In the group of young gay males my student observed, there was much more varied expression of sexual affection alongside friendship expression. Relationships ranged from "being married" to "having an affair" to "occasionally having sex." None of the "married" members were exclusively faithful; indeed, two of them were rather promiscuous, or, to use a less derogatory word, pluralistic. The group's sex network is shown in Figure 2.

Not all the members of this group shared a "gay liberation" consciousness, and some of the pluralism was creating tension between those who defined it as immoral, or at least troublemaking, and those who defined the *objections* to pluralism as old-fashioned and moralistic.

In a gay commune, the process is taken one step further: The acceptance of sexual interaction as a legitimate expression of various dyadic relationships crosscutting the membership of the commune is combined with common residency. This can lead to really complex problems of interaction, such as those Rimmer (1968, p. 276) attempted to solve for his corporate family, by a new type of housing. In one Toronto commune, for example, six gay males lived together as a close, almost familylike group but also enjoyed sleeping with each other. However, the complications arising from bed hopping led to the posting of a list of "who will be in each bed" for the week.

Figure 1. Expected sexual relationships in a group of 14 gay males, according to the Forest Hill code.

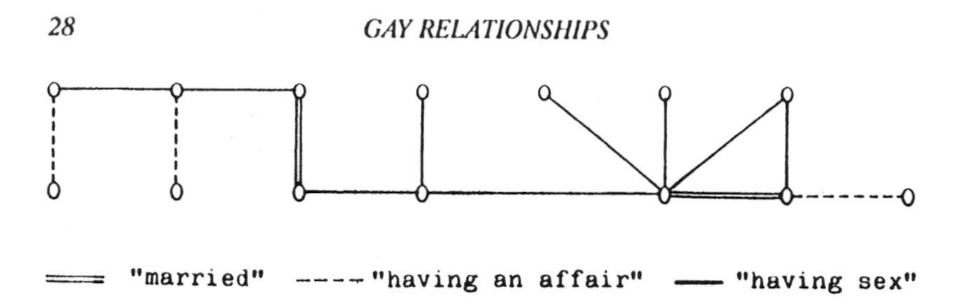

Figure 2. Actual sexual relationships in the group of 14 gay males.

While these communes as corporate entities have shown a surprising ability to survive over a period of years, there has been a tendency for members to pair off and move off on their own, so that few members of the commune remain in it for the whole of its life. But some do, and in the case of one surviving commune they continue to make it work.

Gay males who have fully internalized the gay consciousness and are truly "proud to be gay" are less likely to suffer the lack of self-esteem that is a common predisposing factor toward a manic love style. There is clearly an ideological relationship between gay liberation and a less jealous, less possessive, more playful love style. For example, Carl Wittman's (1972, p. 162) *Gay Manifesto* urges:

The things we want to get away from are

1. exclusiveness, propertied values toward each other, a mutual pact against the rest of the world;
2. promises about the future, which we have no right to make, and which prevent us from growing.

These values are synonymous with those advocated by George and Nena O'Neill (1972) for the heterosexual "open marriage." Clearly a gay commune, in which such values find social support within a legitimating ideology, can help each individual member to enjoy an intimate paired relationship without converting this to closed couple marriage.

The second pattern occurring in the interplay of gay liberation and styles of loving is that of a more honest intimacy in the gay subculture, whether intensely passionate dyadic unions ("gay marriages") are involved or more casual "seeing someone" relationships.

When an *Advocate* advertiser pleaded, "Isn't there anyone who is tired of the phony games in the bar scene, and ready to settle down to a sincere, loving relationship?" he was voicing a complaint often heard among gay males. Many gay liberationists deliberately eschew the bar scene, finding it oppressive and dishonest, and even destructive of integrity. Of course much of this is a function of self-oppression, as noted by *Downcast Gays* (Hodges & Hutter, 1974).

The problem of the gay bar and similar environments is that of an intersection of social environments most conducive to two different, and often fundamentally opposed, love styles: eros and ludus. The emphasis on physical appearance is a natural consequence of the diversified constituency of most gay bars. Perhaps all that the guests have in common is their sexual orientation. Their educational qualifications, vocations, incomes, political and religious views, and indeed their moral values in general, may cover the gamut of social possibilities. All that the guests may have to go on, in deciding (and it is often a painful and hesitant decision) to make the first move in initiating acquaintance, is the other person's "looks."

Thus there is a strong social pressure to maintain a casual, easily detached, noncommittal manner in the bar—in short, a pressure toward a playful or ludic style of love. One must learn to avoid over-optimistic evaluations such as follow on the sudden, exciting encounter with someone who seems to be the ideal partner. Bar people are all too familiar with the syndrome "Lovers who just met tonight, and tomorrow are not even friends."

A successful mixture of ludus and eros is a tightrope act (Lee, 1973, p. 112, 1974, p. 49). The art of passionate caution is not easily acquired. The ludic-erotic lover must combine the ecstatic intimacy of eros with the playful pluralism of ludus. He must be truly with the present partner in the here and now, fully enjoying today's intimacy, yet capable of detaching himself from the partner painlessly.

Paul Rosenfels (1971, p. 101) captures the paradox nicely: "The ability to make romantic attachments as if they were permanent and complete, and at the same time to retain the capability of dissolving such an attachment. . . . If an individual cannot dedicate himself to romance without reserve, he imposes qualifications which undermine the experience he seeks to have."

What is advocated here is definitely *not* a Don Juan syndrome of manipulative exploitation (Rosenfels, 1971, p. 94). Don Juan conned his victims into intimacy by persuading them that he was willing to marry. Rather, the ludic-erotic lover is fully open and honest about his intention to engage in a noncommitted relationship. There can be mutual enjoyment, trust, and comradeship, but without a promise about the future. The second relationship, between David and Jason, in Christopher Larkin's film *A Very Natural Thing* attempts to walk this tightrope. We are left uncertain but optimistic about their capacity to keep the balance, but the film is sociologically insightful in relating David and Jason's intentions to a gay liberation experience.

The ideology of gay liberation groups, at least in Toronto, is clearly that of intimacy among friends, including erotic ecstasy and sexual playfulness, without the necessity of lifetime commitment in imitation of heterosexual marriage. Likewise, the separation of intimates is not expected to be a bitter divorce, but a friendly disengagement in which the partners can continue to relate to each other as fellow members of the gay liberation movement.

As Andrew Hodges and David Hutter (1974, p. 8) note in one of the most emphatic British statements of gay liberation:

> Gay people have no reason to envy the institutionalized sexuality available to heterosexuals, cluttered as it is with ceremonies of courtship and marriage . . . [Our] heterosexual detractors betray their limited vision by their mistaken assumption that promiscuity is incompatible with lasting relationships. Homosexuals are in the happy position of being able to enjoy both at once.

However, they suggest that intimate roles that combine "promiscuity" (I prefer the term *pluralism*) with intimate relationships lasting (at least as continued friendship) for a long period of time are roles that come easier to homosexuals than to heterosexuals. I think they are mistaken. Both gay and straight share socialization into the same "romantic" heritage that emphasizes the search for one fulfilling relationship, a possessive coupling with that person, and a residual bitterness if the relationship does not work out. Gays need liberation from this traditional world view before they can enjoy satisfying ludic-erotic relationships.

Heterosexuals need such liberation too, and as George and Nena O'Neill (1974) admit in their second book, *Shifting Gears*, the transition will not be an easy one. It may well be that gay liberation is pioneering a new model of intimate relationship on the margins of society, which will eventually resolve the problems of a larger society. "The love which has no name" may give new names for love, new love styles to all humanity.

REFERENCES

Abbott, S., & Love, B. *Sappho was a right-on woman.* New York: Stein & Day, 1972.

Ashley, M. *The Stuarts in love.* London: Hodder & Stoughton, 1963.

Belkin, A. I want a lover. *The Body Politic,* October 1975, p. 15.

Berger, P. *Invitation to sociology.* New York: Anchor, 1963.

Burgess, E. W. *Engagement and marriage.* New York: Lippincott, 1953.

Capellanus, A. *The art of courtly love* (J. J. Parry, Ed.). New York: Columbia University Press, 1941.

Chaytor, H. J. *The troubadours and England.* Cambridge: Cambridge University Press, 1923.

Cohen, A. *Deviance and control.* New York: Prentice-Hall, 1966.

Constantine, L. *Group marriage.* New York: Macmillan, 1973.

Fromm, E. *The art of loving.* New York: Bantam, 1963.

Goodman, P. Memoirs of an ancient activist. In L. Richmond & G. Noguera (Eds.), *The gay liberation book.* San Francisco: Ramparts Press, 1973.

Hazo, R. *The idea of love.* New York: Praeger, 1967.

Hodges, A., & Hutter, D. *Downcast gays.* London: Pomegranate Press, 1974.

Humphreys, L. New styles in homosexual manliness. In J. McCaffrey (Ed.), *The homosexual dialectic.* New York: Prentice-Hall, 1972.

Hunt, M. *The world of the formerly married.* New York: McGraw-Hill, 1966.

Kammeyer, K. *Confronting the issues.* Boston: Allyn & Bacon, 1975.

Krich, A. M. (Ed.). *Anatomy of love.* New York: Dell, 1960.

Lee, J. A. *Colors of love.* Toronto: New Press, 1973.

Lee, J. A. Styles of loving. *Psychology Today,* October 1974, pp. 43-51.

Lee, J. A. Meeting males by mail. In L. Crew (Ed.), *The gay academic.* New York: Etc. Publications, 1975.

Lehne, G. Gay male fantasies. *The Body Politic,* September 1974.

Libby, R. *Renovating marriage.* San Ramon, Calif.: Consensus Publications, 1973.

Martin, D., & Lyon, P. *Lesbian woman.* New York: Bantam, 1972.

McKinney, J. *Constructive Typology.* New York: Meredith, 1966.

Merton, R. *Social theory and social structure.* Glencoe, Ill.: Free Press, 1949.

Mishima, Y. *Forbidden colors.* New York: Avon, 1970.

Moller, H. The social causation of the courtly love complex. *Comparative Studies in Society and History,* 1959, *1,* 137-144.

O'Neill, G., & O'Neill, N. *Open marriage.* New York: Evans, 1972.

O'Neill, G., & O'Neill, N. *Shifting gears.* New York: Evans, 1974.

Ramey, J. W. Emerging patterns of behavior in marriage. *Journal of Sex Research,* 1972, *8*(1).

Reik, T. *Of love and lust.* London: Farrar, Straus, Cudahy, 1949.

Richmond, L., & Noguera, G. (Eds.), *The gay liberation book.* San Francisco: Ramparts Press, 1973.

Rimmer, R. *Proposition 31.* New York: Signet, 1968.

Rimmer, R. *Adventures in loving.* New York: Signet, 1973.

Rosenfels, P. *Homosexuality, the psychology of the creative process.* New York: Libra, 1971.

Rossner, J. *Looking for Mr. Goodbar.* New York: Simon & Shuster, 1975.

Slater, P. Social limitations on libidinal withdrawal. *American Sociological Review,* 1963, *28,* 339-345.

Stendhal (H. Beyle). *De l'amour* (H. Martineau, Ed.). Paris: Le Divan, 1957.

Westley, W., & Leznoff, M. The homosexual community. *Social Problems,* April 1956.

Wittman, C. Refugees from Amerika: A gay manifesto. In J. McCaffrey (Ed.), *The homosexual dialectic.* New York: Prentice-Hall, 1972.

Research on Homosexual Couples: An Overview

Letitia Anne Peplau, PhD
University of California, Los Angeles

During the past decade, a research literature describing the intimate relationships of lesbians and gay men has slowly emerged. Several books devoted to homosexual couples have recently been published, including those by Mendola (1980), Silverstein (1981), and Tanner (1978). Other empirical studies of homosexuality increasingly include investigations of personal relationships. Examples are found in the recent Kinsey Institute study (Bell & Weinberg, 1978) and in other research-based books (e.g., Harry & DeVall, 1978; Jay & Young, 1977; Spada, 1979; Wolf, 1979) published in the last five years. Empirical articles on couples have also begun to appear with increasing frequency in this and in other scholarly journals. Indeed, sufficient empirical research has accumulated to permit the publication of four comprehensive review articles on gay male and lesbian relationships (i.e., Harry, 1983; Larson, 1982; Peplau & Amaro, 1982; Peplau & Gordon, 1982). This Symposium is intended to call attention to the growing research focus on couples and to encourage its expansion.

The origins of increased interest in homosexual couples are diverse. Harry (1983) has suggested that the rise in the study of gay and lesbian relationships in the 1970s is closely tied to the rise of the Gay and Women's Movements which emphasized the need to examine the full spectrum of lesbians' and gay men's experiences. Publications such as *Positively Gay* (Berzon & Leighton, 1979) and *Our Right to Love* (Vida, 1978) include discussions of relationship issues. Changes within the social sciences have also been important.

Gay and feminist caucuses within professional organizations have drawn attention to homosexual issues and have provided forums for the presentation of research findings. In the field of sociology, a growing recognition of the diversity of contemporary life-styles has broadened the traditional focus on "marriage and the family" to a concern for more varied forms of relationships. Thus, there has been a shift in sociology from studying homosexuality exclusively from the perspective of "deviance" toward studying homosexuality as part of work on "alternative life-styles" or sex roles. Similar trends can be found in psychology, where a shift has occurred from studying etiology and psychopathology toward viewing homosexuality in the context of intimacy and close relationships. The result of such changes has been to broaden the nature of scientific research on homosexuality. Today, empirical work on lesbian and gay male couples is well underway.

The current literature on homosexual couples has focused on several aspects of gay and lesbian relationships. As Reece suggests later in this issue, a major accomplishment may have been simply to document that lesbians and gay men often *do* develop lasting relationships—a fact that runs counter to prevailing stereotypes of homosexuals as involved only in fleeting encounters. But research has gone well beyond this observation. It is worth highlighting some of the prominent issues that are being addressed in current work and identifying some of the directions for needed future research.

Relationship Models. Of the fallacious myths about homosexual couples, none is more persistent than the belief that gay and lesbian partnership always mimic heterosexual marriage, with one partner playing the traditional "feminine" role of wife and the other assuming the "masculine" role of husband. According to this view, rigid butch-femme roleplaying pervades many aspects of homosexual relationships including the pattern of couple decision-making, the division of household tasks, and sexual behavior in the relationship. Empirical studies (see reviews by Harry, 1983; Larson, 1982; Peplau & Gordon, 1982) have consistently debunked this myth. Most contemporary gay relationships do not conform to traditional "masculine" and "feminine" roles; instead, role flexibility and turn-taking are more common patterns. Only a small minority of homosexual couples engage in clearcut butch-femme roleplaying. In this sense, traditional heterosexual marriage is not the predominant model or script for current homosexual couples.

This finding has led to several questions about homosexual couples. First, if homosexual partnerships are not based on a model of traditional heterosexual marriage, what pattern do they follow? It has been suggested (e.g., Harry & DeVall, 1978; Peplau, 1981) that many gay and lesbian relationships more closely resemble a model of best friendship, with the added element of romantic attraction. Second, if gender and traditional sex roles do not provide the basis for structuring homosexual relationships, what factors do determine the balance of power or the division of activities in a couple? Later in this issue, Harry presents data indicating that age may be a significant factor in the pattern of decision-making in gay male couples. (For a discussion of factors affecting power in lesbian relationships, see Caldwell & Peplau, 1984.) Finally, why is it that a minority of gay male and lesbian couples do engage in masculinefeminine roleplaying? This question is addressed in the article by Marecek, Finn, and Cardell in this issue.

Relationship Values and Goals. Research is beginning to document the diverse goals and desires that lesbians and gay men bring to their primary relationships. Evidence (e.g., Bell & Weinberg, 1978) indicates that most homosexuals want to have a steady love relationship and find this preferable to having only casual liaisons. Research also shows that lesbians and gay men look to their relationships primarily for affection and companionship—goals much like those of matched groups of heterosexuals (e.g., Peplau & Cochran, Note 1; Ramsey, Latham, & Lindquist, Note 2). Beyond these areas of commonality, important individual differences have been found in the relationship values of homosexual women and men. In particular, several writers (e.g., Peplau & Cochran, 1981; Peplau, Cochran, Rook, & Padesky, 1978; Sang, Note 3; Silverstein, 1981) have suggested that important individual differences exist in the value placed on two themes, conceptualized as intimacy, togetherness or dyadic attachment versus independence, separateness, or personal autonomy. This topic is examined in the article by Jones and De Cecco.

The Quality of Homosexual Relationships. An important line of research concerns the nature and quality of homosexual partnerships (e.g., Bell & Weinberg, 1978; Mendola, 1980; Silverstein, 1981). Just as some early studies of homosexual individuals examined personal psychological adjustment, so recent studies of homosexual partnerships have examined the "adjustment" of lesbian and gay male couples. Two studies (Cardell, Finn, & Marecek, 1981; Ramsey et al., Note 2) compared lesbian, gay male, and heterosexual couples on measures of relationship adjustment. In both studies, the homosexual couples scored in the "well-adjusted" range and were indistinguishable on this basis from the heterosexuals. Peplau and Cochran (Note 1) compared matched samples of lesbians, gay men, and heterosexuals on measures of love and liking for their primary partner; again, no significant differences were found among groups. Other research has begun to look at factors that contribute to the quality of homosexual relationships. Currently, research on the quality of gay partnerships is in its infancy. In the future, studies are needed that examine a broader range of factors that contribute to the quality and stability of homosexual couples. We have little research on the issues and problems faced by homosexual couples, and on the solutions that couples create in building successful relationships.

Sexuality. Scientific research refutes the myth that sex is the sole basis for gay and lesbian relationships. While not discounting the significance of sexuality, studies are beginning to put sex in its place alongside other basic components of enduring relationships such as love, commitment, and companionship. One current controversy concerns the impact of sexual exclusivity versus openness on homosexual couples. Although in popular thinking "infidelity" is often construed as a sign of serious problems in a relationship, the causes and consequences of sexual openness in homosexual couples may be more varied. For example, one study (Peplau et al., 1978) found that whether lesbians have sex outside their primary relationship depends on their personal values, not on their satisfaction or dissatisfaction with the relationship itself. Some (e.g., Harry & DeVall, 1978) have suggested that for homosexuals, perhaps especially for gay men, a desire for sexual exclusivity may actually inhibit the development of a long-term relationship. In this view, exclusivity may be part of the early stage of a relationship, but sexual openness may be more compatible with enduring homosexual commitments. We need to know more about this basic issue.

Gender Differences. The literature has also begun to identify gender differences in the relationship experiences of lesbians and gay men (see reviews by Harry, 1983; Peplau & Gordon, 1982). For example, research suggests that lesbians are more likely than gay men to live with their primary partner; lesbians may also be more likely than gay men to be in a steady relationship. The relationships of lesbians are more likely than those of gay men to be sexually exclusive. In addition, lesbians may place greater importance on emotional intimacy and equality in relationships than do gay men. The most common explanations for such sex differences focus on cultural sex-role socialization, possible differences in the norms of the gay male and lesbian communities, and the impact of feminism on lesbian relationships. Further research is needed to clarify whether such gender differences are "real" rather than artifacts of biases in the recruitment of lesbians and gay men for research studies and, assuming the differences are genuine, to identify their origins.

Limitations of Existing Research. Existing empirical studies provide a good beginning toward describing and understanding homosexual couples. While many of the findings, such as the general absence of butch-femme roleplaying, may hardly be surprising to those familiar with the gay community, empirical results provide a scientific basis for debunking common stereotypes and provide empirical validation for more impressionistic depictions of homosexual relationships. Nonetheless, existing research has several major limitations.

One limitation is that most studies are based on small samples of younger, white, middle class individuals. While it may never be possible to obtain a truly representative sample of homosexual couples, studies could be designed to sample a broader spectrum of lesbians and gay men. Second, research has largely relied on questionnaires and surveys, methods that assume that respondents are aware of and can accurately report about issues in their relationships. Although surveys have proved extremely useful, the effects of social desirability pressures on survey responses in homosexual samples are unknown. There is a need for a greater range of research techniques, including ethnographies, in-depth interviews, and observational studies. Greater confidence could be placed in findings that were replicated in different studies using different methods. Third, most studies of homosexual relationships have involved only one member of the couple. While this is a convenient recruitment strategy, studies obtaining independent information from both partners in a couple will enhance the research literature.

Finally, research has of necessity addressed only a limited range of topics. There is need for research on a variety of issues. We know little about the long-term relationships of older lesbians and gay men. It would be useful to determine how relationships may vary across the life cycle of the individual, and to learn whether there are predictable stages in the developmental course of homosexual relationships. It will be important for researchers to be sensitive to individual differences among lesbians and among gay men in the nature of their relationships; the development of relationship typologies may be one approach to this issue. Most of the research to date has been "basic research"; it would be helpful to have more applied studies of the problems encountered by homosexual couples and their varied solutions. In this vein, studies of approaches to couples counseling would also be valuable.

Research on homosexual couples promises to inform several audiences. Studies of gay male and lesbian couples serve to discredit myths about homosexuals that have been prevalent in both professional and folk thinking and provide the basis for a factual depiction of homosexual relationships. For members of the gay and lesbian communities, such studies provide an opportunity to put one's own relationship experiences in the context of the spectrum of possible relationships. Studies of homosexual couples also provide an opportunity to test the generality of social science theories of "human behavior" which have been derived almost exclusively from heterosexual models and tested on heterosexual samples. In this way, research on lesbian and gay male couples contributes not only to our knowledge about homosexuality but also to our more general knowledge about close human relationships. . . .

REFERENCE NOTES

1. Peplau, L. A., & Cochran, S. D. Sex differences in values concerning love relationships. Paper presented at the annual meeting of the American Psychological Association, Montreal, September 1980.

2. Ramsey, J., Latham, J. D., & Lindquist, C. U. Long term same-sex relationships: Correlates of adjustment. Paper presented at the annual meeting of the American Psychological Association, Toronto, August 1978.

3. Sang, B. E. Lesbian relationships—a struggle toward couple equality. Paper presented at the annual meeting of the American Psychological Association, San Francisco, 1977.

REFERENCES

Bell, A. P., & Weinberg, M. S. *Homosexualities: A study of diversity among men and women.* New York: Simon & Schuster, 1978.

Berzon, B., & Leighton, R. (Eds.). *Positively gay.* Millbrae, CA: Celestial Arts, 1979.

Caldwell, M., & Peplau, L. A. Balance of power in lesbian relationships. *Sex Roles*, 1984, *10*(1), 587-599.

Cardell, M., Finn, S., & Marecek, J. Sex-role identity, sex-role behavior, and satisfaction in heterosexual, lesbian and gay male couples. *Psychology of Women Quarterly*, 1981, *5*, 488-494.

Harry, J. Gay male and lesbian family relationships. In E. Macklin (Ed.), *Contemporary familes and alternate lifestyles: Handbook on research and theory*. Beverly Hills, CA: Sage, 1983.

Harry, J., & DeVall, W. *The social organization of gay males.* New York: Praeger, 1978.

Jay, K., & Young, A. *The gay report*. New York: Summit, 1977.

Larson, P. C. Gay male relationships. In W. Paul & J. D. Weinrich (Eds.), *Homosexuality as a social issue*. Beverly Hills, CA: Sage, 1982.

Mendola, M. *The Mendola report: A new look at gay couples*. New York: Crown, 1980.

Peplau, L. A. What homosexuals want in relationships. *Psychology Today*, March 1981, 28-38.

Peplau, L. A., & Amaro, H. Understanding lesbian relationships. In W. Paul & J. D. Weinrich (Eds.), *Homosexuality as a social issue*. Beverly Hills, CA: Sage, 1982.

Peplau, L. A., & Cochran, S. D. Value orientations in the intimate relationships of gay men. *Journal of Homosexuality*, 1981, *6* (3), 1-19.

Peplau, L. A., Cochran, S. D., Rook, K., & Padesky, C. Loving women: Attachment and autonomy in lesbian relationships. *Journal of Social Issues*, 1978, *34*, 7-27.

Peplau, L. A., & Gordon, S. L. The intimate relationships of lesbians and gay men. In E. R. Allgeier & N. B. McCormick (Eds.), *Gender roles and sexual behavior*. Palo Alto, CA: Mayfield, 1982.

Silverstein, C. *Man to man: Gay couples in America*. New York: Morrow, 1981.

Spada, J. *The Spada report: The newest survey of gay male sexuality*. New York: New American Library, 1979.

Tanner, D. M. *The lesbian couple*. Lexington, MA: D. C. Heath, 1978.

Vida, G. (Ed.). *Our right to love: A lesbian resource book*. Englewood Cliffs, NJ: Prentice-Hall, 1978.

Wolf, D. G. *The lesbian community*. Berkeley: University of California Press, 1979.

II. WHERE TO LOOK FOR LOVERS

Finding a gay lover is complicated by the fact that open displays by one man of physical and emotional interest in another man are not welcome in ordinary work or social settings. Whereas a straight man can brazenly ogle the woman classmate or workmate he finds attractive and an emancipated straight woman can, with a few choice looks and words, let a man know she thinks he's a fox, gay men must often be more furtive and even cunning. In conventional settings the gay man must try to figure out who the likely prospects are, that is, who is gay or bisexual, in the first place, or, at least, *willing to explore* (as we beguilingly say in California) their gay feelings. If you're so totally disclosing of your homosexuality that you add the information that you're gay to every introduction to every male, you might scare away prospects who would prefer to remain in the shadows cast by their closet doors. Often the price a gay male must pay for admission to "polite" society is that he is not "blatant," that is, he settles for tacit tolerance of "the love that dare not speak its name."

Occasionally, in more congenial society, coupled straight friends will introduce their "single" gay friends to likely male prospects, but such matchmaking is rare and often based on the gross misconception that *any* man who is gay, ipso facto, should grab at the opportunity to form a relationship with *any other* gay man. Be spared this supreme misunderstanding and leave the matchmaking to your gay friends who know all too well and respect the odds and idiosyncrasies of taste and disposition involved in the quest for a gay lover.

In the last decade the organizational, professional, business, and social settings in which gay men can meet and assess lover prospects have multiplied at an astounding rate so that, in cities like Atlanta, Boston, Chicago, Dallas, Los Angeles, Miami, New York, and San Francisco, the plethora of opportunity can almost obviate participation in straight society. This proliferation of settings, combined with the increasing willingness of gay men to be more casually open about their interest in other men, has immensely increased the prospects of finding lover material.

The research on where to look for lovers has lagged behind gay social inventiveness and reveals more about where we once looked and less about where we are likely to discover them in the future. Neil Tuller, in his study of lesbian and gay couples living in the San Francisco Bay Area, found that social settings, like college classes, meetings of gay organizations, and gay friends' homes, offer more hope for finding a lover than bars, parks, and the baths of the ancient pre-AIDS gay regime. This stands to reason, since a commonality of background, interests, sensibility, and lifestyle seem to be more crucial when you look for someone with whom to share your life, which involves the mind as well as the body.

Where to look for lovers, however, is not the major theme of Tuller's article, which mostly concerns where the relationship heads after you've found "him." These questions about gay relationships arose at the end of the first decade of Gay Liberation and are still around today: trying to restrict all sexual conduct to your lover (incorrectly and *heterosexually* phrased as the "monogamy" issue), rearing children (no longer the exclusive prerogative of heterosexuals), and attempting to avoid the rigid assignment of a feminine role to one partner and a masculine to the other. All these burning and apparently eternal issues are explored in greater detail in Section IV, How to Maintain a Gay Relationship.

In the suburbs and locales remote from the gay urban meccas and for men who are impatient with the stylized maneuvering of the gay bar or gym and their exclusionary focus on physical attraction (especially if you yourself are not a youthful "doll"), one way to look for a lover (or sex partner) is to use the media. *Media* is a little pretentious here, since all I mean is the telephone or the gay newspaper or magazine. (There are also the dating and matching services, more or less computerized, such as *David's* in California, but, as far as I know, no one has published a systematic evaluation of their effectiveness.)

Two articles that follow, the first by Michael Lumby, the second by Mary Laner and Levi Kamel, have analyzed the classified ads that appear in the gay print media and continue to flourish even in the era of "safe sex." There are two categories of such ads. First, there are those placed by "models" who offer an hourly rate for services that range from nitty-gritty genital sex (safe or unsafe), to massage, acting as your party escort, enacting an S&M scene (verbal, physical, or both), letting you watch while they perform with someone else (a package deal) and in the era of AIDS, masturbate themselves for your visual titillation from across the great, protective expanse of a king-size bed. Second, there are the "personal ads," more germane to this book, in which people who are looking for a lover list the desired physical, mental, and social characteristics as well as their own presumably matching set (which is often a duplication of the former). The more confident or conventional advertizers also list disqualifying features (e.g., no "fats" or "femmes" or "smokers") and the more skeptical, lascivious, or beautiful require an exchange of photographs.

There is, of course, always the issue of "truth in advertizing," although, to my best knowledge, no gay paper or individual advertizer has been sued by a disgruntled responder for lying. Lying, of course, or at least *embroidering* the truth, is present in most advertizing, particularly that connected with love and sex, where outright prevarication often combines with impenetrable self-deception. It is so common in the ads that it necessitates the inclusion of the word "sincere" by those who would like to present an honest picture and, very likely, have been "burnt" in the past.

Lumby, who analyzed the self-descriptions of advertizers in over 1,000 ads, found that both the model and the personal ads manifested a major interest in having sex. Those listed under "models" more than suggested payment for sexual services they promised, while the "personals" did not entail upfront fees. In both groups there was a striking emphasis on masculinity, often narrowly defined as penis size, although the particular sexual expertise of the advertizer was usually left to his readers' steaming imaginations. Although the advertizers in the personal ads were hardly indifferent to having sex, other interests, esthetic, athletic, and social, were also mentioned.

Whereas Lumby's analysis concentrated on the ads of models, Laner's and Kamel's dealt only with the personal ads. Still, in approximately 350 of them, they found that the advertizers were occupied with the virility of their prospective partners. Particular physical traits (e.g., body types, penis size) outweighed by far other considerations, although general social appearance (i.e., foxy, good-looking), personality, and interests were also important. Laner and Kamel also compared the ads of heterosexual and homosexual men. Their findings are flattering for gay men whom they describe as refreshingly more frank about the kind of sex they prefer and the goals of relationships they seek and, suprisingly, a little less physical in their requirements of men than straight men are of women.

Couples: The Hidden Segment of the Gay World

Neil R. Tuller

Until the early 1960s, little was known about homosexuality or homosexuals. Most of the knowledge came from psychiatrists who based the majority of their studies and findings on their homosexual patients. The views presented by these psychiatrists naturally reflected the specialized group that they had studied and, therefore, were largely misrepresentative of those who were not under psychiatric care. In the past few years, a great deal has been written about homosexuality. Most of this writing, however, has been more on a macrocosmic rather than a microcosmic level. In other words, most recent studies of homosexuality have been general, examining the whole of homosexuality rather than isolating its specific elements or subgroups. Even those studies most recently done that have been concerned with specific elements of the gay community have concentrated almost exclusively on homosexuals vis-à-vis homosexual institutions, such as gay bars and baths, and other gay organizations. There has also been more interest and study of homosexuality in establishments that are not necessarily designated "homosexual," such as prisons. One large segment of homosexuals, however, that has been virtually ignored in the research is that group whose members do not necessarily frequent various homosexual meeting places and, at the same time, are involved in long-term gay "marriage" relationships. Gay couples are a less visible portion of the gay community and cannot always be found in the conventional meeting places of the homosexual.

The purpose of this study is to examine the lives of 15 gay couples in the San Francisco Bay Area and, in doing so, to generate interest and to serve as an impetus for further, more sophisticated research on the microcosmic level.

METHOD

The initial contacts for this study were made through gay friends of the interviewer: I initially interviewed two couples and then from them received the names of several other couples whom I then contacted and interviewed; from them I ascertained the names of several other couples, and so on. Because of the reluctance of many homosexuals to be identified as such, it is difficult to obtain a random sample of gay couples, or of any other gay group. Because the participants in this research were not chosen at random, they cannot be said to represent all gay couples.

This study is limited to couples who have been together and thought of themselves as couples for at least 1 year. Members of each couple were interviewed and asked a series of questions pertaining to their individual relationship as well as to gay relationships in general (see Appendix A). I attempted, through the interview questions, to find out what kind of relationship each couple had and how their relationship was integrated into the whole of their lives. I interviewed a wide variety of people, and although I found many differences among the couples, I also found some significant similarities. A total of 15 couples, 5 female couples and 10 male couples, were interviewed. All but 1 of these couples had been together for at least 1 year. The exception, a female couple who had been together for 7 months, was included because both members had been in previous long-term gay marriage relationships.

THE SAMPLE

The male couples I interviewed ranged in age from both males being 19 to one male being 34 and the other 48 (see Table 1). They ranged politically from a couple who had written a book on gay liberation to an older, more moderate couple who believed it was very important to "go along with the heterosexual society" and hide their own homosexuality.

TABLE 1

Biographical Information

Age	Birthplace	Profession	Years Together
		Males	
23	Los Angeles, Calif.	Factory worker	1½
23	Sacramento, Calif.	University student	
25	Chicago, Ill.	University student	2
28	Oakland, Calif.	Chemical engineer	
28	Cleveland, Ohio	Filmmaker, author	2
21	New York, N.Y.	Phone operator, author	
23	New York, N.Y.	Student teacher	4
27	Philadelphia, Pa.	Student teacher	
34	Red Bluff, Calif.	Reference librarian	1½
48	New Castle, Ind.	Railroad worker	
28	San Diego, Calif.	Actor	3
23	Iowa City, Iowa	Artist	
32	Pittsburgh, Pa.	Clerk	4
23	San Diego, Calif.	Community worker	
27	Oakland, Calif.	Craftsman	2½
25	Maryland (raised in Panama)		
21	San Francisco, Calif.	University student	1
25	Rochester, N.Y.	Electronics technician	
19	Los Angeles, Calif.	University student	7
19	La Salle, Ill.	University student	
		Females	
24	Vallejo, Calif.	Elementary school teacher	5½
24	Arcada, Calif.	PE teacher	
42	Des Moines, Iowa	High school teacher	13
39	Portland, Oreg.	PE teacher	
40	Germany	Teacher	9½
44	Denver, Colo.	Teacher	
24	Shelton, Wash.	Stenographer	2½
36	New York, N.Y.	Licensed marriage counselor	7 mos.
27	Oakland, Calif.	Doctor	

Approximately an equal number of the gay males were from metropolitan areas as were from "small" towns (see Table 1). I interviewed males who were born in the East, the Midwest, and on the West Coast. For the purposes of this report, the most obvious differences between the males born and raised in the small towns as opposed to those raised in metropolitan areas was that many of those raised in the small towns experienced more problems as teenagers since homosexuality was more socially unacceptable.

The occupations of the gay men varied. Some of the younger men were university students. Other occupations included student teacher at the elementary school level, actor, filmmaker, chemical engineer, employee for a railroad company, artist, telephone operator, electronics technician, clerk, factory worker, and author. The majority of the employers of the males did not know about their employee's sexual preference. None of the male couples seemed especially concerned about hiding their homosexuality, but they generally did not discuss it with heterosexual co-workers or bosses. The couples who felt they were able to reveal the fact that they were gay without losing their jobs had done so. As a matter of fact, two of the men, both actors, were in a play in which most of the actors were openly gay. The younger couples seemed much less concerned about hiding their homosexuality than did the older couples.

In contrast, most of the female couples I interviewed were over 30. Specifically, their ages ranged from 24/24 to 27/50. Again, the division between those born and raised in small towns and those born and raised in metropolitan areas was about equal. In addition, most of the female couples had professional careers and seemed to fit well into society. Six of the women, for example, were teachers at the high school level. These three couples were friends (and the first provided me the contact with the other two), having met through their teaching jobs. Both members of the fourth female couple, the 24- and 36-year-olds, had had a variety of jobs including their present employment as a stenographer and an answering service operator. None of the female couples were openly gay at work because of fear of losing their jobs. It should be pointed out, however, that I was unable to interview several of the younger, more radical female couples that I had initially contacted because they felt that as a male interviewer I could not objectively understand or report on their life-styles, beliefs, and feelings. This situation undoubtedly accounts for some of the differences found between the male and female couples. Nonetheless, age differences in both the male and female couples seem to have little relation to the attitudinal similarities between the members of the couples.

Of all the couples interviewed, only 2 (male couples) had met at places where most gay people go specifically for the purpose of finding a sexual partner. One of these couples had met in a park; the other couple had met at a gay bar. The remaining 13 couples had met on a more socially, less sexually oriented basis. For example, some of the places where they had met were: high school class; Gay Students' Union meeting; friend's home; gay liberation meeting; Metropolitan Community Church; acting in a play; and watching television at a student union. It would seem from the experiences of these couples that the social nature of these meeting places seems to indicate that although it is possible to meet a compatible partner at a bar or a park, it is more likely that compatible mates will be found where the first encounter is not a sexual one but rather a social one.

Most of the male couples had been together from 2 to 4 years, with the longest being 7. The female couples had been together from 7 months to 13 years, and had been together, on an average, longer than the males (see Table 1). There are at least two possible reasons for this. First of all, the particular females that were interviewed were generally older than the males and simply had had more adult years than the males in which to develop their relationships. Another possible reason is that female relationships in general may be longer-lived than comparable male relationships. Obviously, with a small sample such as this, a definite explanation of this phenomenon cannot be proposed.

SOCIAL INTERACTION IN AND OUT OF THE "MARRIAGE"

When I asked how many other couples the 15 interviewed couples knew, I got a wide range of answers. The majority of the males knew 5 to 10 couples, whereas most of the females knew 20 to 50 couples. The exception was 1 male couple who knew 100 to 200 other couples, as at least acquaintances, and approximately 50 of those as good friends. The men in this couple had done a good deal of acting in gay shows and had met many couples through their work. The women, nevertheless, knew more couples than did the men. This may be due to the fact that a single individual is more likely to seek single friends than "married" friends, and since the female couples had generally been together longer, they probably had been seeking "married" friends longer.

When asked if most of the friends of each couple were homosexual or heterosexual, the majority of couples said that their friends were mixed, but added that their closer friends were definitely gay.

The percentages that males gave concerning the number of their friends who had at one time or another entered into a gay marriage varied. (Gay marriage used in this context was defined to mean two gay males or females who feel a sexual and emotional bond between themselves that they intend to last permanently.) Responses from 60% of the male couples indicated that from 20% to 50% of their friends had entered into a gay marriage; the remaining male couples said about 95%. Many of the males who gave the lower figures felt that more of their friends had not entered into such relationships because they were still young and not ready for a permanent, long-term relationship.

The females all claimed that 80% to 100% of their female friends had been in a gay marriage at one time or another, or still were. Two couples said, however, that they believed that of their male friends only about 25% had at one time been in a gay marriage situation.

The question of whether or not monogamy is necessary or desirable in a marriage relationship was one on which I received a great deal of disagreement among the couples (although the two members of each couple generally agreed with each other, as they did in their responses to most of the other questions). The question of monogamy is probably more likely to come up in a homosexual relationship than in a heterosexual one because homosexuals have no model to imitate as do heterosexuals. Further, the socialization process does not teach what a good gay marriage should be like as it does with heterosexual marriages. Some gay people use the heterosexual model and remain monogamous; some are influenced by religious doctrines and remain monogamous; and others simply do whatever works best for their particular relationships. There were basically three different views expressed on the monogamy question. All of the female couples felt that monogamy was very desirable in a gay relationship. One member of a female couple said that her relationship with her lover was constantly growing and that they were building and sharing a life together in which monogamy was an essential part. Another female couple felt that women's relationships need monogamy more than men's do because women are more jealous than men. The other couples did not distinguish between male and female couples when answering the monogamy question. Four of the male couples expressed the opinion that monogamy was very necessary in keeping their relationship together, though most agreed that monogamy was fine for those couples who want or need it, but undesirable and sometimes disastrous for others. Three of the male couples felt that monogamy was boring and disastrous for all relationships. One of these couples said, "We treasure each other's freedom." Two of the male couples discussed the importance of a "basic monogamy." For one of these couples, this meant that as a rule, if they had sex with another person, they did so as a trio. Another couple, also using the term "basic monogamy," said that once in a great while one or both members of the couple could have a sexual one-night stand with another person. However, one member of this male couple quickly added, "But I would sure be mad if I got syphilis after he had an affair!" There was no correlation between the age of the members of the couples and whether or not they were monogamous.

MARRIAGES AND CHILDREN

I asked all the couples if they would like to have children. I also asked what they thought of the idea of using a friend of the opposite sex to have a wanted child. About half of the male couples said they would like to have children; however, most of them said that they would like to wait until they were older and more economically stable. One male thought that he would like to adopt a child later in life out of a feeling of responsibility to help those who are in need. The males who did not want children offered various reasons: one member of a couple did not like children; both members of a couple had enough of children all day while student teaching in an elementary school; and another couple simply did not want the responsibility. A majority of the males felt that it was all right for a gay person to use a member of the opposite sex to have children as long as both parties had a clear understanding of the situation. Several couples did not approve of the idea, feeling that there was enough of a population problem in the world and that people should adopt children. One male supposed that if a woman wanted a child, it was all right for her to use a male friend, but if a male wanted a child, it would not be fair to the woman involved because she would be risking her life by giving birth.

In contrast, none of the five female couples I interviewed wanted children. Two female couples said that they would not want the responsibility of a child and it would not be fair to the child because he or she would have too many problems trying to adjust to gay parents in our society. Two other couples said that they did not have enough patience with children and that they would not want the responsibility, and the fifth couple said that they simply did not like children. Four out of the five female couples felt that using a person of the opposite sex was all right, providing both parties were agreeable and understood the situation. One of these four, however, felt that adoption was a better way of getting a child. The fifth female couple thought that having a child by using a person of the opposite sex was immoral.

I asked the platonic marriage question in two ways: (a) what the couples' opinions were of a relationship where a gay man and a heterosexual or gay woman marry because they are fond of each other although not sexually attracted, and (b) what they thought of such an arrangement for the purpose of putting up a social front in order to keep a job or for some other sociopolitical reason. Twelve of the couples felt that if a man and a woman wanted to marry for either companionship or social acceptance it was all right. The other three couples felt that, on the one hand, it was all right, but at the same time it was giving in to an oppressive society at the expense of one's own happiness, and, therefore, not very desirable. One of the males said that no one should get into such a situation because it is appeasing an oppressive society at one's own expense, and added that gay people must fight back at society, not appease it. Although several couples approved of convenience marriages, they thought that the marriage would be much more successful if it were entered into for companionship. One female felt that this sort of relationship could never work, regardless of the reason for its formation, because some vital elements necessary for a successful marriage would be absent.

When I asked what advantages heterosexual couples have that gay couples get cheated out of, all but one female couple, and ironically one that was having financial problems, said income tax benefits, referring to the fact that they could not file joint tax forms. Another equally stressed disadvantage was that of not being socially accepted. Four couples mentioned, for example, that they could not show their affection in public because of social pressures and acceptance. Other disadvantages that were brought up included: not receiving religious recognition; having to lead a double life for the sake of keeping a job; having problems getting home insurance; not having job security; problems getting joint charge accounts; and problems getting through United States customs (declaring common purchases).

MALE VERSUS FEMALE "MARRIAGES"

Of the 15 couples intervewed, 14 believed that women's relationships last longer. The exception (a monogamous female couple) thought that it was "up for grabs" although both believed that a male's physiology makes him more inclined to be promiscuous and to have more one-night stands. When asked why female relationships last longer, I got a number of different responses. Several couples said that there is less pressure from society on two females who live together than there is on two males in the same situation. They believed that society can much more easily accept the idea of two, older female "roommates" than they can the idea of two older male "roommates." Another reason given by three couples was that they felt that women have a greater need to settle down with another person than men do. Some of the couples believed that this was due to the way females are raised and taught to think in our society, whereas others felt that it was more of an inborn trait, or perhaps a combination of both. The members of one monogamous female couple said that women are more faithful to each other, and therefore it is less likely that another person could come into the relationship and break it up. One of the younger male couples felt that women are much more interested in an emotional, less physical relationship than men are and, therefore, are less likely to view each other as sexual objects, and more as whole human beings. There was an agreement among several of the younger male couples, and one member of a female couple, that with women's liberation becoming stronger, women will no longer be forced into feeling that their place is in the home and that they must settle down into a marriage. Instead, they will become more equal to men in their social roles, and as a result the number of gay female marriages will equalize with the number of male marriages.

The 15 couples gave a broad range of answers to the question of what percentages of all gay people they believed enter into gay marriages at one time or another. The male couples gave estimates of 50% to 90%, with the majority of estimates being between 75% and 90%. Most of the female couples, on the other hand, gave percentages in the 90s, with one exception. This female couple thought 30% was a more realistic estimate. Another female couple felt that most gay women enter into gay marriages, and that only about 25% of gay males do so. After I asked what percentage of gay people enter into gay marriage relationships, I asked why the percentage was high, if a high figure was given, or why more gay people did not enter into such relationships, if a low figure was given. The couples who believed that most gay people enter into gay marriages at one time or another felt so because, first of all, people want security, and secondly, they want to try it to see if it is preferable to a single life. When asked why more gay people do not enter into gay marriages, two couples thought that the pressures against such a relationship in our society are so great that many gay people decide not to face them and so do not attempt long-term relationships. Both members of one male couple, which was monogamous, believed that most people are too promiscuous for such a relationship. Two people further pointed out that coupled relationships are very difficult to form whether they be of a homosexual or heterosexual nature. In comparison, one of the female couples, the most religious of all the couples (and one that had gone through the Metropolitan Community Church marriage ceremony), claimed that more gay coupling does not occur simply because many people do not have faith in God. One of the younger male couples felt that younger gays are looking for new life-styles and rejecting the idea of living with one person in a marriage-type relationship.

ROLE PLAYING

When questioned about the prevalence of role playing in gay marriages, including their own, 14 of the 15 couples felt either that the dominant-submissive, "butch-femme," role playing is not and never has been adhered to or that it used to be in some cases but is no longer customary. One of the female couples, on the other hand, felt that role playing can still be found in 90% of gay marriages, including their own. Both of them added, however, that if the role playing were extreme, a relationship would probably not last. Most of the couples agreed that whenever two people have any kind of relationship, there is usually one personality that is more outgoing or more prominent, but that this "dominance" certainly does not necessarily indicate that one partner plays the masculine, or butch, role while the other plays the submissive, or femme, role. In fact, many couples agreed that there is probably more of an equality between the partners in homosexual couples than in heterosexual couples because homosexuals are not forced into the kinds of roles to which many heterosexuals feel bound. When I asked the older couples who play butch-femme roles if they were simply "aping" heterosexual relationships, 5 of the couples felt that they definitely were, whereas the others felt that it was not a matter of copying heterosexual relationships but rather was due to individual personality traits that seem masculine or feminine. One woman mentioned that she did not believe that even all heterosexuals followed this dominant-submissive model and used the henpecked husband/dominant wife as an extreme example of some heterosexual couples' relationships.

All the couples claimed that they themselves did not have any butch-femme roles in their relationships – that, in fact, they shared household tasks and definitely did not sexually imitate conventional heterosexual roles.

ELEMENTS OF A SUCCESSFUL "MARRIAGE"

Most of the couples claimed they were very happy with their relationships. All the women described their relationships as "very wonderful" or "very good," and one female couple, both members being teachers, said, "You can give us an A!" Another female couple said that their relationship had been wonderful, but that it had been rough because of financial problems. Likewise, most of the male couples also described their relationships as "excellent," "fantastic," and "fun," although others said things like "It's had its ups and downs," "We've gone through a lot of different stages," and "The good has outweighed the bad." All the couples admitted having had problems at one time or another, but most of them expressed great satisfaction with their relationships.

When asked about what could possibly break up their relationships, about one-third of the couples answered "nothing," some of them adding that because they had gone through so much already (usually outside pressures from society and family), they were strong enough to take anything. Three of the couples, however, said that perhaps a third person could break up the relationship, and the older man of the 34/48-year-old couple said that perhaps a younger man could break up his relationship someday. Juxtaposed with this couple was another male couple who insisted that the only way a third person could break them up would be if they did not all get along. They left open the possibility of someday becoming a trio, saying that they know of some "trio marriages" that work very well. One of the female couples, the one that had had financial problems, said that perhaps serious enough financial problems could break them up. All expressed hopes that their relationships would last, and, in general, the majority of the couples seemed stable and happy.

Fifty-five percent of the men and 70% of the women had been in previous gay marriages. The longest of these marriages was a male marriage that had lasted 11 years and had ended with the other man's death. The shortest (also a male couple) had lasted 3 months and had ended because the two men found that they did not have enough common interests. Some of the reasons the women gave for the breakup of their previous gay marriages were: the other woman returned to a former male lover; they did not have enough in common; they were incompatible; one woman tried to put the other into an unwanted role; the other woman (a devout Catholic) had problems of conscience over being homosexual; both were too young and did not know what they were getting into; the other woman had a drinking problem; and the other woman returned to a younger former lover. In contrast, some of the reasons men gave for the breakup of their previous gay marriages were: they "drifted apart"; they were not honest with each other and had melodramatic fights; one member left for a younger man; they disagreed over the issue of monogamy; they were socially incompatible; there were too many pressures from society; and they failed to communicate. Most of the reasons given by both the men and the women had to do with the fact that the partners were not socially compatible, they did not have enough common interests, or one of them felt that she/he could be happier with someone else. It should be emphasized, however, that these are all reasons that could break up any marriage relationship, homosexual or heterosexual.

One of the males and one of the females I interviewed had been heterosexually married. Both of them had broken up their marriages because of "physical and social incompatibility." Some of the other people I interviewed, both male and female, had been engaged but had never married.

There was almost complete agreement on the factors that are necessary in the making of a successful marriage. These included: understanding, love, mutual interests, caring, communication, honesty, openness, lack of extreme possessiveness, integrity, sensitivity, mutual respect, accenting and building on a partner's strengths and playing down his or her weaknesses, tolerance, sharing, being direct, and having faith in one another. The only point that was disputed was that of monogamy. Almost all of the couples mentioned that the same factors keep both gay and straight couples together or break them apart.

CONCLUSIONS

Based on the responses given by the 15 couples interviewed, there seem to be several patterns common to almost all the relationships. All but 1 of the couples indicated that their relationships were free from a stereotypical kind of role playing or aping of heterosexual roles sometimes associated with gay couples. They all agreed that there has been a trend in recent years away from this sort of role playing. It should also be noted that in recent years, with the advancement of the women's movement, the traditional role playing in heterosexual marriages has also begun to break down. There have been many parallels between the women's movement and the gay liberation movement, and this is perhaps one of them.

Almost all of the couples that I interviewed had met in more of a social setting than a sexual one. Two people must be compatible in a social, nonsexual way as well as on a physical sexual level for a happy, long-term marriage relationship. Gay people are beginning to form more social groups that operate out in the open within society. This, perhaps, will facilitate the forming of more long-term gay marriages.

On the question of monogamous relationships it seems that monogamy was desirable, and indeed necessary, for some of the relationships involved in this study, whereas it could possibly be fatal for others. As to be expected, there was a great variance of opinion on this issue. Again, there is a close parallel between the opinions of these couples and heterosexual couples in our society. The question of monogamy has become one that has generated a great deal of controversy and debate, especially in the past few years.

Although there seem to be many stable gay relationships, some never last past the first week or month. Social incompatibility accounts for many of these failures, but social pressures are to blame for a large number of others. Society's intolerance of homosexuals has caused many problems for gay people. It is responsible for the isolation and loneliness felt by some, and the anger and militancy felt by others.

As noted above, some interesting patterns common to all or most of the gay couples in this study have become evident. This study brings up some questions that require further, more sophisticated research: Are the common patterns seen in these couples common to all gay couples? Are they common to heterosexual couples as well? In what ways do society's pressures affect gay marriages? What percentage of the total gay population is coupled in long-term relationships? Are female gay marriages more successful than male gay marriages? If so, why? A great deal may be learned about homosexual coupling as well as heterosexual coupling if we investigate the subject of gay marriages.

APPENDIX A
Interview Questions

Biographical data: age, place of birth, occupation.

Where and how did you meet? How long have you been together?

How many other gay couples do you know? Are most of your friends straight or gay? What percentage of your gay friends would you say are or have been in a gay "marriage"?

Do male or female "marriages" last longer? Why? What percentage of all gay people do you think at one time or another enter into gay "marriages"? Why not more (or why so many, depending on the response)? What are some of the advantages that heterosexual couples have that gay couples get cheated out of?

Have you been in any previous gay "marriages"? How long did it (they) last? What caused it (them) to break up? Were you ever married heterosexually? If so, for how long? What caused the marriage to break up?

Would you have children if you could? What do you think of the idea of using a friend of the opposite sex in order to have a child?

In your gay "marriage" as well as others, do you think that one partner is generally dominant and the other submissive? Is there any role playing?

What is your opinion of so-called platonic or convenience marriages, usually between a homosexual man and a heterosexual woman or a homosexual man and a homosexual woman?

Do you feel that monogamy is necessary and/or desirable in a gay "marriage"?

Would you say that your "marriage" has been good? Do you think it will last? What, if anything, could cause your "marriage" to break up?

What advice would you give to gay couples? What helps to make a gay couple successful? Any other questions or comments?

Men Who Advertise for Sex

Malcolm E. Lumby, PhD
Alhambra, CA

> "CALIFORNIA KID!" . . . is back 'n' purring to perfection. My sleek and undented frame is in A-1 shape and my super-delux shifter is fully in gear. Call Skip, the exceptionally young kid at . . .
>
> TO A VERY SPECIAL YNG GUY. If you are sincere, honest & loving (like me) and want a decent, caring friend, write . . . My aim is happiness for both of us. I'm educated, discreet & stable. Beginner o.k. No dopers, please.
>
> DETROIT SEEKS LOVER/FRIENDS. Am tired of 1 night games. Sincere, sensitive, oversexed guy desires to meet same. Am vers, wl/blt, W/m, 29. No fats, fems, S&M.

Men all over American are advertising for sex. "Hot," "handsome," and "well-endowed" homosexuals – if their self-descriptions are to be believed – from Los Angeles to New York City are selling their sexual services or just giving them away. To learn about the special interest, whereabouts, and personal descriptions of homosexual men who advertise in a national gay newspaper, this researcher conducted a content analysis of 1,111 classified advertisements appearing in the *Advocate*, a biweekly gay newspaper with a circulation of 57,000 (Ayer, 1977).

In addition to reporting the gay scene on a national basis, the *Advocate* includes an extensive classified advertising supplement called "Trader Dick." The supplement provides a forum for men who advertise for business partners, erotic toys and literature, as well as sex, companionship, and love. (Although the *Advocate* has a

"Trader Dick" section for women, very few of them take advantage of the opportunity to advertise. For example, in the February 22, 1978 issue, only two ads for women appeared in the 32-page supplement, now called the "Second Section.")

Lee (1976) has already analyzed 240 "Personals" ads in the *Advocate* and described dominant characteristics of sought-for partners (exclusive of sadomasochistic appeals). The present paper, on the other hand, delineates advertisers' self-descriptions.

The study is important because the advertisements were written by homosexuals themselves, reflecting their particular sexual concerns, interests, and values. By tabulating their dominant interests, one is able to draw advertiser profiles and to note those values emphasized most frequently and those of little overall import.

METHOD

Two 1976 issues of the *Advocate* were selected at random and each word categorized to identify 17 dominant themes in the "Models, Masseurs, and Escorts" (MME) and "Personals" (PER) portions of the "Trader Dick" supplement. Categories were determined in a pilot study of *Advocate* advertisements. The frequency of each word was recorded and tabulated by percentage as reported in Table 1. Reliability was established by two coders who independently rated a data sample. A composite reliability coefficient of .89 was achieved between raters (Holsti, 1969).

FINDINGS

Within the *advertiser seeks/provides* category—as stated in a headline or first sentence—281 (62%) of 450 MME mentioned escort, masseur, or model services, presumably provided in return for a financial consideration; another 165 (37%) included stated or implied sexual services; and 4 others (1%) offered sexually oriented objects for sale. In the PER group, on the other hand, 8 (1%) of 661 offered to serve as escorts, masseurs, or models, whereas 384 (58%) included direct sexual invitations. Unlike MME, 142 (22%) PER advertisers sought lovers, 29 (4%) pen pals, 13 (2%) missing

TABLE 1

Percentage of Male Sex Ads Containing 17 Categories

Item	MME (n = 450)	PER (n = 661)
Advertiser seeks/provides	100	100
Means of contact	100	100
Location	100	100
Name	66	49
Age	50	64
Appearance	50	23
Adjectives, nouns, and verbs	48	32
Body	47	25
Penis	33	8
Height	33	37
Weight	28	32
Hair	25	14
Sexual interests	18	35
Occupation	14	12
Race/nationality	12	42
Eyes	11	8
Rejected	2	20

friends or lovers, 13 (2%) slaves or guinea pigs, and 72 (11%) business opportunities, invitations to see Accu-Jac (electric masturbation device) demonstrations, and the sale of books, films, and photographs. These findings are itemized in Table 2.

As for *location*, 637 (57%) of the advertisers were in California, 217 (20%) in New York, 235 (21%) in all other states, and 22 (2%) in foreign lands. When breaking down the results by categories it is

TABLE 2

Advertiser Seeks/Provides

Item	MME (n = 450)	%	PER (n = 661)	%
Escort/model/masseur	281	62	8	1
Sex	165	37	384	58
Lover			142	22
Friends, pen pals			29	4
Seek missing friends			13	2
Slaves/guinea pigs			13	2
Miscellaneous	4	1	72	11

notable that only 8% of MME were from states other than California and New York, whereas 21% of PER were located in other states.

The *means of contact* for 444 (99%) of MME was by telephone. Of those listing their *names* 275 (93%) gave first names and 22 (7%) last names. Only 207 (31%) PER preferred telephone calls, leaving 454 (69%) to list addresses, mostly post office boxes. Of PER, 184 (57%) listed a first name and 98 (31%) first and last, leaving 40 (12%) to use initials or pseudonyms such a "Euripides," "Master Butch," and "Graphic Guy."

Fifty percent (n = 225) of all MME ads mentioned both *age* and *appearance*. The mean MME age was 24.7, mode and median 23, with a range of 18 to 51. Two others listed themselves as "mature," whereas 81 said they were "young."

Of those MME describing physical appearances, 149 (41%) characterized themselves as attractive (good/nice looking or handsome). Another 149 (41%) used strikingly masculine terms of self-description, including "all-man," "butch," "humpy," "hunky," "jock," "manly," "rugged," or "straight acting/looking." Only 25 (7%) categorized themselves as adonis, that is "beautiful," "cute," "gorgeous," "pretty," or "striking." Twenty-eight (8%) claimed to be sexy and 7 (3%) average.

In contradistinction to the above, 64% of PER advertisers listed their ages, and 149 (23%) used a total of 275 words to describe their appearances. The 420 PER ranged in age from 18 to 40, with a mean of 32.6 and both median and mode of 28, constituting the older of the two groups. Nine individuals identified themselves as "mature" and 21 as "young." Nevertheless, 133 (48%) described themselves as attractive, 109 (40%) masculine, 9 (3%) adonis, 7 (3%) sexy, and 17 (6%) average.

The latter five appearance categories were suggested by word groupings derived from a perusal of pilot study data. This section includes only those words directly related to physical appearance and does not include words listed in the following section where grammatical terms are itemized.

Adjectives, nouns and verbs were used by many advertisers to describe themselves. For example, 278 (48%) MME used such words, whereas only 276 (32%) PER used them. Sixty-eight percent of the MME words were sensual, including "hot," "horny," "mouthwatering," and "potent." Among these, 72 said they were "versatile" and 24 "discreet." Only 94 (34%) PER used sensual words. Stability and dependability were mentioned in 42 (15%) of MME ads containing nouns, adjectives, and verbs, but 96 (35%) PER emphasized them. Seventy-four (27%) PER also placed emphasis on tender and loving qualities by using such words as "compassionate," "considerate," "harmonious," "mellow," "pleasing," and "nice." MME referred to these characteristics only 40 (14%) times. Words suggesting extroversion were used by 3% and 4% of MME and PER, respectively. Included were words such as "dynamic," "energetic," and "outgoing."

MME (47%) placed considerably more emphasis on their *bodies* than did PER (25%). Fifty percent of the 213 MME specified body build as important, with "defined," "firm," "muscular," and "well built" being most often mentioned; 35 of them gave exact measurements, such as "chest, 55″, arms 21″, waist 31″, hgt. 6′3″, wht 250#." Sixteen percent used miscellaneous terms to describe themselves, such as "hairy," "smooth," or "tan," and another 16% emphasized body size. Twelve percent said they had the athletic bodies of dancers, gymnasts, or surfers, and 6% characterized their bodies as "beautiful," "first-class," or "super." Of the 165 PER who described their bodies, 42% emphasized size, primarily on being sleek, slim, slender, or medium, with a few "chubbies," for added measure. Another 31% concerned themselves with build – muscularity definition, and firmness being relevant concepts. Twelve percent were athletic, 9% used adjectives for build descriptions, and only 6% used miscellaneous terms.

There were 147 (33%) MME ads containing references to advertisers' *penises* (see Table 3). Of these, 108 (74%) described themselves as "ample," "real (very) well endowed," or "hung nice(ly)." Another 32 (22%) used extravagant terms to characterize their endowments as "exceptional," "huge," "super," or "thick and meaty." Two (1%) listed actual sizes, such as 8″ or 10″, and 5 (3%) identified themselves as "cut" (circumcised) or "uncut" (uncircumcised). In contrast, only 50 (8%) PER referred to their genitals. Of these, 32 (64%) were in the endowed/hung category, 5 (10%) very large, 6 (12%) circumcised or not, and 1 (2%) listed length. Unlike MME, 6 (12%) said they were "average," "not too hung," "small," or "unendowed."

Height, weight, hair, and *eyes* were described by advertisers in descending order of frequency. The 149 (33%) MME and 247 (37%) PER had nearly identical height distributions: range 5′2″ to 6′6″, mean 5′10″, mode and median 6′. Likewise, the 128 (28%) MME and 213 (32%) PER listed similar weight distributions: range

TABLE 3

Penis Size Described

Item	MME (n = 147)	%	PER (n = 50)	%
Endowed/hung	108	74	32	64
Exceptional size	32	22	5	10
Size given	2	1	1	2
Cut/uncut	5	3	6	12
Average			6	12

110-260 lbs., mean 162 lbs., mode and median 165 lbs. Hair was important enough to be mentioned by 113 (25%) MME and 94 (14) PER. About two-thirds of references in both groups were to color (most being blond or brown) or description (big mustache, short beard, etc.). With regard to eyes, 48 (11%) MME and 56 (8%) PER listed eye color. Blue was listed about 50% of the time, with brown, hazel, and green in descending percentages.

Table 4 indicates specific *sexual interests* listed by 81 (18%) MME and 231 (35%) PER. The MME ads mentioned 110 interests, 53 (48%) of which were categorized as sadomasochistic; the PER ads listed 416 sexual preferences, 161 (38%) of which fall into this category. The terms usually were abbreviated as S&M (sadomasochism), B&D (bondage and domination), FF (fist fucking), w/s (water sports – urinating on a person), along with scat (excrement) and spanking.

Clothing and intimate apparel were mentioned by 29 (26%) MME, and most references were to boots, leather, and Levis. Seventy-two (17%) PER included the apparel mentioned above plus military and police uniforms; bras, spike heels, and garter belts; braces, crutches, and belts; nylon, rubber, and plastic shorts.

Sexual roles were indicated in 20 (18%) of the 110 MME references and in 96 (23%) of 416 PER listings. These were in two groups: French (oral copulation) or Greek (anal copulation) and active or passive. For example, some said they were French active, Greek passive, and/or combinations thereof. Others called themselves top or bottom men. A miscellaneous group of 5 (5%) MME and 76 (19%) PER sought dirty talk, enemas, group sex, nipple action, nudism, shaving the body, super fatties, transsexuals, transvestites, verbal abuse, voyeurism, uncut (uncircumcised) penises, dirty (unwashed) scenes, and chicken (males under the age of consent). (In terms of these data, more PER advertisers sought transvestite or transsexual lovers [$n = 4$] than adolescent boys [$n = 2$].) Finally, a number of objects or areas of activity were identified: Accu-Jac demonstrations, game rooms, toys (dildos), Crisco, grease, or oil.

Occupations were listed by 64 (14%) MME and 82 (12%) PER, but the distributions differed between groups. Ninety-one percent of MME who listed occupations claimed to be college athletes, stu-

TABLE 4

Sexual Interests of Advertisers

Item	MME (n = 81)	%	PER (n = 231)	%
Sadomasochism	53	48	161	38
Clothing, intimate apparel	29	26	72	17
Sexual roles	20	18	96	23
Miscellaneous	5	5	76	19
Objects	3	3	11	3
Total	110	100	416	100

dents, or graduates, whereas PER listed themselves as business or professional men 45% of the time, with another 45% identified as athletes or students. An assortment of miscellaneous professions completed the remaining percentages in both groups.

A strikingly unequal distribution was found when considering *race* or *nationality*. Only 42 (12%) MME mentioned such matters, whereas 278 (42%) PER identified their races or those of persons sought (87% listed Caucasian).

The final notable distinction between groups was in the *rejected* category. Only 9 (2%) MME mentioned things they would refuse to do, but 134 (20%) PER noted 295 unacceptable activities or person types, often listing them in clusters. One in five PER rejected S&M, B&D, FF, pain and punishment, scat, or hard leather scenes. "Fems" and "fat" were rejected by 17% and 19%, respectively; 14% outlawed drugs or dopers; 12%, bars, baths, one-nighters, or hustlers; and 11%, miscellaneous (e.g., beards, Blacks, drinkers, smokers, emotion).

DISCUSSION

In discussing the foregoing results, it must be emphasized that this study deals only with homosexual men who advertise for sex. No effort is made to generalize these findings to the much larger population of homosexual men. Nevertheless, advertiser profiles prove interesting in terms of their similarities and differences.

Most models, masseurs, and escorts offer to provide their sexual services, by implication, for money, with most arrangements being made by telephone. First names are often listed, putting conversations on a more personal basis. Thus, these advertisers provide immediacy of contact on a first-name basis. Prospective customers are verbally screened.

In describing themselves, the Caucasian males in their mid-20s place great importance on appearance and youthfulness. The athletic males primarily reside in major American cities, and they are exceedingly masculine – if their reports are accurate. Although their descriptions are elaborate and sensual with considerable emphasis on their penises, advertisers avoid mentioning specific sexual interests. Likewise, they seldom reject specific behaviors, mentioning their versatility instead.

Given the large number of classified advertisements placed in the *Advocate* by homosexual men professing to be models, masseurs, and escorts, one is prompted to inquire about the implied values of those who respond to these fantasy profiles. Respondents apparently seek a pleasing sexual experience with a young, handsome, sexually talented man with a large penis. Value is placed on a short-term relationship, and the customer is willing to pay for what he hopes will be a glamorous product.

Ads in the *Advocate*'s "Personals" section, on the other hand, are not placed there by big-city hustlers only. Advertisers are more widely dispersed nationally and prefer to be contacted by letter. As a group, they are more cautious in granting access to themselves by using mailing addresses, especially post office boxes. Thus, they limit the likelihood that an unexpected visitor will arrive at a socially inconvenient time and reduce the risk of revealing their sexual orientation to heterosexual friends and business associates.

Being Caucasian is important to the majority of these attractive, slim, and masculine males in their mid-30s. One in five seeks personal friends or lovers, but most want sex partners. Many provide elaborate descriptions of their sexual interests and what they will not do.

The striking emphasis on masculinity in both groups is noteworthy, since it contradicts the stereotyped picture of the homosexual male. Traits and descriptions characterized as feminine are seldom mentioned, and "fems" are among the frequently rejected individuals. Further, the rarity of advertisers seeking adolescent sex partners (2 in 1,111 ads) stands in striking contrast to the accusation that homosexuals actively recruit children. What does stand out in this analysis is the homosexual male emphasis on youthfulness, manliness, and a striking physical appearance.

Sadomasochistic ads in this study are often detailed and creative, as exemplified by the following example: "DEFINITION PLUS! 170 lbs, 47*PRL0* c, 27*PRL0* w, blue eyes, brown hair, long tongue, deep throat, long legs. Into everything, hopefully you. I turn on to leather, crotchworn Levis, scat, w/s, FF, S&M & anything you can think of. Weekly medical insp for your and my safety. Call me! I'm hot, horny & ready to?"

Overall, 86 (8%) of 1,111 advertisers mentioned some form of sadomasochism. Kinsey, Pomeroy, and Martin (1948) found that 20% of men were aroused by sadomasochistic fantasies, with the Playboy Foundation reporting 22%. However, only 3% in the *Playboy* sample reported S&M experiences, often in a minor way (Hunt, 1974). The percentage of advertisers mentioning S&M here is 5% higher, perhaps because men with specialized sexual interest find it difficult to locate others with similar tastes and turn to publications, such as the *Advocate*, as a convenient means of making contacts.

One of this project's shortcomings was a failure to tabulate the numerous interests of advertisers in the "Personals" section. That information would have been useful in that some observers say that homosexuals, as a group, have about as much in common as cigarette smokers and coffee drinkers. Many "Personals" advertisers, however (unlike models, masseurs, and escorts willing to travel—for a price), itemized a plethora of artistic, cultural, recreational, religious, and social activities of interest to them. Thus, they attempted to communicate with those having common values in addition to their shared sexual orientation. Future research in this medium might verify this observation.

Although this content analysis describes men who advertise for sex, and Lee (1976) identified sought-for characteristics, little is known about the people who answer classified ads.

For comparative purposes, it would be more useful to study personal classified advertisements placed in newspapers or magazines by homosexual and heterosexual men. Such a research project could reveal that homosexual men, when describing themselves, are more explicit and detailed than heterosexual men.

REFERENCES

Ayer directory of publications. Philadelphia: Ayer Press, 1977.

Holsti, O. *Content analysis for the social sciences and humanities*. Reading, Mass.: Addison-Wesley, 1969.

Hunt, M. Sexual behavior in the 1970's: Deviant behavior. *Playboy*, 1974, *21*, 54-55.

Kinsey, A., Pomeroy, W., & Martin, C. *Sexual behavior in the human male*. Philadelphia: W. B. Saunders, 1948.

Lee, J. A. Forbidden colors of love: Patterns of gay love and gay liberation. *Journal of Homosexuality*, 1976, *1*(4), 401-418.

Media Mating I: Newspaper "Personals" Ads of Homosexual Men

Mary Riege Laner, PhD
G. W. Levi Kamel, PhD
Arizona State University

Bargaining and the exchange of assets—the so-called marketplace mentality—have long been part of the courtship and mate selection process (Cameron, Oskamp, & Sparks, 1977). Negotiations include institutionalized considerations of potential profit for the self, as well as the expectancy that another will enter into the relationship if she/he also perceives it as potentially profitable (Bredemeyer & Toby, 1960). In Cameron et al.'s (1977) study, newspaper advertisements for heterosexual partners conformed to predictions derived from an exchange theory model. These researchers studied solicitations for dates and mates in one issue of what they called the West's largest "respectable" newspaper for heterosexual singles, the *Singles News Register*. In the main, all of the hypotheses of their study, derived from exchange theory, were supported. The authors also concluded that stereotyped sex role characteristics continue to be valued commodities in these heterosexual ads.

Although Cameron and her co-researchers noted that other publications feature what they call "sexually aberrant ads" (i.e., ads for homosexual dates and/or mates), their study did not include an analysis of these. Lee (1976), however, has reported an analysis of gay male ads in three randomly selected issues of a widely circulated gay newspaper. He developed a typology of five styles of loving relationships to gay men (eros, ludus, storge, mania, and pragma), and while noting the difficulty of classifying advertisements by love style (as well as difficulties of interpreting the shifting homosexual argot), Lee classified the ads he studied according to regularly recurring characteristics mentioned, broadly relating desired characteristics of partners to his typology of love styles. (In a study of male/female differences in conceptualizing "love," Hatkoff & Lasswell, Note 1, who used Lee's five types of love to categorize their respondents, found that, supported by traditional sex role socialization, males in general were significantly more likely to define love in ludic [playful] and erotic [romantic] terms, whereas women were significantly more likely to have storgic [friendship], manic [dependent], and pragmatic [sensible] definitions of love.) Lee's (1976) study of male homosexual ads was not tied in with any theory that might have predicted the characteristic patterns found in his data. For that reason, and because Lee's study excluded some advertisements from his sample as irrelevant to his purposes, we undertook to make a content analysis of the "Personals" advertisements of male homosexuals, utilizing an exchange theory perspective to formulate hypotheses about the nature of the advertisements as they might differ from those of heterosexuals' personal ads.

RESEARCH METHOD AND HYPOTHESES

Following the pattern of Cameron et al. (1977), the research method employed was a content analysis of all personal ads (n = 359) appearing in the "Trader Dick" (classified advertisements) section of the *Advocate*, a gay newspaper that originates in California but has wide national and some international circulation. (This newspaper was also the source of the advertisements analyzed by Lee, 1976. However, Lee excluded both sadomasochistic ads and sexual-service ads, whereas we included all personal ads except those in which someone was seeking to find a former, that is, already known, partner. We utilized the most recent issue available at the time of the start of this study [February 1977]).

Based on exchange theory (see Blau, 1964; Homans, 1961; Thibaut & Kelley, 1959), our first hypothesis was the same as that tested by Cameron et al. (1977):

1. Socially desirable appearance and personality characteristics will be emphasized in the ads, and negative characteristics will be minimized.

The original hypothesis tested by Cameron et al. (1977) used the term "physical" rather than "appearance." However, there is some difficulty with understanding what characteristics they considered to be physical and what ones to be appearance related. We took physical indicators to be such specifics as age, height, weight, hair and eye color, body type, and race. We considered appearance indicators to be those that are evaluative, such as handsome, masculine, Ivy League type.

Cameron and her co-investigators formulated and tested two additional hypotheses derived from exchange theory, dealing with expected differences between heterosexual men and women advertisers; however, these hypotheses were inappropriate for present purposes. Instead, based on the notion of "supranormalcy" of homosexuals, as advanced by Freedman (1975) and others (e.g., Clark, 1975; Hooker, 1957; Horstman, 1972), claiming that homosexuals are more frank, candid, and honest in their interpersonal relationships than are their heterosexual counterparts, we developed an additional hypothesis regarding differences between male homosexuals and male and female heterosexuals:

2. Homosexual males, as compared with heterosexual males and females, will more frequently state explicit goals for their desired relationships.

The basis for our third hypothesis is suggested by Lee (1976) and Humphreys (1972). Lee reported that among the characteristics of the male homosexual ads he studied, he frequently found either the claim of or the request for a partner with a "straight appearance." Lee attributed this both to the stigma attached to homosexual unions and to the increasing "virilization" of the homosexual subculture (see Humphreys, 1972; Lee, 1976, p. 410). Beyond the claim of or request for a straight appearance, we expected that although similar characteristics would be stated by male homosexual and male and female heterosexual advertisers—with the exception of "preferred sex role," which is implied by gender in heterosexual advertisements (Lee, 1976, p. 410)—"virilization" would be indicated by the finding that male homosexuals' emphases on specific characteristics differ from those of male heterosexuals *opposite to* the divergences between heterosexual males and females. At the least, we would expect that there would be statistically significant differences between proportions of male homosexuals and female heterosexuals in terms of claimed and desired characteristics. Simply stated, our third hypothesis was:

3. Homosexual males' advertisements will show evidence of virilization. We expected to find not only the differences indicated above but also claims of or requests for masculinity, in one form or another, in support of our third hypothesis.

RESULTS

Table 1 presents a summary of characteristics mentioned in the personal advertisements (with the exception of preferred sex role or activity, which will be discussed separately). As with heterosexual advertisers, the greatest emphasis was on *physical* characteristics,

TABLE 1

Percentage of Advertisers Mentioning Various Types of Characteristics of Self (Claimed) and of Prospective Partners (Desired)

<table>
<tr><th></th><th colspan="2">Male Homosexuals (n = 359)</th><th colspan="2">Male Heterosexuals (n = 192)</th><th colspan="2">Female Heterosexuals (n = 155)</th></tr>
<tr><th>Characteristics</th><th>% Claimed</th><th>% Desired</th><th>% Claimed</th><th>% Desired</th><th>% Claimed</th><th>% Desired</th></tr>
<tr><td>Personality</td><td>28</td><td>32</td><td>57</td><td>60</td><td>73</td><td>72</td></tr>
<tr><td>Physical traits</td><td>70</td><td>50</td><td>97</td><td>75</td><td>97</td><td>67</td></tr>
<tr><td>Goal for relationship</td><td colspan="2">-- 94 --</td><td colspan="2">-- 61 --</td><td colspan="2">-- 56 --</td></tr>
<tr><td>Recreation/interests</td><td>45</td><td>24</td><td>56</td><td>39</td><td>62</td><td>45</td></tr>
<tr><td>Appearance</td><td>37</td><td>25</td><td>35</td><td>38</td><td>67</td><td>12</td></tr>
<tr><td>Education</td><td>5</td><td>3</td><td>16</td><td>5</td><td>8</td><td>9</td></tr>
<tr><td>Occupation</td><td>13</td><td>4</td><td>46</td><td>3</td><td>20</td><td>24</td></tr>
<tr><td>Financial status</td><td>3</td><td>1</td><td>19</td><td>4</td><td>10</td><td>16</td></tr>
</table>

Note: Heterosexual data are taken from Cameron, Oskamp, and Sparks (1977, p.29). Between male and female heterosexuals, all percentage differences were statistically significant beyond $p < .05$, except for recreation/interests claimed and desired (both ns), physical traits claimed, education desired, and goal for relationship (all ns). Between male homo- and heterosexuals, all percentage differences were statistically significant beyond $p < .05$ except for appearance claimed (ns), and education, occupation, and financial status desired (all ns).

although the percentage claiming and desiring specific physical characteristics was lower ($p < .01$) for homosexual men than for heterosexual men or women. *Personality* qualities, both claimed and desired, which were next most often mentioned by heterosexual women and less frequently mentioned by heterosexual men ($p < .01$ for percentage claiming, and $p < .02$ for percentage desiring), were far less often mentioned by homosexual men ($p < .01$ for all comparisons). *Goals for the relationship* were stated by a majority of all advertisers; however, far more homosexual men than either heterosexual men or women stated specific goals ($p < .01$). Heterosexual men and women did not differ in the proportions claiming or desiring *recreational or other interests*, but fewer homosexual men than heterosexual men specified their own interests ($p < .02$) or specified desired interests in a potential partner ($p < .01$). Differences between homosexual men and heterosexual women were also found ($p < .01$ for both claimed and desired). *Appearance* qualities claimed were about the same for homo- and heterosexual men. However, considerably fewer homo- than heterosexual men stated specifics of appearance desired in a prospective partner ($p < .01$). (One-third of the homosexual advertisers requested a photograph from respondents; unfortunately, we have no comparative data regarding heterosexuals.) Appearance qualities were claimed by far fewer homosexual men than heterosexual women ($p < .01$), and although only a minority of each of these groups stated specific desires for the appearance of a prospective partner, twice as many homosexual men as heterosexual women did so ($p < .01$). *Education, occupation,* and *financial status* received mention, either in terms of claiming or desiring them, from only a minority of all advertisers. Homosexual and heterosexual men did not differ in terms of proportions specifying desires for these characteristics in a prospective partner, but fewer of the homo- than heterosexual men claimed any of these three characteristics ($p < .01$ in all cases). No difference was found between homosexual men and heterosexual women in terms of educational status claimed. However, fewer homosexual men than heterosexual women specified their own occupations ($p < .05$) or their financial status ($p < .01$), and for all three socioeconomic status characteristics, fewer homosexual men than heterosexual women specified their desires in a prospective partner ($p < .01$ for each of the three).

Our first prediction was that socially desirable appearance and personality characteristics would be emphasized in male homosexuals' advertisements, and that negative characteristics would be minimized. All personality terms that could be found in Anderson's (1968) list of likeableness ratings were scored. (Only about half of the personality terms encountered in the ads appeared in Anderson's list. However, with the aid of a thesaurus and a dictionary, we were able to locate synonyms for almost all other personality terms, and to score those on the basis of Anderson's likeableness rating scale. The remainder were terms like "cool" and "groovy.") We found that 23% of the terms scored were strongly favorable (e.g., sincere, honest, mature)–above 5.0 on a 0-6 scale; 42% were moderately favorable (e.g., levelheaded, energetic, generous)–above 4.0; and 21% were below the 3.0 neutral point (e.g., passive, shy, tough). Given that a total of 65% of the personality terms were either moderately or strongly favorable, our first prediction is supported by this finding.

Interestingly, these ratings are not as overwhelmingly favorable as those found by Cameron et al. (1977) using the same likeableness rating scale, who report that 48% of the heterosexuals' personality characteristics claimed were strongly favorable, 38% were moderately favorable, and only 7% fell below the neutral point. Cameron and her associates, however, note that "the Letters to the Editor columns of [heterosexually oriented] singles papers are often focused on the problem of exaggerated self-descriptions in personal ads" (p. 29). Thus, it is tempting to infer that the differences between homo and heterosexuals' personality claims support the notion of greater candor, honesty, and frankness among homosexuals mentioned above.

Recalling that appearance characteristics were also predicted to be favorable, we found that every appearance characteristic claimed also appeared in the list of desired characteristics. Table 2 presents all appearance qualities claimed and desired. Thus, we conclude, in support of our first hypothesis, as predicted by exchange theory, that all appearance characteristics were favorable. (Although it may

TABLE 2

Appearance Characteristics Claimed and Desired by Male Homosexual Advertisers

Characteristics	Claimed	Desired
Masculine (including butch and virile)	26	24
and beautiful or handsome	2	2
and good looking or very good looking	9	3
and "foxy," above average looking, or attractive	9	4
and "not fem" and good looking	--	1
and straight looking or "not fem"	--	6
Straight looking (including "no fems")	4	5
and attractive	1	--
and clean cut	1	1
and average looking	1	--
No fems	--	7
and handsome	--	1
Clean cut	1	2
and good looking or above average looking	2	--
Jr. Executive type	1	--
Ivy League type and good looking	1	--
Beautiful or beautiful and earthy looking	1	2
Handsome, very handsome, super looking, or exotic	12	2
Great looking, very good looking, good looking	31	16
Highly attractive, attractive, "very foxy," foxy looking, cute	23	9
Nice looking, above average looking, modestly attractive, not bad looking	9	--
Fem	--	2
and good looking	--	1
Other	--	1
Total	134	89

be argued that the number of ads that specified "no fats" indicates fatness to be a negative quality, those who desired "no fats" constituted only about 6% of the advertisers. Further, the fact that "fat" people were also mentioned as desirable by some, and not mentioned as undesirable by the vast majority, allowed us to assume that fatness is not necessarily a negative attribute.) Cameron et al.

(1977) report that among the homosexuals in their study, 85% of the appearance traits mentioned were positive, and only 3% for men and 6% for women were negative. These researchers did not indicate how they evaluated appearance characteristics, nor could we locate any external criterion by which to judge them.

Additionally, as with heterosexuals, all male homosexuals who mentioned their own educational level mentioned it favorably (e.g., educated; high IQ). About three-fourths of those who gave their occupation claimed to be professionals or businessmen, paralleling the finding for heterosexuals. Similarly, financial status, when claimed, also paralleled the favorable descriptions given by heterosexuals in that 81% of the homosexual advertisers who mentioned their own financial status claimed to be secure (e.g., wealthy, rich, successful).

Our second hypothesis predicted that homosexual males, as compared with heterosexuals of either gender, would more frequently state explicit goals for the relationships they sought through their advertisements. As seen in Table 1, 94% of the homosexual males did "set the stage for interaction rewarding to themselves" (Cameron et al., 1977) by explicitly mentioning the goal of the desired relationship. Heterosexual men and women far less often specified their desired goals, and the differences between proportions of male homosexuals and heterosexuals of either gender who specified their desired goals were statistically significant beyond the .01 level of confidence in the predicted direction, supporting our second hypothesis (and also supporting the attempt to maximize "profit," as exchange theory would predict). The specific goals for the desired relationships of homosexual advertisers differed greatly from those of both male and female heterosexual advertisers, and provide further explanation for the differences in response distributions between male homosexuals and heterosexuals of both genders. These goals will be discussed later.

Our third hypothesis, based on the notion of virilization among homosexual males, predicted differences between homosexual and heterosexual male advertisers, in a direction opposite to that of differences between heterosexual males and females—or at least statistically significant differences in proportions of respondents within categories. Inspection of the data presented in Table 2 lends partial support to this hypothesis. Forty-three percent of the advertisers claimed some form of stereotypically masculine attributes (e.g., masculine, straight-looking, Jr. Executive type), and 63% desired the same masculine attributes in a partner.

Table 3 presents a partial list of physical specifications claimed, desired, and not desired by homosexual advertisers. The remainder of the physical specifications mentioned were these: 48% of the

TABLE 3

Partial List of Physical Characteristics Claimed, Desired, and Not Desired by Homosexual Advertisers

Characteristics	Claimed	Desired	Not Desired
Body Types			
1. Rugged; hunky; husky; big; strong; very strong	7	10	--
2. Muscular; well defined; solid; hard; athletic/gym body; good or great body; nice build; firm; trim; tight body; swimmer's build	46	47	--
3. Lean, slim or slender body	23	24	--
4. Average or medium build or body	4	3	--
5. Skinny, thin, short, or small body	--	4	--
6. Chubby, fat, or heavy body	4	4	21
7. Miscellaneous body concerns[a]	15	9	--
Sexual specifications			
1. Penis size[b] or type (e.g., circumcised; not circumsised)	27	30	--
2. Other sexual specifications	3	1	--
Other Physical Concerns			
1. Looks younger than actual age	3	1	--
2. Physical qualities are not important	--	5	--
Total	132	138	21

[a]Miscellaneous concerns were: youthful, boyish, or "sexy" body; soft body; complexion type and health considerations; and other measurements (e.g., waist, arms, chest).

[b]An exhaustive list of the qualitative descriptions in this category follows: superhung; well hung; superendowed; horse hung; exceptionally hung; heavy hung; ample endowment; well endowed; heavily endowed; thickly endowed; thick and big; hung.

male homosexual advertisers stated either their own height and/or weight, the desired height and/or weight of the sought-for partner, or both; 70% stated their own age, the age of the partner they desired, or both; race (or ethnicity or nationality) was mentioned by 57% of the advertisers, the great majority of whom were Caucasians searching for other Caucasions; finally, 16% mentioned their own hair or eye color, those desired in a prospective partner, or both, and 17% referred to their own hirsuteness (or lack of it), that desired in their partner (or not desired), or both.

Of body types claimed, 54% were stereotypically masculine (e.g., rugged, very strong, athletic/gym body), as were 56% of those desired, lending support to the assertion that male homosexuals tend toward what has been called virilization. The frequency and type of specifications claimed and desired with regard to penis size also support the notion that male homosexuals have a great deal invested in their maleness (see *Medical Aspects of Human Sexuality*, 1974, p. 53).

The most direct support for our third hypothesis lies in the divergence between directions of homosexual male and heterosexual female proportionate responses within categories, compared with the proportionate responses of heterosexual males. Tests for the significance of differences between percentages were carried out on the data shown in Table 1. (Davies', 1962, method for assessing the significance of differences between percentages was utilized to compute significance levels throughout.) We found that all but one of the differences between percentages claiming or desiring specifics between homosexual men and heterosexual women were statistically significant (the exception being claimed level of education); further, all but claims for occupation ($p < .05$) were statistically significant beyond the .01 level of confidence. Specifically:

1. Personality claims and desires were higher for heterosexual women than for heterosexual men, but lower for homosexual men.
2. Physical specifications claimed and desired were lower for heterosexual women than for heterosexual men, but significantly lower for homosexual men.

3. Goals for the relationship were mentioned about as often by heterosexual women as by heterosexual men, but far more often by homosexual men.
4. Recreational and other interests did not differentiate between heterosexual men and women, but those claimed and desired by homosexual men were significantly fewer than in either heterosexual case.
5. Homosexual and heterosexual men claimed appearance qualities about equally often, but heterosexual women claimed them significantly more often than either group of males. Appearance characteristics desired by heterosexual women were significantly lower than those mentiond by heterosexual men, but more than twice as many homosexual men as heterosexual women stated their desires for the appearance qualities of a sought-for partner.
6. In terms of education, heterosexual women and men did not differ in terms of their desires, but heterosexual women claimed educational characteristics significantly less often than did heterosexual men. Homosexual men did not differ from heterosexual women in terms of claimed educational characteristics (although they claimed them significantly less often than did heterosexual men). The proportion of homosexual men stating desired educational characteristics did not differ from the proportion of heterosexual men; however, only one-third as many homosexual men as heterosexual women stated desired educational characteristics.
7. Occupational claims were significantly lower for homosexual men than for heterosexuals of either gender. Occupational desires did not differentiate between hetero- and homosexual men, but the proportion of homosexual men stating an occupational preference in their partner was significantly lower than the proportion of heterosexual women, whose occupational desires in a partner were, in turn, significantly higher in proportion to those expressed by heterosexual men.
8. Although both heterosexual women and homosexual men claimed financial status significantly less often than did heterosexual men, desires for a partner's financial status were expressed significantly less often by homosexual men than by

heterosexual women. Further, desires for a partner's financial status did not differentiate between homo- and heterosexual men.

In summary of these findings in support of our third hypothesis, out of 15 possible categories (7 categories with 2 subcases, claimed and desired, each, and 1 undifferentiated category), homosexual men showed statistically significant differences from heterosexual men on 11 out of the 15, at or beyond the .05 level of confidence; and homosexual men showed statistically significant differences from heterosexual women on 14 of the 15 categories, largely beyond the .01 level of confidence. Further, the direction of the differences was as predicted, divergent for homosexual men and heterosexual women in 11 of the 15 possibilities.

Goals for Relationships, Recreational and Other Interests, and Preferred Sex Role or Activity

Cameron et al. (1977) found that male and female heterosexual advertisers did not differ in terms of goals specified for the desired relationship. About one-third of them were marriage-minded, almost one-third specified a meaningful relationship, and the remainder were interested in companionship or dating. Male homosexuals' ads showed a markedly different pattern. Advertisements fell into five distinct categories. Permanent relationships were sought in 8% of the cases—which may be considered the counterpart to the heterosexuals' marriage-minded advertisements (Loney, 1972)—and such ads were of the following type: "W/m—35, 168#, blond, muscular, 30″w, gdlkg, hung. If you're 25-33, gdlkng, hairy, sinc., loyal and seeking perm relationship, write w/photo to . . . "

The argot used in these advertisements is sometimes unintelligible to the "uninitiated" and occasionally unintelligible to and even misused by those familiar with the homosexual subculture (see Andreas, Franzini, & Linton, 1974). As Lee (1976, p. 407) pointed out, abbreviated messages are typical, due to line, rather than word, rates in the *Advocate*. The advertisements we present here for illustrative purposes are more likely to be intelligible than many, with the possible exception of "Fr. a/p, Gr. act," which indicates that the writer both gives and receives oral/genital sex, and prefers to be the inserter, rather than the insertee, in acts of anal intercourse.

A second category of advertisements sought meaningful relationships (30%), that is, a companion, pal, or friend, and the following advertisement is illustrative: "I'M A BEAUTIFUL GUY–GRAD STUDENT into various sports, music, arts, fitness, 5'9", 160, lt br/blue. Never part of bar or bath scene. Seek sim type athletic buddy, sim age, 18-27, prefer blond guy into outdoors and loyal friendship. I can relocate. Please send photo."

The largest proportion of advertisements were for a sexual relationship (47%), as in the following typical ad: "BASKET HAPPY! Well hung W/m into skin-tight faded Levis and corduroy. Fr. a/p, Gr. act. Reply (photo a must) to . . . " (Relationships per se were unspecified in an actual total of 13% of the advertisements. However, more than half of this group stated either their preferred sex role or activity or that desired in a partner. Thus, although the goal for the relationship was not explicitly stated, these advertisers indicated implicitly that a sexual relationship was wanted. Such ads, then, were added to the group of sexual relationship ads, leaving a residual of 6% of the total number in the unspecified group.)

Some form of exchange characterized 9% of the advertisements, such as the following: "SKI BUDDY WANTED FOR ASPEN W/M. Wk late Feb. Transp/lodge paid for fun masc guy. Write . . . "

The smallest proportion of advertisements, 6%, left the goal for the relationship unspecified, as in the following example: "W/m–20, br, bl eyes, 6', 150 goodlooking–looking for someone 18-25 in Washington DC area but will answer all. Photo given priority." Within this group of advertisements, there were 14 placed by couples, that is, two men advertising for a third or for another couple.

The preponderance of advertisements specifying a sexual relationship may leave the impression of wantonness or promiscuity, but it is also possible to see the tendency of the homosexual men to be explicit about sex in another light. A sexual relationship is possible, of course, in any encounter, heterosexual or homosexual, regardless of goals specified in personal advertisements. It may be that homosexual males are simply more open and explicit about a topic that heterosexuals tend to gloss over. Further evidence for this explicitness is found in the statements of recreational or other interests made by male homosexual advertisers. For both claimed and desired interests, specifications tended to fall into one of three groups: (a) those who mentioned their sexual interests only (49% of those claimed and 39% of those desired); (b) nonsexual interests only, such as hiking or movies) (41% of those claimed, 52% of those desired); and, less frequently, (c) a combination of sexual and nonsexual recreational and other interests (10% of those claimed and 9% of those desired).

Lee's (1976) typological study of male homosexuals' advertisements suggested that among homosexuals "the search for a suitable mate becomes that for a partner with an appropriate love style" (p. 403). As noted earlier, gender implies preferred sex role or activity for heterosexuals (although the implication may be inaccurate for any particular pair), but among homosexuals such matters must be made specific in advance, or a rewarding encounter is less likely. Yet the majority of advertisements (almost 67%) stated no preference for any special sex role or activity, and an additional 3.5% either stated that the advertiser was "versatile" sexually or specified that the desired partner must be versatile, or both. Dominant/submissive relationships were specified in about 15% of the ads, and of the remainder (about 15%), sex *role* was left unspecified, but preferred sexual *activity* was mentioned, for self or other or both. These findings suggest that rigidity of sex role (e.g., dominant/submissive) is uncharacteristic of the vast majority of homosexual male advertisers, but that sexual activity type (i.e., love style) is of somewhat greater concern. Two French passives, for example, are unlikely to find themselves compatible; similarly, one who is interested only in mutual masturbation would prefer not to be contacted by a potential partner who characterizes himself as "Greek active only."

These data confirm the suggestion of Freedman (1975, p. 30) who holds that sex role dichotomies are not as important to homosexuals as to heterosexuals, and that the gay life leads to a high degree of honesty and straightforwardness in terms of making the social arrangements that lead to interpersonal relationships. Further, as Lee (1976) has noted, "there is now a positive emphasis on sex (one or several encounters) as a legitimate and desirable part of the process of becoming better acquainted'' (p. 413). Finally, combining sexual explicitness with the proportions seeking permanent and/or meaningful relationships affirms that homosexual males, like heterosexual males, tend to ludic (playful)/erotic (romantic) in orientation (Hatkoff & Lasswell, Note 1).

The advertisements of the ''men's men'' we have studied and reported here lead to an additional conclusion that helps to explain the many statistically significant differences between homosexual males and heterosexual of either gender (but especially heterosexual women); namely, it is more important, among homosexual males, to make explicit at the outset what one wants, looks like, and does (sexually) than to specify other qualities or characteristics (such as personality traits or nonsexual interests) since, once a sexually compatible partner has been located, personality traits will become evident and recreational or other interests can be negotiated. Speculatively, heterosexuals who tend to disguise their sexual interests or preferred sexual activities (and even, sometimes, their preferred sex roles) might take a cue from the frankness of the homosexuals we have studied. Should they do this, which is highly unlikely in the foreseeable future, it might be that fewer heterosexual pairs would find themselves seeking counseling or other help for sexual incompatibilities after a relationship negotiated on the basis of other criteria is already developed.

CONCLUSIONS

Content analysis of 359 male homosexual personal advertisements, and comparison of the findings with those of 192 male heterosexual and 155 female heterosexual advertisers, was carried out within a pattern of eight common themes—personality, physical attributes, goals for relationship, recreational and other interests, appearance, education, occupation, and financial status (Cameron et al., 1977). It was predicted, in accordance with exchange theory, that homosexual male advertisers would, like their heterosexual counterparts, present themselves to advantage in their ads in an attempt to maximize rewards in any ensuing relationship. It was also hypothesized that goals for the relationships sought would be specified significantly more often by homosexuals than by their heterosexual counterparts, based on the assumption of greater candor and honesty among homosexuals, and (again according to exchange theory) in an effort to set the stage for a self-rewarding interaction. Finally, on the basis of the assumption of a tendency toward virilization among homosexual males, it was hypothesized that the advertisements of male homosexuals would differ more from the specifications found in the ads of female heterosexuals than from those found in male heterosexual ads, tending to emphasize one or another form of masculinity. (Masculinity, as used here, indicates "normative masculinity" of one type or another, and not the exaggerated "supermasculinity" such as might be found in a leather-and-chains subculture.) Each of these hypotheses was supported.

Finally, we found that homosexual male advertisers were more open and specific about the sexual nature of the relationships they sought, and although only a small minority stated specific sex *role* requirements, advertisers often made a note of the type of sexual *activity* in which they had interest. These findings are explained on the basis of the need of same-sex persons to be "up front" about such matters, which are typically taken for granted (with or without cause) in heterosexual pairings, rather than to indicate mere wantonness among homosexuals, as is sometimes attributed to them.

REFERENCE NOTE

1. Hatkoff, T. S., & Lasswell, T. E. *Male/female similarities and differences in conceptualizing love*. Paper presented at the meeting of the National Council on Family Relations, New York, October 1976.

REFERENCES

Anderson, N. H. Likeableness ratings of 555 personality-trait words. *Journal of Personality and Social Psychology*, 1968, *9*, 272-279.

Andreas, V. R., Franzini, L., & Linton, M. A comparison of homosexual and heterosexual response to the Menninger Word Association Test. *Journal of Clinical Psychology*, 1974, *30*, 205-207.

Blau, P. *Exchange and power in social life.* New York: Wiley, 1964.

Bredemeyer, H., & Toby, J. *Social problems in America.* New York: Wiley, 1960.

Cameron, C., Oskamp, S., & Sparks, W. Courtship American Style: Newspaper ads. *Family Coordinator*, 1977, *26*, 27-30.

Clark, T. Homosexuality and psychopathology in nonpatient males. *American Journal of Psychoanalysis*, 1975, *35*, 163-168.

Davies, V. *A rapid method for determining the significance of differences between two percentages* (Rev. ed.). Pullman, Wash.: Institute of Agricultural Sciences, 1962.

Freedman, M. Far from illness, homosexuals may be healthier than straights. *Psychology Today*, 1975, *8*, 30-31.

Homans, G. *Social behavior: Its elementary forms.* New York: Harcourt, 1961.

Hooker, E. The adjustment of the male overt homosexual. *Journal of Projective Techniques*, 1957, *21*, 18-31.

Horstman, W. *Homosexuality and psychopathology*. Unpublished doctoral dissertation, University of Oregon, 1972.

Humphreys, L. New styles in homosexual manliness. In J. McCaffrey (Ed.), *The homosexual dialectic*. New York: Prentice-Hall, 1972.

Lee, J. A. Forbidden colors of love: Patterns of gay love and gay liberation. *Journal of Homosexuality*, 1976, *1*, 401-418.

Loney, J. Background factors, sexual experiences, and attitudes toward treatment in two "normal" homosexual samples. *Journal of Consulting and Clinical Psychology*, 1972, *38*, 57-65.

Medical aspects of human sexuality. August 1974.

Thibaut, J., & Kelley, H. *The social psychology of groups.* New York: Wiley, 1959.

III. WHOM TO CHOOSE AS A LOVER

The question of where you look for a lover is inextricably involved with the question of whom you find desirable. The individuality, even the irrationality, of need and desire is impossible to catalogue. Choosing a lover, as the articles in this section suggest, seems at least to involve physical attraction, personality traits (liking the person for himself), and sharing moral values (e.g., trust, loyalty). The priority individuals assign to these categories is highly varied. Some rare people, for example, rank moral values and personality above physical attraction. As the relationship unfolds, there can be shifts among categories. When we say that beauty is only skin deep, we imply that a relationship requires more than a handsome appearance and generous genital endowment. But without those initial enticements, some relationships would never have gotten started.

The not insignificant part that physical attraction plays in the choice of lovers is an underlying theme in the articles in this section. Paul Sergios and James Cody, sampling participants in the public, gay social life of Los Angeles, found that men expected partners to be more physically attractive than themselves. Such attraction increased "liking" and led to dates. As patrons of gay bars know, in the sometimes grim competition for foxy-looking men, some individuals try to make up in social aggressiveness for what they believe they lack in physical attractiveness. The authors have an interesting revelation about the effectiveness of that strategy. They also deal with *the* burning issue pertaining to physical attractiveness: Does it lead to long-term relationships?

Physical attraction, it might appear for many individuals, is tied to femaleness and maleness in the way that Freud believed anatomy was destiny. First you ascertain whether you like men or women (or both) and then you look for particular men or particular women. As Gisela Kaplan and Lesley Rogers argue, doing that may be putting the cart before the horse or, more precisely, giving more importance to the genitalia than to the person. Also, as they suggest, assigning priority to biology may more accurately describe what we have done in the past in pursuing partners than what we are likely to do now and in the future. At an unconscious level, where it is possible to distinguish men to whom we are actually attracted from men whom we are cruelly fated to pursue, we may discover that we are drawn to those who are not paragons of unblemished masculinity. Instead, those individuals we find irresistibly intriguing may represent unique amalgams of physical and psychological femininity and masculinity, what the authors call *androgyny.*

Age is a crucial ingredient of sexual attraction and in the choice of partners for enduring relationships. Until the last two centuries in western history, affluent parents often unilaterally arranged the marriages of young daughters to older men who had the financial means or civic stature to promise a materially secure family life. The extra-marital lovers chosen by these future husbands were often still younger than their wives. In ancient Greece they were often adolescent boys or girls. The tradition of the man marrying a slighter younger woman persists today. However, when the ages of partners are widely separated, there is now the lingering suspicion that the husband will tyrannize over the wife (or younger partner, who could be the husband).

With social egalitarianism as an ideal of the 18th century Enlightenment, the approximate equality in the ages of marital partners became a normative guarantee that husband and wife would share the power to make decisions. It was blithely assumed, however, that this power would be exercised within a rigidly defined feminine role for the woman that did not tread upon masculine prerogatives. It is in the latter part of our century that there has been the widespread expectation of women that there be a single standard of equality that extends to all areas of marital decision-making.

The idea that equality of age leads to equality of power has become a normative requirement in gay relationships, as we see in the article by Joseph Harry. There are still exceptions: Very young gay men may still seek older partners and older gay men younger ones. By calling this requirement "age egalitarianism," Harry shows that it is related to a burning issue in gay relationships, that lovers avoid the trap of playing husband and wife, the feminine role assigned solely to one partner, the masculine to the other, with power concentrated in the hands of the would-be "husband."

The quest for lovers, either of the same or opposite sexes, involves an ingenious combination of deceptive public relations and searching for someone you can like, respect, and trust. Mary Laner found that two sets of traits are exhibited in this quest, the "attraction traits" and what she calls "companionship traits." Such attributes as good looks, a sense of humor, and money attract partners in the competitive social market, but it takes more than these (she lists particular companionship traits) to be able to live together in a relationship that has a future. The artful intermingling of surface and substance in the courtship process, Laner shows, often leads to considerable misperception of prospective partners.

Importance of Physical Attractiveness and Social Assertiveness Skills in Male Homosexual Dating Behavior and Partner Selection

Paul Sergios
James Cody
Los Angeles

We all grew up in a society that offered competing messages about beauty and physical attractiveness. On the one hand, our elders preached: "Beauty is only skin deep and mostly in the eye of the beholder." Simultaneously, we were exposed to advertising that reinforced ideal male caricatures, great looks and sleek physiques. For homosexual men, the double binding dissonance is further complicated. While their heterosexual counterparts enjoy a wide diversity of environments in which to initiate relationships, homosexuals are still limited in their choice of settings. The importance of physical attractiveness seems to become even more relevant when homosexuals consider that in being socialized as males, they are taught to compete and openly display their masculinity. Somehow, though, they know the importance of beauty is in fact a compromise between the two extremes. And yet many homosexuals find themselves competing for male "trophy beauties" and feeling rejected if *they* themselves are not beautiful enough. Objectively, is it possible to determine to what extent "beauty is only skin deep" in contemporary homosexual culture and to what degree it may be in the eyes of the *beheld*? More importantly, is there a way to determine how significant physical attractiveness is in contributing to the initiation and perpetuation of dating behavior and relationship formation among homosexual men?

Walster, Berscheid and Dion (1966) evaluated a sample of heterosexual college students on the dimension of physical attractiveness by having a panel of four confederates rate each student on a 1-8 scale. The students were randomly matched in pairs and then sent on a staged "computer dance date" the following weekend. Immediately after this two-hour interaction, subjects indicated how much they liked their matched partner. The experiment showed that in heterosexual dyads, the most important determinant of a person's like for his or her date in a simulated computer dating situation was the date's physical attractiveness.

Using a similar design, Berscheid (1973) later found that males' and females' levels of dating aspiration are not affected by their perception of their own attractiveness. Individuals who are fully aware of their own inadequacies on the "physical attractiveness hierarchy" prefer social contact with those persons *more*, but not less, attractive than themselves. This fails to support Lewin's "level of aspiration" hypothesis (1944) that one's realistic social choices should be less socially desirable than one's fantasy choices due to the competition involved in gaining such a potential romance partner.

In a self-critique of her own work, Walster (1971) writes that if her subjects had been older than 18 years of age, had been given more than 2-1/2 hours to get acquainted, and had met in a more conventional single dating setting, rather than in groups, other variables besides physical attractiveness might have had a greater effect on the subjects' liking and further dating behavior. It is important to note, however, that youth, limited time periods for partner selection, and group partner selection setting (e.g., bars and discos) are all factors male homosexuals commonly deal with in dating and courtship situations. Although several studies have replicated Walster's findings within the heterosexual culture (Byrne et al., 1971), none have been attempted with male homosexual dyads.

Walster also offers specific criticism about the use of computer dating methodology. Walster noted that in the environment of the manufactured "computer date," individuals may not be affected by whether or not their dates like them because the dates are so polite that is impossible for the individual to know if he or she is accepted or rejected. Such misperceptions may be less likely to occur in an actual disco and bar setting, as Walster points out, since partners are not "required" to remain in a specific pair, but may instead choose their prospective partner and more easily express rejection.

Walster also considered such variables as assertiveness and self-esteem as influential factors on liking among heterosexuals. In measuring self-esteem and assertiveness, Walster asked her subjects how popular they considered themselves within groups of both sexes, how easy it was for them to get a date with a very attractive counterpart, and how many dates they had experienced in the past year. Walster also obtained a measure of the subject's intelligence, nervousness, fear of rejection, and emotional involvement in social situations. The results showed no direct correlation between these measures and the subject's self-esteem or their expressed preferences in partner selection and subsequent dating behavior. Walster concluded that, regardless of the subject's own assertiveness and attractiveness, the largest determinant of how much a partner was liked and how much a subject wished to date the partner again was the partner's *physical attractiveness.*

Focusing on the attractiveness variable, Hagen and Symons (1979) found that there is one group of men who are exceptionally concerned with their facial looks and bodily appearance: homosexual men. Fully half of the homosexual men surveyed had below average images of their looks and bodies while only one-tenth of the heterosexual subjects held such a perception. The researchers suggested that homosexual men exist in a sub-culture with higher standards for attractiveness and that they assess themselves based on this standard.

The importance of physical attractiveness may also extend to long-range relationship formation among homosexual men. Clark (1977) suggested that when choosing lovers, many homosexual men have been programmed to be attracted to a limited variety of body types, and to place the standard of "body beauty" above all others. Through informal interviews, Clark found that intense competitive mechanisms have been internalized by some homosexuals as a function of their being socialized as males. These mechanisms, according to Clark, affect partner selection in longer term relation ships; a homosexual man is apt to pursue avidly a male more physically attractive than himself because he has learned to desire such a symbol of attractiveness.

Based on Walster and Byrne's findings, the present study hypothesized that among male homosexuals, physical attractiveness would prove to have more influence on liking and dating behavior than either the independent effects of social assertiveness skills or the combined effects of attraction and assertiveness. It is proposed that a homosexual man will be more likely to pursue both an immediate short-time and long-range relationship when he is matched with a partner on the basis of physical attractiveness and not social assertiveness.

These specific predictions were examined. First, an individual who is either high or low in physical attractiveness would expect a date to be as attractive or more attractive than himself. Second, an individual would *express the most liking* for a partner who had a high physical attractiveness, regardless of the individual's own physical attractiveness. Third, an individual's level of social assertiveness would not be expected to affect significantly his liking of his matched partner nor to interact with physical attractiveness to produce liking.

The design of the experiment permitted us to examine the effects of physical attractiveness and social assertiveness on long-term liking. However, because of the small number of subjects who actually experienced a subsequent date with their matched partner in an eight-week follow-up, it was not possible to confirm or disprove a formal hypothesis on long-term liking. It was our supposition that all of the predictions offered for short-term liking may also be extended to long-term follow-ups of dating behavior.

METHOD

On the basis of an assertiveness questionnaire and physical attractiveness rating, homosexual men were matched with particular partners and required to spend two hours interacting with that person in a gay disco. After this interaction period, participants rated their reactions to their date, and to the experience. Eight weeks later, participants were contacted by telephone to determine whether they had had further contact with their assigned partner or with anyone else from the dance.

DESCRIPTION OF VARIABLES

The variable of "social assertiveness skills" was assessed through a questionnaire which measured specific personality traits that prior researchers have found seem to predict success in dating and courtship settings. Traits included introversion and extroversion, self-esteem, and personal initiative. The variable of physical attractiveness was assessed based on assistants' ratings of each subject's appearance.

A one-factor, 16-level design was used; the one independent variable manipulated was the degree of matching partners on physical attractiveness and assertiveness. Physical attractiveness and social assertiveness were assumed to be independent of each other. A subject who fell in the top 40% of scores on physical attractiveness was considered a "high attractive" while a subject who fell in the bottom 40% was considered "low attractive." The middle 20% of scores were considered intermediate values and subjects obtaining such scores were dropped from the study. A subject was assigned to one of *four* possible groups based on his own attractiveness and social assertiveness skill scores: (High-High/High-Low/LowHigh/Low-Low) with the first letter representing social assertiveness skills and the second physical attractiveness. . . .

Social Assertiveness Questionnaire

During the first phase of the study, subjects completed a 200-item questionnaire. Items were selected from diverse sources and were intended to provide an index of social assertiveness skills.

The questionnaire included items from Walster's experimental version. The subjects were asked how physically attractive, how personally attractive, and how considerate they expected their computer date to be. The subjects were also asked how popular they were among groups of both sexes, how easy it was to get a date with a very attractive counterpart, and how many dates they had experienced in the past year. Items from the Minnesota Multiphasic Personality Inventory (1982) inquired into the subjects' emotional involvement in social encounters. Finally, a fear of rejection scale dealt with the ability of the subjects to execute risk-taking behaviors in threatening social settings.

Sample

The sample consisted of 225 male homosexuals ranging in age from 21 to 35. Men were recruited from gay communities in the Los Angeles area. Advertisements and other promotional materials presented in the gay press described the "Computer Dating Study" as involving a "systems-based dating assignment process." Men who met the general requirements of being "between 21 and 35 years of age, not presently involved with a lover, and able and willing firmly to commit themselves to four hours of research" were encouraged to contact the experimenter by telephone. Over 300 calls were received. The researchers also visited numerous rap groups to publicize the study. Bar posters and windshield flyers were distributed twice weekly and the study was announced on a local gay radio program. Through this extensive effort, a cross section of homosexual males from varying economic backgrounds, ethnicities, and levels of education was obtained.

A pre-screening procedure insured that all subjects were complete strangers at the start of the study. Thus, although 225 completed the questionnaire during the study's first phase, 25 did not take part in the dance interaction because they knew other participants.

The experimenter ultimately used only those subjects with the most extreme scores on both the physical attraction and social assertiveness dimensions. One hundred additional subjects were dropped after the pre-test because they received "intermediate" test scores on one or both of the dimensions. Thus, 100 subjects actually participated in the pairing process and were invited to attend the afternoon tea dance.

Procedure

The experiment consisted of three main phases: pre-testing, the dance interaction, and the follow-up.

Pre-testing. Two-hundred-and-twenty-five 21-35 year-old males were pre-tested in a large classroom located in the L. A. Child Development Center Complex. Four homosexual male assistants were seated at a table as the subjects entered. The assistants helped the subjects fill out a brief data sheet and release form, and assigned each a numerical code. It was explained that to insure complete anonymity, the number represented the sole means of identifying the subjects once the study was in progress.

Surreptitiously, the four assistants rapidly and individually evaluated each man's physical attractiveness on an 8-point scale, going from 1 (''Extremely Unattractive'') to 8 (''Extremely Attractive'').

Once all the subjects were seated, the researcher gave a brief introduction explaining the background of the research and answered any questions or concerns the subjects expressed. After completing the questionnaire, subjects were told that based on their responses to the ''general information'' questions in the test packet, a computer would assign each with a partner from the group and the two would interact at an afternoon tea dance scheduled for the following weekend.

In actuality, the subjects were assigned to one of four classifications according to their responses in the social assertiveness questionnaire and, by their physical attractiveness ratings. As explained earlier, subjects were considered as high or low on these dimensions, based on their scores. Subjects were finally matched with a date similar or complementary to themselves on either variable of assertiveness or attractiveness; 10 possible dyad combinations resulted. (See design section.) Throughout the study, the subjects were unaware of this manipulation, thinking instead that they were matched based on their responses to the ''general information'' section of the questionnaire.

Before being dismissed from the pre-test, the subjects were told that they would meet their partner at the dance site on the following Saturday and would spend approximately two hours with *only* this person at the dance site.

During the week that elapsed between the pre-test and the dance, the experimenter carried out the pairings using all of the data provided. As mentioned earlier, all those subjects who fell within five points of either direction of the group mean in attractiveness or assertiveness (100 in all), were dropped from the study. These persons were called on Tuesday evening, thanked for their participation, and told a bogus story about the study's cancellation.

Dance interaction. Subjects began arriving at Flamingo's Disco in the Silverlake area of Los Angeles at 11:30 a.m. The experimenter took charge of placing the men into their assigned pairs by verbally calling out the code numbers and having each subject raise his hand to acknowledge his presence to his partner. Once the subjects were paired, they were sent inside the disco.

At approximately 1:45 p.m., the subjects were taken out of their dyads. Half remained in the disco and the second half were escorted to the outside patio area. At this point, each of the subjects was given a short questionnaire and asked to indicate their responses honestly and completely. The questions were designed to measure immediate liking, asking the subjects the following: (a) how much the subject liked his date; (b) how "physically" and "personally" attractive the date was perceived to be; (c) how similar the date's values, attitudes, and beliefs seemed to be with his partner's; (d) whether or not the subject would like to date his partner again; (e) the number of other men observed during the course of the dance; and (f) those specific personal and physical traits the subject found most attractive and unattractive in his matched partner. After completing the questionnaires, the subjects were thanked and told they could say good-bye to their dates before leaving; many of the subjects exchanged telephone numbers.

Follow-up. Eight weeks after the dance, subjects were called, thanked for their continued participation, and asked a few questions about their most recent involvement with their computer date. Each participant was also asked if he had become involved with any other member of the 100-person sample. The extent of the subjects' involvement was assessed, as well as those traits subjects found most attractive and unattractive in their matched date, traits which were not readily apparent at the tea dance.

RESULTS

Sample Description

Of the 100 subjects who participated in the afternoon tea dance, the range of physical attractiveness scores went from 1.7 to 7.8. The interrater reliability between the four confederates was .59. The mean of the attraction scores was 4.7. The range of the social assertiveness scores went from 244 to 353 on a 1-450 scale (with 450 representing the most assertive). The mean of the assertiveness scores was 298.

The 100 subjects who were dropped after the pre-test had scores that ranged from 4.0 to 5.0 on the physical attractiveness scale and scores that ranged from 293 to 303 on the social assertiveness scale. This cut-off allowed for a five-point margin on either side of the mean, eliminating those intermediate scores on both dimensions. Thus, subjects who received scores of 292 and below on the questionnaire were considered as "low" on the social assertiveness skills dimension, while subjects who scored 303 and higher were considered "high" on this trait. Subjects who received physical attractiveness ratings of 4.0 and below were considered "lows" on the attractiveness dimension; subjects with scores 5.0 and above were counted as "highs."

Short Term Impact of Attractiveness and Assertiveness

Date's expectation. It was predicted that very attractive subjects, as well as those who were not very attractive, would expect an acceptable date to be more physically attractive than themselves. During the pre-test, each subject was asked how physically attractive he expected his date to be. The correlation between a subject's physical attractiveness and total expectations in a date was .35. This small correlation suggests that subjects of all physical attractiveness rating groups expected their dates to be more attractive than the ratings would suggest they were themselves.

Attractiveness. The second hypothesis was that a subject would express the most liking for a partner more physically attractive than himself. An initial method of testing this hypothesis involved an examination of the mean differences in liking scores of subjects in several of the treatment groups.

A 30-point scale was used to measure liking (on the post-dance questionnaire), with 1 representing "Dislike Extremely" and 30 representing "Like Extremely." Differences in liking scores were determined by subtracting the higher liking score of one partner from the lower score of his counterpart.

As Table 1 illustrates, subjects who were similar in that they were both either high or low in attractiveness, manifested very level and equivalent differences in liking. Subjects matched on the basis of complementary attractiveness, by comparison, manifested more extreme differences in liking. Mean differences levels shot up from 2.0 and 3.0 to 5.2 and ultimately 15.5.

The most extreme example of this was evident in the High Assertiveness/Low Attractiveness matched with High Assertiveness/High Attractive group. Of these six pairs of subjects, 80% of the High Assertiveness/Low Attractive subjects expressed a greater degree of liking for their High Assertive/High Attractive counterpart than the High Assertive/High Attractive partner expressed for his High As-

Table 1

Mean Differences in Liking of Matched Dyads

Subjects who liked their date more	Subjects who liked their date less	Mean difference in liking	Range
HH	HH	2.0	18-21
LH	HH	2.0	20-21
LH	LH	3.0	17-23
HL	HL	3.0	15-23
LL	LL	3.0	15-20
HL	LL	3.5	13-23
LL	HH	4.4	17-26
HL	LH	5.2	10-21
LL	LH	6.2	12-25
HL	HH	15.5	8-28

First letter represents Social Assertiveness Skills (High/Low)

Second letter represents Physical Attractiveness (High/Low)

Differences in liking are based on a 30-point scale

sertive/Low Attractive date. In fact, a mean difference in liking for the highly attractive men amounted to 15.5 with a range in scores for 8 to 28. These last results were especially significant. In almost every single instance of the last four groupings in Table 1, the subject low in physical attractiveness liked his highly attractive date more than the highly attractive man liked his low attractive partner—regardless of the subject's social assertiveness level.

A separate 2 × 2 ANOVA was conducted for both attractiveness and assertiveness. The ANOVA showed that physical attractiveness was significant. $F(3,28) = 7.574$ $p \geq 05$. One main effect exists in physcial attractiveness: liking increases, regardless of the physical attractiveness of the subject, as the physical attractiveness of his partner increases. (See Figure 1.)

Assertiveness and assertiveness/attractiveness interaction. The third hypothesis was that an individual's level of social assertiveness will not affect significantly his liking of his matched partner, nor will it interact with physical attractiveness to produce liking. The results supported both predictions. The summary statistics suggested that social assertiveness alone did not work to produce differences in liking. The 2 × 2 ANOVA showed that social assertiveness was not significant. $F(3,28) = .3872$ $p \geq .05$. The summary statistics also suggested that there was no interactive effect between the variables of social assertiveness and physical attractiveness. Since there was an unequal number of subjects in each cell, and because reciprocal scores were not possible in 4 of the 16 dependent cells, a 16 × 1 Newman-Keuls ANOVA was used to determine the interaction affects. The A × B interaction was not significant. $F(16, 74) = 2.35$ $p \geq .05$.

Long Term Effects

Follow-up. It was predicted that the same pattern that was found during the computer dance would also be found in long-term partner selection. Specifically, it was expected that those men matched with a partner HIGH in attractiveness would pursue further dating with that person. The results did *not* support this hypothesis. Of the 50 couples surveyed, only 12 had seen each other since the time of the

FIGURE 1.

MAIN EFFECT OF PHYSICAL ATTRACTIVENESS ON LIKING

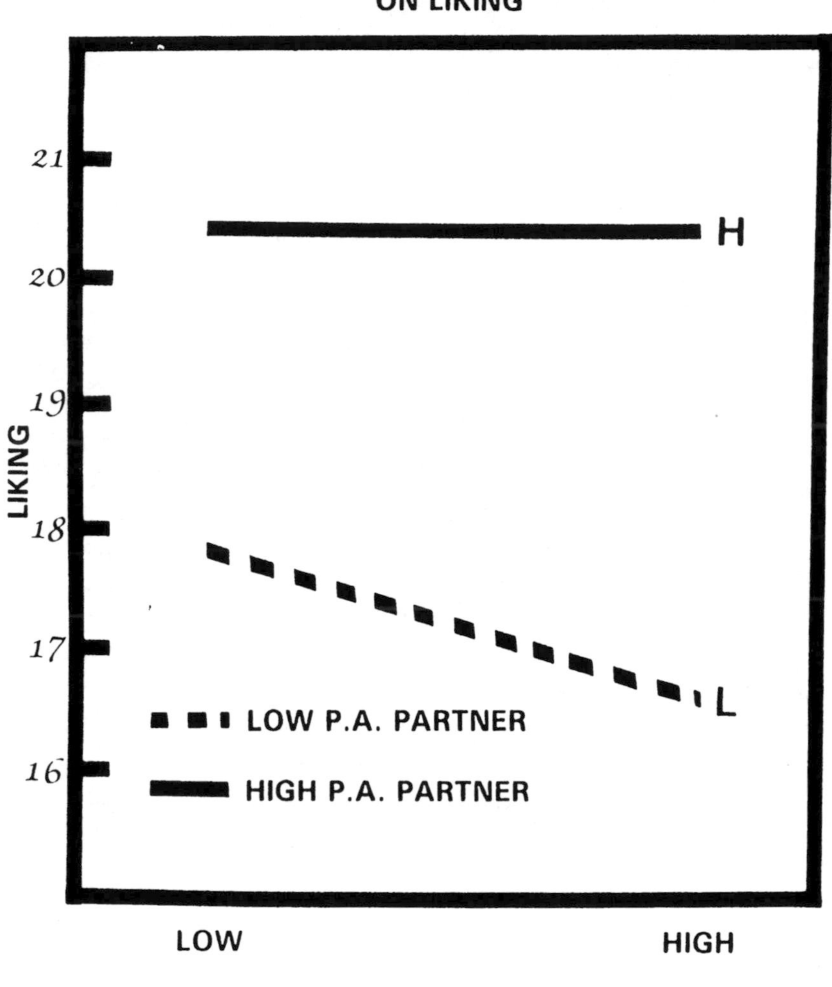

dance. There were an equal number of low attractives who initiated dating behavior with high attractives as there were high attractives who initiated such behavior with low attractives. In addition, there were an equivalent number of low attractives who attempted contact with their low attractive dates as there were high attractives who sought out their high attractive partners for another visit.

Also, four men chose not to remain in their assigned dyads, and pursued dating behavior with *another* member of the 100-person sample. One would expect that each of these would have been dissatisfied high attractives seeking out an equally attractive male. But only one of these four represented an attractive subject who sought a highly attractive partner. (He was initially matched with a low attractive.) In fact, two of the subjects who initiated such behavior were high attractives who sought out low attractives. The fourth man was a low attractive who made contact with another low attractive. (He was initially matched with a high attractive.) Among these four changes, there was no discernible pattern in social assertiveness skills. In two cases, the men sought similar assertives (L-L, H-H), and in the other two cases, the men found complementary assertives (L-H, H-L).

DISCUSSION

The present study clearly supported the notion that homosexual men, regardless of their own attractiveness, preferred partners more attractive than themselves. As Walster (1966) found for heterosexuals, individuals low in desirability will not necessarily feel more comfortable nor actually like or prefer equal counterparts. The present study supported the idea that social assertiveness skills have less impact on liking, and that assertiveness does not interact with attrac tiveness to affect liking. This agrees with the original correlational findings of Walster that self-esteem and assertiveness do not provide any prediction of liking for heterosexual couples.

The most surprising results concerned long-range partner selection. It was predicted that the same factors that affected the initiati on of short range associations would also contribute to long-range liking, and the formulation of enduring relationships among homosexual men. This does not appear to have been the case. We speculated that in telephone conversations or other types of meetings that occurred days after the tea dance, the men had additional time to discover characteristics of their assigned partner other than physical attractiveness, which apparently influenced liking and dating behavior. The results suggested a similar pattern among those men who chose not to remain in their assigned dyads. Thus, on a long-range basis, for certain individuals, regardless of their own attractiveness and assertiveness skills, physical beauty in potential mates may not be as significant a factor as it is in settings that perpetuate short-range dating behavior.

These results may be of limited scope. The oldest participant in this study was 35 years of age. Perhaps as homosexual men grow older, the importance of physical attractiveness in initial dating decreases. It may also be that in the artificial computer date situation, individuals were not very affected by their date's liking of them because the dates were so polite that it was impossible for the individual to know whether the date accepted or rejected him. For instance, numerous subjects may have exchanged telephone numbers as a gesture of courtesy but with no intention of ever calling their partners back. Or perhaps, individuals were so eager to be liked that they incorrectly perceived the available cues. It is possible that many subjects did not call each other back because they incorrectly perceived rejection on each other's part. The low correlation between the partner's stated liking for the subject and the subject's perception of the partner's liking for him is less likely to occur in an actual disco or bar environment. In such a setting, subjects are not "required to interact with a specific person for a given time" and thus may be more willing to display rejection.

Finally, it might be that if subjects went on a different kind of date (in a non-traditionally gay setting, as in outside of the group-meeting situation of a bar or disco), then other factors such as social assertiveness might become just as significant as the physical attractiveness variable.

Further research needs to be directed at similar populations of homosexual men of larger sample sizes and in varying social environments. Factors other than social assertiveness and physical attractiveness must be pre-evaluated in a rigorous and precise fashion to determine their respective importance in the schema of male homosexual short-term dating behavior and long-range relationship formation.

REFERENCES

Berscheid, E., & Walster, A. (1973, July). The body image report. *Psychology Today, 7,* 119-131.

Byrne, D. (1971). *Attraction paradigm.* New York: Academic Press.

Byrne, D. (1977). Continuity between the experimental study of attraction and real-life computer dating. In S. S. Duck (Ed.), Theory and practice in interpersonal attraction (p. 285). New York: Academic Press.

Clark, D. (1977). Loving someone gay. Milbrae, CA: Celestial Arts.

Hagen, J., & Symons, A. (1979). Beauty report. In S. Sprecher & E. Walster, *Mirror, mirror on the wall* (p. 25). Honolulu: University of Hawaii Press.

Hathaway, S. R., & McKinley, J. C. (1982). A Minnesota multiphasic personality schedule (III) (Rev. ed.). *Journal of Psychology, 14,* 73-84.

Hooker, E. (1983, March 12). Personal communication.

Lewin, K., Dembo, T., Festinger, L., & Sears, P. (1944). Level of aspiration. In J. Hunt (Ed.), *Personality and the behavior disorders* (p. 46). New York: Ronald Press.

Peplau, L. A. (1981, March 12). What homosexuals want in relationships. *Psychology Today,* pp. 28-38.

Walster, E., Berscheid, E., & Dion, T. (1966). Importance of physical attractiveness in dating behavior. *Journal of Personality and Social Psychology, 54,* 210-215.

Breaking Out of the Dominant Paradigm: A New Look at Sexual Attraction

Gisela T. Kaplan, PhD
University of New South Wales
Australia

Lesley J. Rogers, PhD
Monash University
Australia

Focus on the physical sex of the partner of choice has anchored views of human sexuality to genital structure and imposed severe limitations, both methodologically and theoretically, on any study of sexual relationships. To date, theoretical frameworks of sexuality, as De Cecco and Shively (1983/1984) observed, have been based on a dichotomous biological concept of male versus female. Sexual identity, considered to be an internal aspect of the individual, is defined in terms of the physical sex of sexual partners. Moreover, since the assignment as male or female is made purely on the basis of genital morphology, the concepts upon which we construct theories of sexuality are confined to the physical sex of the partners of choice. Definitions of heterosexuality and even bisexuality are based on this one criterion. Therefore, it is no surprise that theories of homosexuality and bisexuality, which are based on biological determinism, win easy acceptance even in the absence of supporting evidence. As De Cecco and Shively (1983/1984) state, this is a consequence of the definitional emphasis on physical sex of partners. Birke (1982) recognizes the dangers of the use of gender dichotomy in research because this becomes a principle upon which sexuality research is based.

Because of the biological pitfall, De Cecco and Shively suggest a shift away from the focus on sexual identity to an examination of the structure of sexual relationships. Such a shift would allow consideration of similarities that may exist between homosexual and heterosexual relationships by circumventing the male-female dichotomy.

Because the genital categories are still incorporated into our living and thinking, we do not believe that their elimination would lead the way to studies that would have theoretical and methodological importance. The psychological, economic, and social consequences of defining relationships as either heterosexual or homosexual are as yet too important to eliminate or minimize. However, we concur with Birke and De Cecco and Shively that the dichotomies created on the basis of genital sex are not a sound basis for the scientific investigation of human sexuality.

The structure of sexual relationships includes the actual quality and intensity of personal interaction. In our view, this structure exists both independently of, and in conjunction with, sexual identity (Blumstein & Schwartz, 1977). We are prepared to go further than De Cecco and Shively by arguing that genital concepts of sexual identity mask real questions of sexual attraction.

The inherent contradiction between the customary research emphasis on genital morphology and actual sexual experience could not be more clearly highlighted than by pointing to sexual attraction. Whereas research on human sexuality constructs its hypotheses and tools on the foundation of genital morphology, sexual attraction may operate on quite a different basis. To some bisexuals or transsexuals (Srensen & Hertoft, 1982) the genitalia may be extraneous to their sexual attractions (Ross, 1984). Even in ambisexual individuals sexual attraction may be governed by nongenital traits. Fast and Wells (1975), for example, in an interview with a bisexual male, asked what his new male lover was like. His answer: "A lot like Linda physically—slight and dark."

The ideal male and female, stereotypically portrayed in the media, are extremely rare individuals. Most people possess an intermingling of masculine and feminine attributes. Bem (1974) has argued that masculinity and femininity should be measured as separate dimensions, not as opposite poles of a single continuum, so that individuals may display behavior that is both very masculine and very feminine. Such a case could be argued for many of the physical characteristics that play a part in sexual attraction. Individuals may possess some physical characteristics considered feminine and others masculine. The combined physical characteristics, including secondary sex characteristics, of males and females significantly overlap. Physical characteristics are linked to the choice of clothing that the individual uses to portray his or her identity. The form of dress can either exaggerate, conceal, or be incongruous with male or female physical characteristics, as judged on the basis of the individual's particular make-up and the contemporary cultural norms (Harré, 1981).

Initially, sexual attraction does not focus on the genitalia of the partner. The genitalia become important if the attraction leads to sexual intercourse. We do not usually decide whether an individual is a male or female by observation of the genitalia. This assignment is based on clothing, secondary sexual characteristics, and behavior (Kessler & McKenna, 1978). In a similar vein, sexual arousal is usually not initiated by sight of the genitalia but by secondary sex characteristics as hair, bosom, buttocks, thighs, hips, hands and a range of less sexually specific characteristics such as eyes, voice, smile, or smell. Each secondary sex characteristic could perhaps be placed along some continuum from pure maleness to pure femaleness.

Even the least sex specific characteristics have been culturally divided into "female" or "male" attributes. The individual is a complex collection of all these characteristics and may be more or less male or female in any one of them. No matter what we define or try to measure as sexual attraction, or what we describe as a sexual relationship, to base our conceptualizations on the male-female dichotomy is clearly an over-simplification. It has served as a basis for discrimination and an agent of social control. As Ross (1983/1984) asserts, these categories have little to do with actual interaction and initial sexual arousal. Paul (1983/1984) argues that we should view the "bisexual option" as third sexual identity. His position, however, rests on the same dichotomy.

Western society stylizes and channels sexual practice into rigid "norms" by focusing on genital sex and, in doing so, fosters heterosexual practice (Ross, Rogers, & McCulloch, 1978). Research on human sexuality has been dogged by the same rigid constraints (Rogers & Walsh, 1982; Rogers, 1982, 1983). Few scientific studies have explored arousal to a variety of erotic stimuli (Sigusch, Schmidt, & Reinfeld, 1970; Steele & Walker, 1974). Fewer discuss partners of choice except by genital sex. Why, one may ask, is this so? Hoffman (1983/1984) has presented evidence that sexually ambiguous individuals are considered to be abominations in monotheistic cultures. One of the few studies of the sexual partners of transsexuals (in this case female-to-male transsexuals) found that female partners were more frequently orgasmic in intercourse with transsexual males than they had been in the past with biological male partners (Steiner & Bernstein, 1981). All transsexuals in this study had undergone mastectomy but nonphalloplasty. Sexual ambiguity apparently increased the arousal of female partners. Clearly, more research is needed on the precise nature of sexual attraction and arousal. Whether or not such attraction is followed through to sexual intercourse is yet a different matter because here social sanctions play into individual choices. We also suggest that oppression of homosexuality has largely worked successfully by a concentration on the genitalia.

Cultural uneasiness with sexual ambivalence and ambiguity, we propose, may result from the premonition that an amalgam of male and female attributes may be more sexually arousing. In art and the media, the portrayal of sexual ambivalence has always paid dividends. Being part of an audience, we suggest, provides the individual an anonymous, stylized opportunity of experiencing arousal by performers portraying the mix.

The current popularity of transvestite performers has its historical antecedents. The dance of the pantomime was by a man dressed as a woman. Shakespeare used cross-dressing in several of his plots, for example, in *Twelfth Night*, in which a female character poses as her twin brother. Transvestism in the Shakespearean theatre was particularly convoluted because female characters were often played by males. Opera frequently uses cross-dressing. *Der Rosenkavalier*, for example, opens with a love scene between two sopranos, one playing an older woman and the other a young man. It also involves a woman playing the role of a man disguised as a woman. Cross-dressing was one of the disguises popular in the comic scenes of 17th-century opera. The intrigue of transvestites was enhanced by castrati singing both male and female roles.

Theatrical interest in transvestism is not confined to Western culture. In Japanese Kabuki theatre the female role, the *onnogata*, is played by a male, who is highly skilled and completely convincing as a female. Subtle hand movements let the audience know that the performer is indeed male. The *onnogatas* have many cult followers who may be sexually attracted to them. Widespread enjoyment of performers who portray a mixture of femaleness and maleness may well extend to life outside the theatre where it is less openly expressed.

Based on our assumption that sexual attraction is not primarily anchored to female and male genitalia, the structure of sexual relationships could be investigated in new and challenging ways. Detailed studies of partner choice by individuals classified as bisexuals or transsexuals would be particularly promising.

The purely sensual side of human sexuality is little concerned with the classification of people as male or female. These categories are meaningful for procreation but inadequate for understanding the complexity of sexual relationships, i.e., sensual and sexual behavior in the dialectical relationship of the individual to the world.

REFERENCES

Bem, S. L. (1974). The measurement of psychological androgyny. *Journal of Consulting and Clinical Psychology, 42,* 155-162.

Birke, L. (1982). Cleaving the mind: Speculations of conceptual dichotomies. In S. Rose (Ed.), *Against biological determinism* (pp. 60-78). London: Allison and Busby.

Blumstein, P. W., & Schwartz, P. (1977). Bisexuality: Some social psychological issues. *Journal of Social Issues, 33*(2), 30-45.

De Cecco, J. P., & Shively, M. G. (1983/1984). From sexual identity to sexual relationships: A contextual shift. *Journal of Homosexuality, 9*(2/3), 1-26.

Fast, J., & Wells, H. (1975). *Bisexual living.* New York: M. Evans & Co.

Harré, R. (1981). The dramaturgy of sexual relations. In M. Cook (Ed.), *The bases of human sexual attraction* (pp. 251-274). London: Academic Press.

Hoffman, R. J. (1984). Vices, god and virtues: Cosmology as a mediating factor in attitudes toward male homosexuality. *Journal of Homosexuality, 9*(2/3), 27-44.

Kessler, S. J., & McKenna, W. (1978). *Gender: An ethnomethodological approach.* New York: Wiley.

Paul, J. P. (1983/1984). The bisexual identity: An idea without social recognition. *Journal of Homosexuality, 9*(2/3), 45-63.

Rogers, L. J. (1982). The ideology of medicine. In S. Rose (Ed.), *Against biological determinism* (pp. 79-93). London: Allison and Busby.

Rogers, L. J. (1983). Hormonal theories for sex differences – Politics disguised as science: Reply to DeBold and Luria. *Sex Roles, 9,* 1109-1113.

Rogers, L. J., & Walsh, J. (1982). Shortcomings of the psychomedical research of John Money and co-workers into sex differences in behavior: Social and political implications. *Sex Roles, 8,* 269-281.

Ross, M. W. (1984). Beyond the biological model: New directions in bisexual and homosexual research. *Journal of Homosexuality, 10*(3/4), 63-70.

Ross, M. W., Rogers, L. J., & McCulloch, H. (1978). Sex, stigma and society: A new look at gender differentiation and sexual variation. *Journal of Homosexuality, 3,* 315-330.

Sigusch, V., Schmidt, G., Reinfeld, A., & Weidman-Sutor, I. (1970). Psychosexual stimulation: Sex differences. *The Journal of Sex Research, 6*(1), 10-24.

Srensen, T., & Hertoft, P. (1982). Male and female transsexualism: The Danish experience with 37 patients. *Archives of Sexual Behavior, 11*(2), 133-155.

Steele, D. G., & Walker, C. F. (1974). Male and female differences in reaction to erotic stimuli as related to sexual adjustment. *Archives of Sexual Behavior, 3,* 459-470.

Steiner, B. W., & Bernstein, S. M. (1981). Female-to-male transsexuals and their parents. *Canadian Journal of Psychiatry, 26,* 178-182.

Decision Making and Age Differences Among Gay Male Couples

Joseph Harry, PhD
Northern Illinois University

The present work assesses the extent to which age and age preferences serve as criteria influencing the selection of sexual/romantic partners among gay males. We also explore whether age differences and similarities between partners affect power and decision making among couples. These questions are examined in a sample of 1,556 gay men from the Chicago area.

Gender-Structured Relationships. There appear to be three major forms according to which male homosexual pairings have been structured in various historical cultures. Carrier (1971, 1977) has reported that heterosexual gender roles appear to have served as the models for structuring homosexual pairings in a Latin American tradition of homosexuality, although that tradition is not limited to Latin American countries. Within this tradition, participants in homosexual encounters model their behaviors around traditional heterosexual roles and thereby tend to emphasize differences between partners. In these cases gender role determines dominance in the relationship; the "masculine" partner is more powerful. The case of the *berdache* among American Indians is another instance in which heterosexual roles have informed homosexual pairings (Kessler & McKenna, 1978, pp. 24-25).

While earlier writers on homosexuality such as Bieber, Dain, Dince, Drellich, Grand, Gundlach, Kremer, Rifkin, Wilber, and Bieber (1962, pp. 232-234) and Socarides (1968, pp. 73-76) have suggested that contemporary gay male couples model their relation ships on traditional heterosexual gender roles, empirical research has found little support for such a formulation. Westwood (1960, p. 119) reported little evidence among English homosexuals that masculine and feminine men were mutually attracted to each other. Rather, the very large majority preferred masculine partners. Haist and Hewitt (1974) were able to classify their gay male respondents into inserters and insertees, but their questions obliged the respondents to choose only one of the activities and precluded the choice of both or neither. Saghir and Robins (1973, pp. 74-75) found that few gay persons patterned their relationships on an approximation of a husband-wife model. Similarly, Bell and Weinberg (1978, p. 93) reported "very little evidence of a 'masculine/feminine' sex-role dichotomy in the performance of household tasks." Although a rather small minority of gay male couples may organize their relationships around the traditional gender-role dichotomies, the evidence seems fairly clear that gender roles do not structure the large majority of pairings of gay men in Western non-Latin societies.

Age-Inegalitarian Relationships. A second cultural pattern which has sometimes structured male homosexual relationships involves an older adult male who establishes a relationship with an adolescent or preadolescent male. The best known example of this pattern is from ancient Greece in which an older male assumed a dominant mentor relationship with a preadult male (Dover, 1978, pp. 84-87). In this pattern, age rather than gender appears to define dominance in the relationship. This form of institutionalized homosexuality also occurs in some non-Western societies as well as among several groups in New Guinea (Herdt, 1980, pp. 318-320). Although age differences serve as a principal criterion around which such homosexual liaisons are structured, there is often an accompanying cultural belief that the younger partner benefits from the relationship in ways that will enhance his future masculinity as an adult heterosexual.

Research findings on the extent to which age differences structure homosexual liaisons in Western societies are mixed but generally suggest that pairings between partners of significantly different ages are not the majority case. In a study of the demographic characteristics of homosexual partners, Cotton (1972) reported age differences in a majority of the cases. His sample was small, however, and he did not indicate what constituted an age difference. Cotton found greater similarity in demographic characteristics, including age, between close homosexual friends than between sexual partners. This suggests that the degree of similarity between partners in demographic characteristics may depend on the emotional closeness of the relationship. The sexual relationships studied by Cotton may or may not have involved emotional closeness. Since very few of them involved living together, it is possible that most of the partners were not particularly close. When discussing differences and similarities between partners it may be important to specify whether the partners have a close relationship. There may be greater dissimilarity between parties to temporary sexual encounters than among those involved in more enduring relationships.

Bell and Weinberg (1978, p. 319) reported that 50% of their gay males involved in a current relationship were within 5 years of their partner in age, suggesting some tendency for age similarity. Westwood (1960, p. 117) reported no clear tendency for gay males to have affairs with or be attracted to persons outside their own age group. Harry and DeVall (1978, p. 124) found that men in their early 20s preferred older men as sexual partners; those from 25 to 34 preferred same age partners, and those over 35 preferred younger or same age partners. Harry and DeVall also showed that a preference for younger partners was associated with a preference for being dominant in decision making, while a preference for older partners was associated with a preference for being subordinate. Although these data suggest the possibility that age differences can structure decision making among some gay male couples, almost half of their respondents preferred same-age partners and the association between decision making and age preference, while statistically significant, was not particularly strong (gamma = 0.22). Since Harry and Devall's respondents were asked only if they preferred sexual partners "younger" the "same age," or "older" than themselves but were not asked about specific age differences, it is also not known from their data just how large age differences must be to affect decision making.

Age-Egalitarian Relationships. The rather mixed findings on age preferences in gay relationships suggest an alternative model. Although a minority of gay persons in modern Western societies may prefer age-different partners, the majority case may be one of a preference for age-similar partners. In this pattern, men of approximately the same age are attracted to each other and create relationships with egalitarian decision making. This egalitarian pattern appears to be largely lacking, or at least invisible, in those cultures that have structured homosexual relationships around the Greek model (Dover, 1978, pp. 86-87; Herdt, 1980). In contrast, the pattern of egalitarianism may be found more commonly in modern societies which emphasize individual happiness and democracy in intimate relationships. These gay relationships may resemble contemporary heterosexual pairings by involving considerable similarity of partners in demographic characteristics but may differ from heterosexual pairings in that neither age nor gender differences can operate to create the inequality often found in heterosexual marriages. The present study analyzes the extent to which age affects gay men's stated age preferences for sexual partners and the degree to which age preferences are related to decision-making differences in actual relationships.

METHOD

The data for the present work consist of responses from 1,556 gay men from the Chicago area, the central city plus suburbs. The very large majority of these respondents—1,515—were obtained through *Gay Life*, the major Chicago area gay newspaper. This publication, with a distribution of approximately 18,000, is a "throwaway" rather than a subscription publication. It is distributed to nearly all of the gay establishments in the area. Piles of the paper are placed weekly in 104 gay establishments, although this number varies slightly from month to month. These 104 places include 56 gay bars, 5 gay organizations, 7 steam baths, 2 gay hotels, 17 adult bookstores and arcades, 17 restaurants, a movie house, and a medical clinic. *Gay Life* is also distributed at a number of nongay supermarkets and restaurants located in or near the Newtown "gay ghetto" of Chicago.

A total of 17,600 questionnaires were distributed along with the regular copies of two issues of the paper during November 1978. These questionnaires contained prepaid return envelopes and had stamped on their covers in large letters, "Lifestyle Study of Gay Men," to increase visibility. Since *Gay Life* is not a subscription publication, the usual sampling biases toward the more educated in readership surveys do not obtain. Likewise, it should be noted that the *Gay Life* respondents do not constitute a readership survey since the questionnaires could have been picked up by anyone, regardless of whether he read *Gay Life*.

It was anticipated that the respondents obtained through *Gay Life* would underrepresent homosexual men over 50 years of age. All major studies of homosexual males to date appear seriously to underrepresent older homosexuals if we assume that the age distribution of adult gay men should approximate that for the general male population (Saghir & Robins, 1973, p. 15; Weinberg & Williams, 1974, pp. 95-96; Harry & DeVall, 1978, p. 25; Bell & Weinberg, 1978, pp. 274-276). In order to obtain greater numbers of older respondents, questionnaires were mailed to the 275 members of a Chicago organization for gay men over 40 years of age; 62 were returned. The median age of these respondents was 50.3 years as compared with 29.7 for the *Gay Life* respondents. (There is reason to believe that the actual membership of this group is rather less than 275 and that a sizable although unknown percentage of this number are members in name only who have been retained on the mailing list long beyond their last dues payment.)

A total of 1,770 questionnaires were returned from the two sources. Of this total, 214 questionnaires were excluded because they did not meet at least one of several predetermined criteria. Twenty-one were excluded because they were incompletely answered. Twenty-nine were excluded because they were from exclusive or near exclusive heterosexuals (Kinsey Os and 1s). Forty-eight were excluded because they were received after our cutoff date for returns of February 1, 1979. Finally, 116 were excluded because they did not meet our geographic criterion of living within the City of Chicago or its suburbs. Our geographic area of acceptability was defined as a "social Commuting area," an area within which one might reasonably commute to the central city on a weeknight for purposes of recreation and return home in time for work. While 10% of the questionnaires distributed were returned, it is not possible to calculate a traditional response rate because of the modes of distribution. In the case of the *Gay Life* distribution it is unknown how many questionnaires actually got into the hands of potential respondents.

The resultant sample of 1,556 men had the following demographic characteristics. Most men (91%) were white, 7% were black, and 2% were "other." The median age was 30.1 years with a standard deviation of 9.7 years. Median education was 15.6 years with a standard deviation of 7.8 years. Eighty-four percent were never married, 2% married, and 14% separated/divorced or widowed. Forty-eight percent had incomes under $15,000 and 9% reported incomes of over $30,000. Seventy-nine percent were residents of Chicago with the remainder being from the suburbs or nearby Indiana. These respondents are quite similar in their demographic characteristics to the groups studied in the other major studies of gay men. Probably underrepresented are less educated, older, or nonwhite men.

RESULTS

Age Preferences and Age. Table 1 presents the relationship of a man's own age to his preferred age for a sexual partner. The question on preferred age was "My usual preferred age for the man I like to relate sexually to is:______." A scale of response categories with five-year intervals ranging from 10 to 75 or older was provided. Respondents were also provided the alternative response category of "Age is not important to me." Of the 1,556 respondents, 19.6% indicated that age was not important. The measure of preferred age is taken to reflect preferences for sexual partners but may also reflect preferences of partners for an enduring liaison.

In broad outline the data of Table 1 support the idea that gay men prefer partners of ages similar to their own; as respondent age increases so does preferred partner age. Similarity is more pronounced among those of ages 25 to 34. It is also apparent, however, that preferred partner's age does not increase in a one-to-one ratio

Table 1

Preferred Age of Sexual Partner by Respondent's Age (Percent)

Preferred Age of Sexual Partner	Respondent's Age: Under 25	25-29	30-34	35-39	Over 39
Under 25	20%	8	11	12	9
25-29	46%	41	28	20	15
30-34	25%	34	40	35	26
35-39	7%	13	17	20	27
Over 39	2%	3	4	13	23
n	276	344	265	161	243

$X^2 = 223.29$ df = 16 $p < .001$

Note: Table excludes men who indicated having no age preference.

with age of respondent. The modal preference for somewhat older partners exhibited by men in their early 20s changes to a preference for partners of the same age among men from 25 to 34 and subsequently to a preference for somewhat younger partners among those over 35. If the 40 and older group is broken down more finely, the percentages within the more finely divided groups remain substantially the same as those for the 40 and older group in Table 1.

The data suggest that both age-egalitarian and age-inegalitarian preferences are quite common and that preferences for age inequality are most common among the oldest and the youngest groups. However, preferences for age-different partners do not often reach beyond ten years except among the oldest age group; the median preferred difference for the sample as a whole is 4.9 years. Hence, while choice of age-different partners is common, such choices do not conform very closely to the Greek model in which an older man associates with an adolescent or preadolescent partner who is many years his junior. Indeed, less than 2% of the respondents preferred a partner under 20 years of age. This tiny percentage seems to bear on the occasional claim that male homosexuals are sexually interested in the young.

Table 2 examines preferred age differences for respondents of various ages and shows that preferences for men of significantly different ages than the respondent's age are strongly concentrated among those under 25 and those over 39. Of those under 25, two-fifths want someone six or more years older than themselves while among those over 39, two-thirds are interested in men more than ten years younger than themselves. It seems that interest in age inegali-

Table 2

Difference Between Respondent's Age and Preferred Age of Sexual Partner by Age (Percent)

Age Preferred-Age Difference	Respondent's Age: Under 25	25-29	30-34	35-39	Over 39	Total %
Partner's Age is:						
Over 10 years older	12	4	1	1	0	4
6 to 10 years older	29	14	4	4	1	11
1 to 5 years older	47	38	21	9	2	26
0 to 5 years older	12	39	43	38	11	28
6 to 10 years younger	1	6	23	20	21	13
Over 10 years younger	0	0	8	27	65	17
n	276	344	265	161	243	1289

$X^2 = 940.18$ df = 20 $p < .001$

Note: Table includes only men who stated an age preference.

tarian couplings is strongly age-related. Still, a majority (54%) of the respondents prefer a partner within five years of their own age.

While it is possible to interpret the relationship between respondent's age and preferred age of sexual partners in terms of age preferences changing as the respondents grow older, a much different interpretation is possible. Men under 25 appear to be interested in men somewhat under 30 years of age. Those 25 to 34 are interested in men about 30 years of age. Those over 40 find men in their 30s attractive. It thus seems that age preferences do increase with age but extremely slowly. This is clearly shown if preferred partner age is regressed on age. The slope of the regression line is 0.22 with an intercept of 22.4 years. The Pearsonian correlation is 0.34 while the respective means for preferred partner age and respondent's age are 29.4 and 32.4. The corresponding standard deviations are 6.1 and 9.7 years. There is considerably less variation in the ages of the respondents' erotic visions than there is in their own ages. As the respondents grow older, their erotic visions age at the glacial rate of one-fifth as fast. This indicates that while one may grow old and wrinkled, one's erotic ideals seem forever embalmed in eternal youth.

Since the data of Tables 1 and 2 are based on stated preferences, one may wonder about the extent to which these preferences are realized. Those attracted to a given age group may not have their attractions reciprocated. Table 3 presents age differences in current relationships. A relationship is operationalized as having a "current lover or sexual partner with whom you are going or living." Among all respondents 51% report a current relationship, 38% report having had past relationships, and the remaining 11% indicate that their sexual encounters have been too brief to include any that might be called a relationship. The median age difference among current partners is 5.0 years, a figure virtually identical with the median age difference between the respondent and his preferred partner. Table 3 indicates substantial similarity between the ages of current partners. For age groups up to 35 years the majority of respondents are in relationships in which the partner is no more than five years older or younger than themselves. Beyond age 35 this pattern tends to break down, and larger percentages of the two older age groups

Table 3

Age of Current Partner by Respondent's Age (Percent)

	Respondent's Age				
Partner's Age	Under 25	25-29	30-34	35-39	Over 39
Under 25	36	17	18	21	8
25-29	28	35	28	15	7
30-34	18	27	27	30	16
35-39	10	13	17	18	13
Over 39	7	8	10	16	56
n	135	214	163	95	118

$X^2 = 195.21$ df = 16 $p < .001$

<u>Note</u>: Table includes only those men currently in a relationship

are coupled with men ten or more years younger than themselves. Among men over 40, 56% have a partner also over 40. However, since some of these men are in their 50s and 60s the actual similarity of ages is less than it appears. The data of Table 3 are generally quite similar to those of Table 1 and show that age preferences appear to be reflected in actual relationships.

Age Differences and Decision Making. While approximate similarity of ages among partners both actual and preferred is the dominant trend, a substantial minority of men prefer partners older or younger than themselves. For this subgroup, age differences may serve as a factor around which relationships inegalitarian in dominance or decision making may be organized. Further analyses explore the extent to which preferences for age-different partners are also preferences for more or less dominant partners. Table 4 represents a log-linear analysis of preferred dominance in sexual partners by preferred partner age and the respondent's own age. A readable introduction to log-linear analysis may be found in Reynolds

(1977). The analyses in the present work were done by the BMDP computer package (Brown, 1977). The measure of dominance in the respondent's preferred partner is a five-point rating scale running from "Dominant" to "Compliant" and the object being rated is "the man to whom I like to relate sexually." It should be noted that for all age and age preference groups, a large majority of the respon-

Table 4

Log-Linear Analysis of Preferred Partner Dominance by Preferred Partner Age and Own Age

Partial (1st Order) Associations				Marginal (0-Order) Associations	
Effect[a]	df	LR Chi-squared	p	LR Chi-squared	p
DP	3	24.92	.001	13.78	.003
DA	4	26.16	.001	15.03	.005
PA	12	191.92	.001	180.78	.001
DPA	12	13.49	.335		

Own Age (A)	Preferred Partner Age (P)	Preferred Partner Dominance (D) Low	High	n
-24	-24	70	30	53
	25-29	72	28	120
	30-34	67	33	66
	35+	64	36	25
25-29	-24	93	7	27
	25-29	84	16	135
	30-34	70	30	116
	35+	63	37	51
30-34	-24	93	7	28
	25-29	86	14	72
	30-34	78	22	99
	35+	68	32	57
35-39	-24	78	22	18
	25-29	94	6	32
	30-34	70	30	53
	35+	65	35	52
40+	-24	80	20	20
	25-29	89	11	37
	30-34	81	19	58
	35+	83	17	118

Note: Table includes only those who indicated an age preference in partners.

a. Variables are referred to by single capitalized letters. Relationships between variables are referred to by combinations among those letters with the term "DPA" referring to the interaction term.

dents prefer nondominant partners. This is consistent with Peplau and Cochran's (1981) finding that 92% of their gay male respondents said both partners in a relationship should have "exactly equal say." Table 4 reveals that all zero-order and first-order partial associations are significant with no significant interaction. Younger men and men who prefer older partners are more likely to prefer dominant partners. These associations of age and age preferences with desired partner dominance seem to indicate that the relatively visible characteristic of age may be taken by potential parties to a relationship as one indicator of the expected dominance structure in that relationship. Hence, it can serve as a sorting mechanism helping persons to identify candidates for both egalitarian and inegalitarian relationships.

Although the measure of desired dominance in a partner shows sizable associations in Table 4 with both respondent's age and preferred partner age, it remains somewhat unclear what forms of dominance are tapped by this measure. In order to assess the extent to which age differences in actual relationships influence dominance or decision-making structures, Table 5 presents reported decision-making differences by age differences for current and past relationships. The past relationship in question is the respondent's longest lasting relationship. The question measuring decision-making differences is "In our relationship I make (made) the decisions: Always, Mostly, Half and Half, Occasionally, Never." Not included in Table 5 are the 11% of respondents who said their sexual encounters had been too brief to include any which might be described as a relationship. Table 5 shows that older partners in both past and present relationships are reported to make decisions more often. Hence, age differences or similarities seem a significant factor around which dominance and decision making are structured in gay relationships. It is worth noting that there appears to be some asymmetry in the association between age differences and decision making. While the percentage differences found when predicting from age differences to decision making are of modest to moderate magnitudes, the percentage differences (in parentheses) predicting from decision making to age differences are much larger. Among current relationships, 30% of respondents who said they made the

Table 5

Log-Linear Analysis of Decision Making by Partner Age Difference by Current versus Past Relationships

Partial (1st Order) Associations				Marginal (0-Order) Associations	
Effect[a]	df	LR Chi-squared	p	LR Chi-squared	p
DA	4	90.35	.001	90.09	.001
DC	2	17.65	.001	17.39	.001
AC	2	0.51	.774	0.25	.882
DAC	4	1.95	.745		

		Decison Making (D)			
Relation-ship (C)	Age-Difference (A)	I made Decisions	Half & Half	He Made Decisions	n
Current	Respondent 3 or More Years Younger	16(30)	69(44)	15(74)	339
	Zero to 2 Years Age Difference	24(24)	72(25)	4(12)	184
	Respondent 3 or More Years Older	32(46)	64(29)	4(14)	255
Past	Respondent 3 or More Years Younger	18(26)	60(46)	22(67)	243
	Zero to 2 Years Age Difference	28(23)	62(26)	9(19)	141
	Respondent 3 or More Years Older	44(50)	50(29)	5(14)	190

Note: Table excludes those who had never had a relationship.

a. Variables are referred to by single capitalized letters. Relationships between variables are referred to by combinations among those letters with the term "DAC" referring to the interaction term.

b. Row percentages are outside of parentheses; column percentages within categories of the relationship variable are within parentheses.

decisions had older partners versus 74% of those whose partners made the decisions. The corresponding percentages for past relationships are 27 and 70. Hence, if a gay relationship is inegalitarian in decision making, it is likely to be a relationship between age different persons. However, a difference in age is not sufficient to ensure an inegalitarian relationship.

Table 5 also shows that current relationships differ significantly from past ones in that current ones are reported to be more egalitarian. This difference is largest for the egalitarian category and minimal for the two inegalitarian categories. Such an association is consistent with the notion that inegalitarian relationships may be more fragile than egalitarian ones. However, there remains the alternative interpretation that respondents may have reworked their remembrances of past relationships to recall them in a less than satisfying manner.

DISCUSSION AND CONCLUSIONS

The results of this study have shown that age seems to be a major criterion defining pools of potential erotic and romantic partners among gay men. Age also serves to define the expected dominance structure in a relationship. This appears to be true in both actual relationships and in terms of stated erotic partner preference. Age seems to define expected dominance structures for both erotic encounters and more enduring liaisons, although the earlier stated rationale suggests that partner selection criteria which favor cultural and demographic similarity between partners might be more operative in selecting men for enduring relationships than for erotic encounters. Attempting a reformulation of the partner selection process, we suggest that the selection of sexual partners may differ from the selection of enduring partners only in the number of selection criteria employed. Under this hypothesis, both sexual partners and enduring partners must pass the tests of age and physical attractiveness. Hence, one would expect to find the same patterns of association for both types of partners. However, enduring partners must meet other criteria of personality, masculinity, or social roles. Further research would be useful to identify additional criteria used in partner selection and the order in which they may be invoked.

While there appear to be some similarities between the age-different pairings found in the data and the Greek model of same-sex relationships, the differences seem at least as great as the similarities. The Greek model involved liaisons between adult men and adolescent or preadolescent youths. In this study, an interest in adolescent males is virtually nonexistent. Of course, some adult gay men are principally or exclusively interested in adolescents (Silverstein, 1981, ch. 8), but they appear to be sufficiently rare that they were not detectable in the present survey in notable numbers.

The data suggest that homosexual relationships in modern societies differ substantially from both the gender-role defined form found in the Latin American model and from the Greek model. The Latin American and Greek forms of relationships seem severely inegalitarian. In contrast, in the modern model the large majority of gay men believe in decision-making equality in a relationship, whatever their actual practice may be. Such egalitarianism in gay relationships seems to be facilitated economically by the rarity with which one partner in a relationship financially supports another. Another study (Harry, 1979, p. 623) found that only 1% of gay male Detroit respondents were economically supported by another man; none at all was found in the present data. Since both parties to gay relationships are typically employed, total financial dependency as a basis for inequality in a relationship does not arise.

In summary, the form of same-sex relationships found in industrialized Western nations seems less severely inegalitarian than either the Latin American or the Greek model and tends to occur between persons of approximately equal ages. The equality of ages in the modern form helps to assure, but hardly to guarantee, equality in decision making. A secondary pattern within modern gay male relationships involves pairings of age-different mates and is associated with inegalitarianism in decision making. However, these age-different pairings do not seem to approximate the Greek model since age differences between partners are commonly only five to ten years. Age in the modern gay worlds appears to operate as an important and visible criterion by which gay men define a field of desirables, whether they are interested in egalitarian or inegalitarian relationships.

REFERENCES

Bell, A., & Weinberg, M. *Homosexualities.* New York: Simon and Schuster, 1978.

Bieber, I., Dain, H. J., Dince, P. R., Drellich, M. G., Grand, H. G., Gundlach, R. H., Kremer, M. W., Rifkin, A. H., Wilber, C. B., & Beiber, T. B. *Homosexuality: A psychoanalytic study.* New York: Basic Books, 1962.

Brown, M. D. (Ed.). *Biomedical computer programs.* Berkeley: University of California Press, 1977.

Carrier, J. Participants in urban Mexican male homosexual encounters. *Archives of Sexual Behavior,* 1971, *2,* 229-291.

Carrier, J. Sex-role preferences as an explanatory variable in homosexual behavior. *Archives of Sexual Behavior,* 1977, *6,* 53-65.

Cotton, W. L. Role-playing substitutions among male homosexuals. *Journal of Sex Research,* 1972, *8,* 310-323.

Dover, K. J. *Greek homosexuality.* London: Duckworth, 1978.

Gagnon, J., & Simon, W. *Sexual conduct.* Chicago: Aldine, 1973.

Haist, M., & Hewitt, J. The butch-fem dichotomy in male homosexual behavior. *Journal of Sex Research,* 1974, *10,* 68-75.

Harry, J. The "marital" liaisons of gay men. *The Family Coordinator,* 1979, *28,* 622-629.

Harry, J., & DeVall, W. *The social organization of gay males.* New York: Praeger, 1978.

Herdt, G. *Guardians of the flute.* New York: McGraw-Hill, 1981.

Kessler, S., & McKenna, W. *Gender.* New York: Wiley, 1978.

Peplau, L. A., & Cochran, S. Value orientations in the intimate relationships of gay men. *Journal of Homosexuality,* 1981, *6*(3), 1-19.

Reynolds, H. T. Analysis of nominal data. Beverly Hills: Sage Publishers, 1977.

Saghir, M., & Robins, E. *Male and female homosexuality.* Baltimore: Williams and Wilkins, 1973.

Silverstein, C. *Man to man.* New York: Morrow, 1981.

Socarides, C. *The overt homosexual.* New York: Grune & Stratton, 1968.

Weinberg, M., & Williams, C. *Male homosexuals.* New York: Oxford University Press, 1974.

Westwood, G. *A minority: A report on the life of the male homosexual in Great Britain.* London: Longmans, 1960.

Permanent Partner Priorities: Gay and Straight

Mary Riege Laner, PhD
Arizona State University

Until very recent years, homosexuals have been somewhat neglected in terms of scientific study, although there has been no lack of speculation in print regarding various aspects of homosexuality. (See Bell, 1971, for an overview of both historical and contemporary treatments.) In large part, focus has been on the "deviant" nature of homosexuals and their life-styles. Recent reports, however, in both the scholarly journals and in papers presented at professional meetings, have suggested not only the essential normalcy of homosexuals but, in some cases, have offered evidence of "supranormalcy." Among these studies are those of Riess, Safer, and Yotive (1974), who found no more psychopathology among female homosexuals than among female heterosexuals and also reported psychodynamic differences between male and female homosexuals. Clark (1975) found no significant differences between any of several categories of male homosexuals and exclusively heterosexual control subjects in terms of either personality or psychopathology, and suggested that homosexuality is simply a deviation in sexual pattern and object choice within the psychologically normal range. Turnage and Logan (1976) maintain that sufficient evidence now exists to warrant considering the term *deviant* a misnomer, and urge that the term *variant* be substituted for it in discussions of nonheterosexual behavior, especially homosexuality.

Evidence for this stance is provided by investigators such as Freedman (1975), who found that in some ways, lesbians seemed to function better than heterosexual control subjects—results that affirmed the previous conclusions of Hopkins (1969) and Siegelman (1972). For example, "creative opposition" to conventionality, Freedman (1975) held, might produce more equalitarian sex roles among homosexuals than among heterosexuals: "The shared wisdom of the gay world is that two men or two women living together as mates quickly see the limitations of stereotyped sex roles. Breadwinner/homemaker and dominant/submissive dichotomies just aren't as important to gays as they are to most people" (p. 30).

Further, Freedman held that as with sex roles, so with sexuality. That is, the gay life may provide certain types of experience that lead to a high valuing of honesty: "For instance, the social arrangements that prepare the way for a homosexual experience are often much more straightforward than in heterosexual situations . . . Gay people don't have to feign love or any other emotion" (pp. 30-31).

Finally, due to social discrimination against homosexuals and the mask of heterosexuality many gay people feel forced to wear as a result, Freedman believed that many gay people become sophisticated about "masks," that is, about the relationship between identity and role. Thus, "many gays have a fairly complex understanding of self-disclosure, both in themselves and in others. Moreover, they are often more candid and open than nongays" (p. 32). Freedman found that his lesbian subjects told fewer lies than did his heterosexual controls, and that they were more candid and less defensive—a finding which supports that of Horstman (1972) who studied matched groups of homosexual and heterosexual males.

Oberstone and Sukonek's (Note 1) comparative study of heterosexual and homosexual women led them to conclude that none of the popular myths about female homosexuals were supported. There seemed to be no "typically lesbian" personality characteristics, and clinical psychologists were unable to differentiate between the personality profiles of homo- and heterosexual women. (Hooker, 1957, found the same inability to differentiate between male gay and straight subjects.) Further, these investigators found that gay women were no more promiscuous than their straight counterparts. They tended to enter and leave romantic liaisons similarly, but more of the lesbians were currently living with their lovers, and were more satisfied with their relationships (in terms of emotion, sex, friendship, and interest levels) than were the heterosexual women studied. These findings are similar to those of Cotten (1975).

While not all investigators would agree (see, for instance, Hassell & Smith, 1975; Myreck, 1974), it is apparent that a body of literature is developing that characterizes both male and female homophiles as equally or more successful at sociosexual relationships than heterosexuals.

One area of sociosexual functioning that has been extensively studied among heterosexuals, but neglected in homosexuals, is that of courtship. Since similarities and differences between heterosexuals and homosexuals in certain aspects of courtship are the focus of the present study, a brief review of relevant literature dealing with heterosexual courtship is presented here.

It has been proposed that cultures such as our own, that prepare their young for successful courtship experiences, do not prepare them equally well for permanent pairing (see Gorer, 1948; Mead, 1949; Waller, 1937). This has been attributed to the competitive nature of courtship as against the cooperative attitudes and behaviors required for permanent partnership. It has been found, for instance, that college students seek the same traits in a date as they do in a mate, even though traits that make for a successful dating relationship and those that make for a successful permanent relationship vary considerably (Christensen, 1958).

The mate selection process is often investigated with regard to traits desired in a permanent partner. Powers (1971) summarized the state of the field in terms of research into "ideal mate" characteristics and concluded that, in spite of a number of methodological limitations, the general consensus across studies is one of high agreement on preferred mate characteristics. Those traits found to be important in an ideal mate were the same for men as for women (although some traits were emphasized more by one sex than the other). Powers summarized his conclusions as follows: "Research reviewed here has covered a thirty year span, 1939-1967, and has included both Depression and post World War II college samples. Traits which have been emphasized by both males and females during this period are largely characteristics which contribute to what has been called the companionship relationship" (p. 214).

More recently, these findings have been confirmed by Laner and Coakley (1974) and Laner (Note 2). Each of these studies added a new dimension—the perception of permanent partner desires both across and within sexes. Laner and Coakley (1974) found that in spite of the similar priorities held by each sex, each manifested considerable distortion of perception of the priorities of both opposite and same-sex peers. Laner (Note 2) found that across three stages of courtship (early, middle, and late) the greatest misperception of priorities occurred in the latest stage, and the least in the earliest stage. These findings are surprising in view of the fact that priorities have been found to be stable over time, highly similar between men and women, and are discussed by the majority of both men and women with same- and opposite-sex peers.

An additional finding of these studies was that the priorities of women were the most inaccurately perceived, by both men and other women.

Laner and Coakley (1974) and Laner (Note 2) explained their findings on the basis of (a) the competitive nature of courtship, (b) the greater pressure on women during the college years to find a permanent partner, and (c) differential socialization of men and women. (See Howe, 1976, for a discussion of the systematic socialization for differences, rather than for similarities, by heterosexually oriented parents, schools, etc.) Further, they held that mass media imagery contributed to the projection onto others of an inaccurate set of priorities, largely oriented to superficial qualities and values linked to a consumer-oriented lifestyle, rather than the companionship traits actually preferred.

In still another dimension, Centers (1975) found that attitudes of his respondents were significantly more alike in the "most preferred date" stage of courtship than they were in the late stage (i.e., during cohabitation or engagement) where attitudes showed a strong *negative* correlation.

The outcomes of inaccurate perception of priorities, increasing over the courtship span, and of attitudinal dissimilarity, in terms of permanent pairing in heterosexual couples, are demonstrated in the findings of Landis and Landis (1973), who reported that their married respondents admitted to not knowing how their partners stood on such critical issues of married life as sex, children, and money until *after* they were married, at which time disagreements caused marital conflict.

As noted earlier, no attention has been paid in the literature to mate selection priorities or to the perception of these on the part of homosexuals. The present study attempts to shed light on similarities and differences between homosexual and heterosexual permanent partner priorities and on the perception of these by gay and straight men and women.

HYPOTHESES OF THE PRESENT STUDY

Unlike heterosexuals, homosexuals of both genders have not been socialized into perceiving their potentially permanent partners as qualitatively different from themselves. Further, as Freedman (1975) and others have asserted, homosexuals of both genders may be more honest and direct in certain aspects of their mating processes than are heterosexuals. However, there is no reason to believe that the courtship of homosexuals is less competitive than that of heterosexuals, nor that homosexuals are not influenced by mass media imagery. These reflections lead to the following hypothetical considerations:

1. If courtship as a competitive institution is saliently responsible for the inaccuracy of perception of permanent partner priorities of others, then both heterosexuals and homosexuals should hold inaccurate perceptions of the priorities of others. (That is, if courtship is a game of jockeying for position and bargaining for the most profitable outcome, "mask wearing" in order to maximize options and outcomes should be characteristic of most courting persons regardless of gender or of sexual orientation.)
2. On the other hand, if differential socialization, that is, socialization for differences between the sexes rather than for similarities, is primarily responsible for inaccurate perceptions,

then homosexual respondents may be expected to show very little inaccuracy of perception, compared with their heterosexual counterparts.

3. If *both* the competitive nature of courtship and differential socialization are factors in distorting the perceptions of those approaching permanent pairing, then homosexuals may be expected to show some inaccuracy in terms of the perception of permanent partner priorities, but not as much as their heterosexual counterparts.
4. In view of the findings of recent studies as to homosexual "normalcy," there is no reason to believe that the permanent partner priorities of homosexuals of either gender differ significantly from the permanent partner priorities of heterosexuals of either gender.

The present study tested the null hypothesis of no difference between the priorities of homosexuals and heterosexuals in traits desired in a mate, and also tested the null hypothesis of no difference between homosexuals and heterosexuals in terms of error in the perception of traits desired by others.

METHOD

In order to provide for comparative data across studies, the questionnaire utilized by Laner and Coakley (1974) and Laner (Note 2), based on the earlier work of Varley (Note 3), was the instrument by which data were collected, with wording modified as appropriate for homo- and heterosexual respondents.

The questionnaire was distributed early in the Spring 1977 semester to students enrolled in a Sociology of Courtship and Marriage class at a southwestern university, and was simultaneously distributed by mail along with the regular newsletter mailing to the membership of a gay service organization on the same campus. Care was taken that responses from the classroom sample, largely but not exclusively heterosexuals, did not overlap with the responses from members of the gay organization, largely homosexual and bisexual men and women. Anonymity of response was guaranteed, and the task was presented as a voluntary one.

Printed instructions asked subjects to rank order six traits in terms of their own priorities in a permanent partner. Respondents were also asked to rank in order the same traits in four other ways: as they perceived others of their same gender and sexual orientation would rank them; as they thought others of the opposite gender but same sexual orientation would rank them; and as they thought others of both same and opposite gender with a different sexual orientation (homosexual or heterosexual) would rank them. Information regarding the respondents' age, sexual orientation, year in school, and marital or courtship status was obtained. Additionally, respondents were asked whether they had discussed their feelings about the kind of person with whom they would like to have a permanent relationship, and if so, with whom; and whether they expected (or hoped) to form a permanent relationship, and if so, when.

In the classroom setting, questionnaires were returned to the instructor in such a manner that no individual questionnaire could be connected to the respondent. Members of the gay campus organization returned their questionnaires to the researcher (also the classroom instructor) by mail in prestamped, preaddressed envelopes.

All but one of the classroom subjects returned their questionnaires, and about half the membership of the gay organization returned theirs. (Regarding the response rate of the homo- and bisexual respondents, Greenberg, 1977, has observed that alienation tends to increase among those who have been members of a gay activist organization for a year or more. In particular, Shilts, 1976, states that the state in which this study was conducted is ultraconservative politically, and homophobic. Shilts cites the concern of a leader of another gay organization in this state that getting local homosexuals to do anything is "like pulling teeth"—attributed to both apathy in the gay community and to the "virulent prejudice of most legislators" (p. 18). Thus, what might be considered a low response rate in other groups may be viewed as a relatively high response rate here).

CHARACTERISTICS OF THE SAMPLES

Usable responses were obtained from 48 heterosexual men, 44 heterosexual women, 69 homo- and bisexual men, and 19 homo- and bisexual women. (For the homosexual-bisexual samples, this is a predictable ratio of male-to-female response, given the findings of Kinsey, Pomeroy, & Martin, 1948, and Kinsey, Pomeroy, Martin, & Gebhard, 1953, regarding the distribution of male and female homosexuality in the general population.)

Ages ranged from 19 to 33 for straight men, and from 16 to 45 for the gay men (homo- and bisexual). (No statistically significant differences were found between responses of those homo- and bisexual men who were outside the age range of the heterosexual men, and those within that age range. For that reason, all responses are reported together.) The age range for straight women was 18 to 28, and for homo and bisexual women, 17 to 35. (The sample of homo and bisexual women was too small for meaningful analysis of differences between those within and those outside the age range of the heterosexual women, but on the assumption that since no differences were found for different-aged males, they would not be found for different-aged females, the responses of the homo- and bisexual women are reported together.)

No statistically significant differences in response style were found between freshmen-sophomores and juniors-seniors, nor between those in college and those who were not presently in school or who had already graduated, nor between those who had already formed a permanent relationship and those who had not. Thus, no subcategorical treatment of these groups was necessitated. One statistically significant difference in response style was noted between bisexual and homosexual males. This difference, however, did not warrant the separate treatment of these groups, and is discussed further below.

Differences were found across groups in terms of relational status (all subjects were unmarried), and between the straight and gay/bisexual respondents in terms of the proportions of each that had discussed their priorities in a permanent partner with members of both sexes regardless of their sexual orientation. There were also differences between straight and gay/bisexual respondents in terms of the proportions of each group that had already formed a permanent relationship. These differences are presented in Table 1.

The first section of the table indicates that nearly twice as many gay/bi women were cohabiting (including a sexual relationship) as were gay/bi men, although a considerably larger proportion of gay/bi women than of other groups were not dating at all. In general, more of the gay/bi groups of both sexes were cohabiting than either straight men or women.

The second section of the table shows that while a large majority of each of the four groups had discussed their desires in a permanent partner, gay/bi men and women had done so far less often with members of both genders, regardless of sexual orientation. Rather, they tended to discuss this topic within gay circles and with members of both genders, regardless of orientation, in about equal proportions.

The third section of Table 1 reveals that while a large majority of all groups, in approximately equal proportions, expect (or hope) to form permanent relationships at some time, considerably more gay/bi men and women than straight men and women had already formed such relationships.

Table 2 displays the stated permanent partner priorities of each of the groups studied. These data indicate that the priorities of gay/bi men and straight men do not differ in terms of rank order. Similarly, the priorities of gay/bi and straight women do not differ from one another. The companionship traits of honesty, affection, and intelligence are ranked in the top half of the priority order for all groups. Men differ from women only in that they place a somewhat greater emphasis on good looks; women place a somewhat greater emphasis on a partner's sense of humor. These findings generally support the first hypothesis of this study—that men's and women's rank-ordered preferences in traits of an ideal mate do not differ, whether gay/bi or straight.

Aside from the similarity in general rank orderings, however, the proportion of gay/bi men's desire for intelligence differs from that of straight men ($p < .05$), and these groups also differ in their relative emphases on good looks ($p < .10$), gay/bi men placing

TABLE 1

Differences in Relational Status, Discussion of Desires in a Permanent Partner, and Formation of Permanent Relationships in Straight and Gay/Bi Men and Women (in Percentages)

	Straight Men	Straight Women	Gay/Bi Men	Gay/Bi Women
Relational Status				
Not dating at all	21	11	12	32
Casual dating	42	43	49	16
Steady dating	17	20	13	5
Promised/engaged	8	18	(Category not relevant)	
Cohabiting	12	8	26	47
Discussed Desires in a Permanent Partner? (With Whom?)				
Discussed	79	91	88	84
With members of both sexes	76	75	41	44
Expect/Hope to Form a Permanent Relationship? (When?)				
Expect or hope to	92	89	91	89
Already have it	19	7	32	47

TABLE 2

Permanent Partner Priorities of Gay/Bi and Straight Men and Women, by Percentage of Each Group That Ranked Each Trait in the Top Half of Their Priority Order

Trait	Gay/Bi Men (_n_ = 69)	Straight Men (_n_ = 48)	Gay/Bi Women (_n_ = 19)	Straight Women (_n_ = 44)
Honest	86	83	94	86
Affectionate	78	79	79	82
Intelligent	72	53	74	70
Goodlooking	33	48	10	16
Has sense of humor	29	37.5	42	39
Has money	1	--	--	7

more emphasis on intelligence and less on appearance than do their straight same-sex counterparts. (Within the male homosexual/bisexual groups, fewer bisexuals valued intelligence than did homosexuals – 45% compared to 79%, $p < .05$ – indicating that in this dimension, bisexual males' preferences more closely approximate those of heterosexual males than of homosexual males, although for all three of these groups, intelligence ranks third in the priority rank ordering.)

Straight women and straight men differ in terms of their desire for intelligence in a permanent partner ($p < .10$) and in their desire for a good-looking partner ($p < .01$). A larger proportion of straight women emphasize their desire for intelligence in a permanent partner than do straight men, and fewer straight women emphasize the importance of good looks than do either straight or gay/bi men (the difference between straight women and gay/bi men on desire for intelligence in a partner is statistically significant beyond the .05 level).

While men and women, regardless of sexual orientation, share a similar set of priorities, where they differ, men, regardless of sex object orientation, are most like other men, and women, regardless of sex object orientation, are most like other women.

Table 3 presents perceptions of gay/bi men's priorities – or rather their misperceptions – by all groups studied. Curiously, both straight women and straight men assess the priorities of gay/bi men somewhat more accurately than do either gay/bi men themselves or gay/bi women. Most errors revolve around the false perception that gay/bi men rank good looks higher than they actually do, and honesty, intelligence, and affection lower than they actually do. While there is little misperception of the priority of both a sense of humor and the importance of money, the proportions of those who think these traits are ranked in the top half of the priority order tend to be higher than the proportion of gay/bi men who actually rank them there.

In Table 4, the actual priorities of straight men are compared with the perceptions of these priorities by all groups studied. Once again, both straight men and straight women are more accurate in their assessments of the priorities of straight men than are either of the

TABLE 3

Priority Misperceptions of Gay/Bi Men, by Gay/Bi and Straight Men and Women, Shown as Percentage of Bach Group Who Think That Gay/Bi Men Rank Each Trait in the Top Half of Their Priority Order[a]

Trait	Actual Priorities of Gay/Bi Men (n = 69)		Perception by Gay/Bi Men (n = 66)		Perception by Straight Men (n = 45)		Perception by Gay/Bi Women (n = 18)		Perception by Straight Women (n = 43)	
	%	Rank	%	Rank	%	Rank	%	Rank	%	Rank
Honest	86	(1)	53	(3)	55	(3)	55	(3)	60	(2)
Affectionate	78	(2)	79	(1)	91	(1)	67	(2)	93	(1)
Intelligent	72	(3)	41	(4)	44	(4)	39	(4)	47	(4)
Goodlooking	33	(4)	77	(2)	60	(2)	72	(1)	51	(3)
Has sense of humor	29	(5)	29	(5)	40	(5)	33	(5)	37	(5)
Has money	1	(6)	23	(6)	9	(6)	22	(6)	12	(6)
Error scores (absolute value of differences between percentages summed across the six studied traits):			131		118		140		103	

[a] In this and following tables, perceiving groups may be smaller than their sample size. This is due to the fact that a small number in each sample did not attempt to make assessments of the priorities of other groups.

TABLE 4

Priority Misperceptions of Straight Men, by Straight and Gay/Bi Men and Women, Shown as Percentage of Each Group Who Think That Straight Men Rank Each Trait in the Top Half of Their Priority Order

	Actual Priorities of Straight Men (n = 48)		Perception by Straight Men (n = 48)		Perception by Gay/Bi Men (n = 66)		Perception by Straight Women (n = 49)		Perception by Gay/Bi Women (n = 18)	
Trait	%	Rank	%	Rank	%	Rank	%	Rank	%	Rank
Honest	83	(1)	56	(4)	48	(3)	50	(3)	28	(5-6)
Affectionate	79	(2)	69	(2)	83	(2)	82	(1)	72	(2)
Intelligent	53	(3)	62.5	(3)	27	(5)	34	(4)	39	(4)
Goodlooking	48	(4)	77	(1)	86	(1)	77	(2)	89	(1)
Has sense of humor	37.5	(5)	27	(5)	44	(4)	32	(5)	44	(3)
Has money	--	(6)	10	(6)	11	(6)	25	(6)	28	(5-6)
Error scores (absolute value of differences between percentages summed across the six studied traits):			97		120.5		114.5		151.5	

gay/bi groups. The primary misperceptions are of the importance straight men are believed to place on good looks, and the reduced importance other groups attribute to straight men in terms of the first three companionship traits. As with the priorities of gay/bi men, most groups accurately perceive the lowest ranked traits, but regarding the relative importance of money, all groups tend to think it is more important to straight men than they themselves say it is.

In Table 5, the actual priorities of gay/bi women are compared with the perceptions of these priorities by all groups studied. Gay/bi men most accurately perceive the priorities of gay/bi women, and straight men perceive these priorities least accurately. Here again, the importance of good looks is ranked higher than it actually is, intelligence is ranked lower by some groups than it actually is, and a higher proportion of all groups judge money to be more important to gay/bi women than it actually is (although all groups correctly perceive money to be last ranked among the studied traits).

In Table 6, the actual priorities of straight women are compared with the perceptions of these priorities by all groups studied. Gay/bi women considerably outdistance all other groups in misperceiving the priorities of straight women. Straight women show the most accurate perception of their own group's priorities. The primary misperceptions, once again, are in terms of the attribution of greater importance to good looks than is actually the case. Similarly, the importance of money to straight women is overemphasized by all groups, including straight women themselves, and the importance of intelligence in a permanent mate is considerably underestimated by most groups.

DISCUSSION

Overall, the most misperceived priorities are those of straight women, while misperceptions of gay/bi women, gay/bi men, and straight men are approximately equal.

The greatest degree of misperception is attributable to gay/bi women. Gay/bi and straight men misperceive the priorities of others in approximately the same degree. The least misperception of priorities is attributable to straight women.

TABLE 5

Priority Misperceptions of Gay/Bi Women, by Gay/Bi and Straight Women and Men, Shown as Percentage of Each Group Who Think That Gay/Bi Women Rank Each Trait in the Top Half of Their Priority Order

Trait	Actual Priorities of Gay/Bi Women ($\underline{n}$ = 19)		Perception by Gay/Bi Women ($\underline{n}$ = 18)		Perception by Straight Women ($\underline{n}$ = 43)		Perception by Gay/Bi Men ($\underline{n}$ = 65)		Perception by Straight Men ($\underline{n}$ = 45)	
	%	Rank	%	Rank	%	Rank	%	Rank	%	Rank
Honest	94	(1)	79	(2)	67	(2)	80	(2)	60	(3)
Affectionate	79	(2)	89	(1)	91	(1)	89	(1)	89	(1)
Intelligent	74	(3)	33	(4-5)	53	(3)	46	(3)	44	(4)
Has sense of humor	42	(4)	33	(4-5)	30	(5)	32	(5)	33	(5)
Goodlooking	10	(5)	44	(3)	42	(4)	40	(4)	67	(2)
Has money	--	(6)	22	(6)	16	(6)	14	(6)	7	(6)
Error scores (absolute value of differences between percentages summed across the six studied traits):			132		121		106		148	

TABLE 6

Priority Misperceptions of Straight Women, by Straight and Gay/Bi Women and Men, Shown as Percentage of Each Group Who Think that Straight Women Rank Each Trait in the Top Half of Their Priority Order

Trait	Actual Priorities of Straight Women (n = 44)		Perception by Straight Women (n = 44)		Perception by Gay/Bi Women (n = 18)		Perception by Straight Men (n = 48)		Perception by Gay/Bi Men (n = 66)	
	%	Rank	%	Rank	%	Rank	%	Rank	%	Rank
Honest	86	(1)	64	(1-2)	55	(3)	54	(3-4)	61	(3)
Affectionate	82	(2)	64	(1-2)	72	(2)	66	(2)	67	(1)
Intelligent	70	(3)	57	(4)	22	(5)	54	(3-4)	42	(5)
Has sense of humor	39	(4)	25	(6)	11	(6)	17	(6)	18	(6)
Goodlooking	16	(5)	59	(3)	89	(1)	73	(1)	65	(2)
Has money	7	(6)	32	(5)	50	(4)	40	(5)	47	(4)
Error scores (absolute value of differences between percentages summed across the six studied traits):			135		233		176		178	

Most misperceptions of priority rankings across groups are seen as an overemphasis on the prestige or courtship-status traits of good looks and money, and an underemphasis on the importance of the primary companionship traits. Thus, to a considerable extent, each group attributes to its own and to all other groups a media-supported set of priorities indicating "marketable" traits of superficial value, and does not perceive the greater value of the subtler, companionship qualities.

It was hypothesized that similarities in terms of misperceptions would characterize all groups studied. This hypothesis is supported, in general, by these findings. Thus, it appears that the competitive nature of courtship, whether heterosexual, homosexual, or bisexual, is the most influential factor accounting for the misperceptions observed.

If members of each group respond to their potential permanent partners according to what each *thinks* the other wants in a mate, the misperceptions found in this study do not augur any better for the smooth functioning of homo or bisexual pairings of a permanent nature than they do for permanent heterosexual pairs. However, as Bernard (1964) has advised, permanent relationships may be of either what she calls the parallel or the interactional type. In parallel arrangements, each partner lives his/her own life in the male or female world. This pattern has also been called the "traditional" model. Conversely, an interactional pattern means togetherness, companionship, and sharing of a single world, and is frequently called the "contemporary" model. Kerckhoff (1974) has pointed out that "value consensus, personality fit, and so on, may well be important in mate selection where the expected marital pattern is interaction. But there is no reason to believe that these factors should affect the choice of a spouse in the same way when the expected marital pattern is parallel" (p. 75).

While Kerckhoff was referring to heterosexual relationships, as was Bernard, these considerations have even stronger implications for permanent homosexual relationships, insofar as homosexual pairings are, according to Freedman (1975) and others, less likely to be of the traditional than of the interactional type. The "shared world" of the interactional pattern probably characterizes more homosexual than heterosexual pairings, at least at present. This implies that value consensus and perceptual accuracy of one another's priorities are perhaps more important in homosexual than in heterosexual pairs. If gays tend to think of one another as more concerned with looks and money than they actually are, and less concerned with traits like honesty, intelligence, and affection, regardless of actual priorities, then attempted permanency may be undermined in more gay than straight relationships by these misperceptions, since straight relationships have additional legal/social sanctions and bonds to hold them together, even in the face of mismatching of understandings, than do homosexual relationships. This may account for the poignant statement of one gay male who was searching for a permanent relationship that "it's hard to find someone who isn't just looking for a trick," as well as for the reputation about and even among gays that stable relationships are rare. In short, the misdefinition of priorities may become a self-fulfilling prophecy.

Whether called dating by those involved, or called courtship by sociologists, it is a process by which mates are chosen (Lowrie, 1951, p. 340). The dating/courtship values of good looks and money, as has been shown, are projected onto others as traits desired in a permanent mate. It is of particular interest to note that the actual priority ordering of traits is the same as that found in earlier studies (Laner & Coakley, 1974; Laner, Note 2; Varley, Note 3), supporting Powers' (1971) contention that actual priorities have tended to remain stable across time. Further, the direction of the misperceptions of priorities has also tended to remain the same across studies using the same instrument, over the last 16 years, in spite of the often mentioned greater openness and "togetherness" of the youth culture.

Since support has been found for the essential "normalcy" of gay/bisexual men and women in that their priorities do not differ from those of heterosexuals, nor are they different in their misperceptions of the priorities of their own and other groups, it remains only to explain why the priorities of straight women are the most misperceived, and why gay and bisexual women misperceive the priorities of others to the greatest extent, and straight women the least:

1. *Misperception of the priorities of straight women*. The cumulative error scores of the priorities of straight women (722) considerably outdistance the cumulative error scores of the perceived priorities of gay/bi women (507), gay/bi men (492), and straight men (483.5). For practical purposes, it may be said that the misperceptions of the three latter groups do not differ.

Since women in general receive primary socialization for marriage, while men in general receive primary socialization for work, and since straight women (rather than gay women) have accepted the traditional "routing" for which they have been socialized, we would expect that they, as a group, would be the most adept at playing the courtship game. (This would be especially true during the college years, during which they are approaching and passing their typical age at marriage.) Playing this game involves marketing oneself to the greatest advantage, parlaying one's physical and lifestyle assets into a profitable outcome in the marriage market, while concealing negative qualities or actual priorities not thought to be valued in the courtship groups as a whole. Their adeptness at playing this game may lead others to suspect that what is valued during courtship is also what is valued in marriage—particularly if Farber's (1964) theory of the permanent availability of married persons is correct. That is, if married women are not actually "off the market" but are in theory (and often in practice, given our high and rising divorce and remarriage rates) still available as potential mates for alternate spouses, then to some extent the courtship game continues to be played even after marriage, regardless of possible desires for marital permanence with the first partner, and regardless of the high value placed on companionship traits over prestige (market) traits. Little wonder, then, that especially in straight women, the actual characteristics desired in a permanent partner are the most misperceived.

2. *Misperceptions by gay/bi women (greatest) and by straight women (least)*. To some extent, the considerations above assist in explaining why gay/bi women misperceive priorities the most, and straight women the least. The cumulative error scores of gay/bi women (656.5) as compared with those of straight men (539), gay/bi men (535.5), and straight women (473.5) may be explained by

the fact that gay/bi women have rejected the traditional socialization for women (i.e., into permanent relationships with members of the opposite sex—marriage). Having taken an alternate route, it is likely that gay/bi women perceive the priorities of others—again largely in terms of the prestige-oriented traits—as shallow, exploitative characteristics of a life-style they themselves reject. Conversely, straight women, who have accepted the traditional routing, are not only skilled at impression management but also develop skill at "seeing through" the facades of others, and thus misperceive actual priorities the least.

Whether these explanations suffice remains to be tested in future research designed to probe further into the causes of accuracy and inaccuracy of cross and intrasex perception.

While Freedman (1975) and others may be correct in their belief that homosexuals are more candid and honest than are heterosexuals, the expected effects of such straightforwardness are not manifested in the findings of this study. Perhaps the greater openness and directness of communication among homosexuals holds primarily for those who are already involved in permanent relationships over time, or for those who seek casual sexual encounters. In terms of the dating/courtship process, gay men and women show no more (and in one case, less) insight into the priorities of others, both gay and straight, than do members of the straight world.

REFERENCE NOTES

1. Oberstone, A. K., & Sukoneck, H. *Psychological adjustment and style of life of single lesbians and single heterosexual women*. Paper presented at the Western Psychological Association Convention, Sacramento, California, April 1975.
2. Laner, M. R. Ideal mate images in college courtship cohorts. *Proceedings of the Fifth Alpha Kappa Delta Sociological Research Symposium*, Richmond, Virginia, 1975.
3. Varley, D. Unpublished study, University of New Mexico, 1961.

REFERENCES

Bell, R. R. *Social deviance*. Homewood, Ill.: Dorsey Press, 1971.

Bernard, J. The adjustments of married mates. In H. T. Christensen (Ed.), *Handbook of marriage and the family*. Chicago: Rand-McNally, 1964.

Centers, R. Attitude similarity-dissimilarity as a correlate of heterosexual attraction and love. *Journal of Marriage and the Family*, 1975, *37*, 305-312.

Christensen, H. T. *Marriage analysis* (2nd ed.). New York: Ronald Press, 1958.

Clark, T. R. Homosexuality and psychopathology in non-patient males. *American Journal of Psychoanalysis*, 1975, *35*, 163-168.

Cotten, W. L. Social and sexual relationships of lesbians. *Journal of Sex Research*, 1975, *11*, 138-148.

Farber, B. *Family: Organization and interaction*. San Francisco: Chandler Publishing Co., 1964.

Freedman, M. Far from illness, homosexuals may be healthier than straights. *Psychology Today*, 1975, *8*(28), 30-31.

Gorer, G. *The American people*. New York: W. W. Norton, 1948.

Greenberg, J. S. The effects of a homophile organization on the self-esteem and alienation of its members. *Journal of Homosexuality*, 1976, *1*(3), 313-317.

Hassell, J., & Smith, E. Female homosexuals' concepts of self, men, and women. *Journal of Personality Assessment*, 1975, *39*, 154-159.

Hooker, E. The adjustment of the male overt homosexual. *Journal of Projective Techniques*, 1957, *21*, 18-31.

Hopkins, J. H. The lesbian personality. *British Journal of Psychiatry*, 1969, *115*, 1433-1436.

Horstman, W. Homosexuality and psychopathology. Unpublished doctoral dissertation, University of Oregon, 1972.

Howe, F. Sexual stereotypes start early. In E. A. Powers & M. W. Lees (Eds.), *Process in relationship* (2nd ed.). St. Paul: West Publishing Co., 1976.

Kerckhoff, A. C. The social context of interpersonal attraction. In T. L. Huston (Ed.), *Foundations of interpersonal attraction*. New York: Academic Press, 1974.

Kinsey, A. C., Pomeroy, W. B., & Martin, C. E. *Sexual behavior in the human male*. Philadelphia: W. B. Saunders, 1948.

Landis. J. T., & Landis, M. G. *Building a successful marriage* (6th ed.). Englewood Cliffs, N.J.: Prentice-Hall, 1973.

Laner, M. R., & Coakley, J. J. Mate selection priorities of college students: A new twist. *Cornell Journal of Social Relations*, Spring, 1974, 149-164.

Lowrie, S. H. Dating theories and student responses. *American Sociological Review*, 1951, *16*, 334-351.

Mead, M. *Male and female*. New York: William Morrow, 1949.

Myreck, F. Attitudinal differences between heterosexually and homosexually oriented males and between covert and overt male homosexuals. *Journal of Abnormal Psychology*, 1974, *83*, 81-86.

Powers, E. A. Thirty years of research on ideal mate characteristics: What do we know? *International Journal of Sociology of the Family*, 1971, *1*, 207-215.

Riess, B. F., Safer, J., & Yotive, W. Psychological test data on female homosexuality: A review of the literature. *Journal of Homosexuality*, 1974, *1*(1), 71-85.

Shilts, R. Fear and faith in Arizona. *Advocate*, February 9, 1977, pp. 6-7; 10; 18.

Siegelman, M. Adjustment of homosexual and heterosexual women. *British Journal of Psychiatry*, 1972, *120*, 477-481.

Turnage, J. R., & Logan, D. L. Sexual "variation" without "deviation." *Homosexual Counseling Journal*, 1976, *2*, 117-120.

Waller, W. The rating and dating complex. *American Sociological Review*, 1937, *2*, 727-734.

IV. HOW TO MAINTAIN A GAY RELATIONSHIP

Once you have found a partner whom you find attractive and companionable, you will probably turn to the inventive and exciting work of building a relationship that lasts. There are no guaranteed formulas for accomplishing this because partners must deal with their own and each other's highly individual and evolving needs, expectations, and sensibilities, which each becomes aware of as the relationship unfolds and in response to the unique and not always predictable circumstances of their lives. Based on gay relationships that have been studied over the past decade, the articles in this section will give you a sense of the issues that emerge, possible pitfalls to avoid, and some general guidelines that may be applicable to your particular relationship.

Perhaps the most global view of gay male relationships is provided in the article by David McWhirter and Andrew Mattison, which was published before the appearance in 1984 of their book, which I briefly described in my introduction to this volume. They have charted a pattern in the temporal evolution of gay relationships as six sequential stages: blending, nesting, maintaining, collaborating, trusting, and repartnering. An underlying theme in their developmental pattern is the need for the partners to recognize and maintain their individuality in the process of merging their interests and resources. In the authors' words: "Maintaining a relationship depends upon establishing balances between individuation and togetherness, conflict and its resolution, autonomy and dependence, confusion and understanding."

Since only males are involved in gay relationships, one might expect that partners would be spared the rigid assignment of feminine and masculine roles, a practice that unwittingly hogties straight relationships. Since heterosexual marriage, however, is the traditional model of intimacy and enduring companionship and the one we generally are reared to believe in, the temptation of gay partners to try to imitate it in building their own relationships is perhaps unavoidable: Any model may seem better than none.

The article by Jeanne Marecek, Stephen Finn, and Mona Cadell sketches some factors that may determine how "gender roles" are assigned in same-sex relationships of both men and women. The article distinguishes between *gender role*, the actual feminine or masculine behavior of partners, and *gender identity*, the internal picture each partner has of the self as masculine or feminine. In theory, since gender identity develops in early childhood, it shapes gender role, rather than the reverse. The authors, however, discuss other factors that influence the adoption of gender roles, such as the practical reality of the partners' lives together and the differences in economic, occupational, and social resources with which each enters and contributes to the relationship.

The determined attempt of gay partners to avoid falling into sex-role stereotypes is *not necessarily* the best way to maintain a relationship. We have heard much about the liabilities of untrammeled masculinity: the destructively competitive quest for power and control; the difficulty in expressing feelings and exposing vulnerability; and the frustrations of adhering to a strict sexual fidelity. This view of masculinity would seem to preclude the possibility of having relationships. It also places a premium on femininity, which contains several ingredients considered to be basic to relationships: emotion, attachment, and trust. It is therefore surprising to learn from the study by Rex Reece and Allen Segrist that more masculine partners had longer relationships than androgynous ones, even though they were less self-disclosing. Another unexpected finding, since it represents a behavioral departure from the male stereotype, was that the more masculine partners were more cooperative than the androgynous.

Along with gender roles, the partners' moral values, the subject of Anne Peplau's and Susan Cochran's research, are crucial to gay relationships. Their study focused on two core values that were found to shape intimate heterosexual relationships. *Attachment* is defined as "the value placed on having an emotionally close and relatively secure love relationship." *Autonomy* refers to the personal independence from the relationship that each partner desires to maintain, particularly with regard to retaining old and developing new friendships. Relationships that emphasize attachment, Peplau and Cochran found, are cast in the traditional marital mold, whereas the predominance of autonomy allows relationships to be "liberal," open to innovation. How these two values relate to others and influence gay relationships is also revealed in their report.

It is commonly assumed that enduring relationships are those that are "closed" rather than "open," words that have become euphemistic short-hand for partners restricting their sexual activity to each other or spreading it around. The irony of the traditional "closed" relationship is that it unwittingly makes sexuality, the very thing it seeks to integrate into the relationship and to control, an ingredient of supreme importance by placing it in its own category of the "exclusive" (What else is "exclusive" in the relationship?) . The question sensibly addressed by Lawrence Kurdek and Patrick Schmitt is whether or not sexual exclusivity makes the relationship *better*, or just last longer. Their results, as you will see, suggest that you can have a lasting and good relationship with or without this restriction but that its observance may safeguard particular qualities of relationships that are important to you as an individual.

During the AIDS epidemic maintaining relationships has been advocated as a way to protect partners from deadly viral infection. This position poses at least two problems. There is the epidemiological fact that one partner can be the source of infection for another. Therefore it may be necessary for the gay couple to avoid the transmission of blood and semen even when they have sex with each other. There is also the psychological issue that, if the partners are seriously incompatible, they may injure each other's mental health while desperately attempting to preserve their physical health. The balance of costs and gains in such tradeoffs, of course, must be determined by each partner, with the decision to break off the relationship remaining a realistic option. There is a serious doubt about the value of a relationship that is originally contracted to provide companionship, comfort, and happiness, but is preserved only as the means to avoid death.

Stages in the Development of Gay Relationships

David P. McWhirter, MD
Andrew M. Mattison, MSW, PhD
University of California
San Diego

Until the end of World War II, the primary focus of psychotherapy was the individual. Starting in the late 1940s, however, there was a gradual inclusion of therapeutic work with couples and eventually with families. A similar pattern of development has occurred in psychotherapy specifically for gay persons, as the early focus of therapy for individuals gradually broadens to include couples' therapy. In fact, the treatment of couples has become a keystone in the psychotherapeutic armamentarium of some therapists. Treatment has assumed many forms, but all are based on or extrapolated from heterosexual dyads, mainly because there is little research with homosexual couples. Although there are many similarities among primary relationships, regardless of the sex or orientation of the participants, same-sex couples do have unique characteristics that must be taken into consideration when theoretical and clinical issues are combined to form a treatment approach.

This paper presents a theoretical construct for the psychotherapy of gay male couples and is based on research and clinical work spanning 10 years. During that time we provided psychotherapy for hundreds of gay men in relationships. We also completed a 5-year research project studying 156 gay male couples who had been together from 1 to 37 1/2 years. With the knowledge and insight gained from this research and from our accompanying clinical experience, we have developed a theoretical model with broad clinical applications in the psychotherapy of gay men.

Two of the more important assumptions to emerge from our work are: (1) each relationship is a separate entity in itself with its own life, history, and development; (2) much like an individual, each relationship passes through a series of predictable developmental stages.

When Dr. Benjamin Spock (1945) popularized the developmental psychologists' discovery of stages of childhood, rebellious, difficult-to-handle 2-year olds suddenly became manageable and acceptable because they were passing through a predictable stage labeled the "terrible twos." Spock introduced a new sanity and calmness into childrearing by assigning characteristic behaviors and factors of physical growth to specific time periods or stages. These observations were not new to Spock's audience, but the commonsense, easy-to-understand way he packaged the information normalized many of the changes of infancy that had previously been so anxiety-provoking to parents.

The same may well be true of our observations about couples: What we describe as stages of the relationships are not really new findings; nevertheless, the formulation of characteristics common to the stages of gay male partnerships offers the potential for understanding the stages better, thereby reducing distress for the individuals and couples. Behaviors, interactions, and feelings formerly considered flaws in the relationships, or individual personality defects, are seen here as merely characteristic of a certain stage.

THE STAGES

Over a 5-year period (1974 to 1979), the authors interviewed in depth 156 gay male couples who were not in therapy and had lived together anywhere from 1 to more than 37 years. Some couples were interviewed once, others many times. The research design was a descriptive study using an interview schedule of 256 single items and 72 open-ended questions. The couples all lived in California, mostly in San Diego County. Men's ages ranged from 20 to 69 years, the mean age being 37.4 years. The mean time in a relationship was 8.7 years, with median being slightly over 5 years.

The significant data relating to stages of the relationships emerged in themes extracted from the interviews. Many factors, such as the age of the partners, their previous relationships, personalities, and backgrounds, affect relationship stages; but considering all the possible variables, there are enough similarities among the couples as their relationships progress to recognize individual stages and to suggest that most gay male relationships pass through them.

We have identified six stages, with the first four occurring within the first 10 years as a couple. The stages are presented as tentative formulations needing further clinical trial and research validation. Even though we have found wide variations within our own practice, the conceptualization of developmental stages has been very helpful in the clinical approach to therapy with gay male couples.

Stage One: Blending (First Year)

Characteristics:

1. Blending
2. Limerance[1]
3. Equality of partnership
4. High sexual activity

Blending is experienced as the intensity of togetherness gay men feel early in their relationships. Their similarities bind them, their differences are mutually overlooked. They tend to do everything together, almost to the exclusion of others. Limerance is intense and most often reciprocal, although there are variations here. Equality is usually manifested in shared financial responsibility and equal distribution of the chores of daily living, but most importantly as a shared attitude of equality. Sexual activity varies but usually includes several encounters weekly and *de facto* sexual exclusivity.

Stage Two: Nesting (1 to 3 Years)

Characteristics:

1. Homemaking
2. Finding compatibility

3. Decline in limerance
4. Ambivalence

During the first year together men appear to have limited concerns about their living environment. By the second year, however, attention to their surroundings takes the form of homemaking activities, decorating a new home or rearranging an old one. Couples in this stage also tend to see each other's shortcomings and discover or create complementarities that enhance compatibility. The partners' decline in limerance is usually not simultaneous and is often a cause for worry and concern. The search for compatibility and the decline in limerance set the stage for the mixture of positive and negative feelings about the value of the relationship that we call ambivalence.

Stage Three: Maintaining (3 to 5 Years)

Characteristics:

1. Individualization begins
2. Risk-taking
3. Dealing with conflict
4. Relying on the relationship

Maintaining the relationship depends upon establishing balances between individualization and togetherness, conflict and its resolution, autonomy and dependence, confusion and understanding. The intense blending of Stage Two clears the path for the re-emergence of individual differences, identified here as individualization. As this process begins, individualization is accompanied by some necessary risk-taking—whether in outside sexual liaisons, more time apart, greater self-disclosure, or new separate friendships. These risks often result in conflicts, including jealousy and differences of opinion, interest, or tastes that are dealt with either by confrontation and resolution or by avoidance. The fourth characteristic of the stage (relying on the relationship) may well be the ingredient sustaining the other three characteristics. After 3 or 4 years together, two gay men tend to look upon their relationship as if it were a third person possessing certain dependable qualities, such as steadfastness, comfort, and familiarity, which sustain the momentum of their partnership. It should be noted here that recognition and support of the relationship by family and friends often begin only after a couple has been together 3 years.

Stage Four: Collaborating (5 to 10 Years)

Characteristics:

1. Collaborating
2. Productivity
3. Establishing independence
4. Dependability of partners

Besides the usual meaning of "cooperation," collaboration also implies giving aid to an occupying enemy. Couples in Stage Four can unwittingly collaborate in this sense and aid the development of boredom and feelings of entrapment. After 5 years together, couples experience a new sense of security and a decreasing need to process their interactions. On the one hand, this decline in communication frequently gives rise to making unverified assumptions about each other. On the other hand, their collaborative adjustments often lead to effective complementarity. This complementarity, combined with the coping mechanisms for dealing with conflict and boredom, yields new energy for enriching their horizons beyond the relationship. This energy leads to mutual as well as individual productivity of a visible nature, such as business partnerships, financial dealings, estate building, or achieving personal gains in professional or academic worlds. The individualization of Stage Three can progress to the establishment of independence, sustained by the steady, dependable availability of a partner for support, guidance, and affirmation.

Stage Five: Trusting (10 to 20 Years)

Characteristics:

1. Trust
2. Merger of money and possessions

3. Constriction
4. Taking the relationship for granted

Trust develops gradually for most people. As the years pass, and as they gain experience, gay couples trust each other with greater conviction. The trust of Stage Five includes a mutual lack of possessiveness and a strong positive regard for each other. The slow merger of money and possessions may be a manifestation of this trust. Among men in the latter half of Stage Five, we also found a gradual isolation from the self as manifested by lack of feelings and inattention to personal needs, isolation from the partner by withdrawal and lack of communication and sometimes isolation from friends in the same ways. We have identified this characteristic as a type of constriction; it may be a result of the men's ages. The attitude of taking the relationship for granted develops as a result of the other characteristics of this stage.

Stage Six: Repartnering (20 Years and Beyond)

Characteristics:

1. Attainment of goals
2. Expectation of permanence of the relationship
3. Emergence of personal concerns
4. Awareness of the passage of time

The twentieth anniversary appears to be a special milestone for gay male couples. We found a surprising number of couples reporting a renewal of their relationship after being together for 20 years or more. Most men's goals include financial security; the men in our sample had usually attained this after 20 years. Other goals included business, professional, and academic success. These couples also assumed that they would be together until separated by death. Most men expressed a series of personal concerns, such as for health and security, fear of loneliness, death of partners or themselves, etc. Most were struck by the passage of time and would reminisce about their years together.

This developmental paradigm of gay male relationships is not intended as a new typology for couples but rather as a broad framework for understanding some of the developmental phases these couples experience. Although stages are organized around time periods and are presented in time-related linear sequence, there are many variations that influence the stages and make them far more dynamic than our brief outline reveals. For instance, men who have had several previous relationships may shorten Stage One to a few weeks or months and move dramatically through Stage Two in a year. Some couples may linger far longer in the warm glow of Stage One because of their similarities, while others with wide age differences may have many Stage Three characteristics after a few months or a year.

Gender Roles in the Relationships of Lesbians and Gay Men

Jeanne Marecek, PhD
Stephen E. Finn
Mona Cardell
Swarthmore College

Gender roles are sets of behavior or functions that society deems appropriate for members of each sex. The conventional female role encompasses such functions as caring for children and a home, nurturing others, and acceding to the wishes of others; it proscribes involvement in public life and assertion of dominance over others. The conventional male role, on the other hand, encompasses assertion of power and physical strength, achievement in public life, and being a "good provider"; it proscribes emotional expressiveness and dependency. Adherence to these roles by women and men was once regarded as healthy and even as necessary for maintaining the social order. Recently, however, critiques by feminists and social scientists have pointed to the limitations that gender roles place on individuals and on society.

In this paper, we consider gender roles in the intimate relationships of lesbians and gay men. Conventionally, gender role expectations govern such aspects of relationships as division of housework, sexual expression, and decision-making. Some lesbians and gay men report patterns of behavior in their relationships that resemble conventional gender roles to some extent (e.g., Cardell, Finn, & Marecek, 1981; Peplau & Gordon, 1983). It is important to note, however, that these reports rarely typify the stereotype of exaggerated roleplaying (e.g., butch-femme relationships) sometimes attributed to homosexual couples, but rather suggest more moderate conformity to gender-role norms. Furthermore, although direct comparisons are hard to draw, studies suggest that traditional gender roles may be less common in lesbian and gay male couples than in heterosexual couples (Cardell, Finn, & Marecek, 1981; Peplau & Amaro, in press). Nonetheless, the evidence that gender roles can occur even in relationships in which both partners are of the same gender leads us to raise three general questions. First, to the extent that it does occur, why does gender-role-playing occur in same-sex couples? Second, on what basis are roles allocated in couples in which roleplaying does occur? Third, what are the implications of gender roles for partners' satisfaction with their relationships?

GENDER ROLES IN LESBIAN AND GAY MALE COUPLES

One possible explanation for the origins of gender-role-playing in couples is that individuals internalize the prevailing cultural models of how to behave in intimate relationships and bring these models to their own relationships. These cultural models are represented in portrayals of intimate relationships in literature, mass media, and even myth and the Bible. To the extent that these representations portray romantic aims as thwarted by violations of gender-role conventions, the opportunities they afford for vicarious learning may be especially potent. In addition, early observations of others' relationships—particularly the observation of one's parents' relationship—may lead to identification and subsequent, perhaps unconscious, imitation.

According to this account, we would expect roughly equal amounts of gender-role-playing among heterosexual, lesbian, and gay male couples. It appears, however, that the relationships of lesbians and gay men involve less gender-role-playing than the relationships of heterosexual couples. Thus, we would have to postulate either that lesbians and gay men have less exposure to cultural representations of traditional gender-role behavior in intimate relationships, or that parents and other significant adults in the early lives of gay men and lesbians are less gender-role-typed than those in the lives of heterosexuals. Neither of these claims seems especially plausible; additional explanatory factors must therefore be sought.

One possible explanation is that most cultural models of intimate relationships (as well as most of the relationships observed directly by children) involve heterosexual couples. Thus, although the processes of internalization of the models may be similar for everyone, the internalized models might be less applicable to same-sex relationships than to heterosexual relationships because the former are more dissimilar to the models. Another possible factor is the endorsement of feminist values, accompanied by efforts to expunge conventional gender-role behavior. Especially among lesbians, the endorsement of feminism may be more widespread than among heterosexuals. A third factor may be espousal of the ideology of gay liberation. Lesbians and gay men who are identified with the gay liberation movement are striving to create new forms of relationships that are distinct from those of heterosexual couples. Though such individuals might not renounce conventional gender roles as such, their relationships would be less likely to embody them.

ROLE ALLOCATION IN LESBIAN AND GAY MALE COUPLES

To the extent that gender-role allocation occurs in heterosexual couples, the woman is expected to play the feminine role and the man, the masculine role. While in practice, reversals of these expectations no doubt occur, they seem to be fairly infrequent. By contrast, in same-sex couples, gender does not provide a basis for the allocation of roles. Thus, for homosexual couples whose relationships do involve gender-role-playing, what might the process of role allocation be?

We suggest three hypothetical models of how roles might be allocated to partners in same-sex couples. The first model proposes that roles are allocated via a two-stage process involving incidental pragmatic factors (such as income disparity, skill differences, or work schedules) and internalized gender-role norms. Initially, pragmatic factors would lead one partner to assume certain tasks or responsibilities in the relationship. Subsequently, additional behaviors that are part of the same gender role as the initial behavior will also be assumed by this partner. For example, differences in partners' work schedules might lead one of them to take responsibility for the preparation of dinner. Meal preparation is a component of the feminine role, and thus is part of a cluster of behaviors including housework, decorating, and purchasing household supplies. Thus, assuming responsibility for cooking might imply assuming responsibility for these tasks as well. In such a way, the initial assignment of cooking responsibilities could be made without reference to gender roles; however, the subsequent clustering of other behaviors would reflect internalized gender-role prescriptions. Furthermore, the nature and salience of the pragmatic factors operative at the first stage would vary from couple to couple. Roles resembling the traditional gender roles could occur in same-sex couples, but there would be no systematic way to predict across couples which roles would be allocated to which partners.

The second model rests on the observation that the masculine role is more valued and more rewarded than the feminine role. Thus, it might be that the claim to the masculine role is the prerogative of the partner who is the more powerful member of the couple. This power could be based on such personality traits as dominance or ability to influence others. Alternatively, it may be based on the higher status afforded by such factors as greater age, higher income, or greater educational attainment.

The third hypothetical model relies on the gender identities of the partners in the couple. Gender identity refers to how "male" or "female" one feels. Except among transsexuals, gender identity typically is closely related to biological sex. However, gender identity need not be simply "male" or "female"; rather it could lie anywhere along a continuum, much as other personality traits. As Money and Erhardt (1972) point out, there is considerable variation among members of each sex in the extent to which individuals identify with that sex. This variation can be observed in individuals' responses to such questions as whether they ever appear as members of the opposite sex in their sleeping dreams or in their sexual fantasies, whether they ever experience a concern or a wish that others will perceive them as members of the opposite sex, and so on (Finn & Mahowald, in press). It is important to note that, as we have construed it, gender identity is not necessarily related to gender-role behavior. Nonetheless, in a culture such as ours, which blurs the distinction between the two constructs, we would expect to find a close association between the two.

There is no evidence to date that gay men and lesbians differ from heterosexual men and women respectively in their gender identities (cf. Bell & Weinberg, 1978). Nonetheless, it is possible that in same-sex couples (in which biological sex provides no cues for role assignment), even small differences in the gender identities of the partners might lead them to play different gender roles. Thus, for example, both partners in a gay male couple may be male identified, but if one is extremely male-identified, he may assume masculine role behavior and functions exclusively. His less-strongly male identified partner may have to assume complementary feminine-role behaviors. This notion that the extremity of one's gender identification may influence one's gender role is a speculative and controversial one. Nonetheless, we suggest that it is worthy of further scrutiny.

GENDER ROLES AND SATISFACTION IN COUPLES

In general, gay couples and heterosexual couples seem to experience similar degrees of satisfaction in their intimate relationships (e.g., Peplau & Amaro, in press; Cardell, Finn, & Marecek, 1981). Furthermore, some lines of evidence suggest that egalitarian or role-free relationships provide greater avenues to satisfaction than relationships that are gender-role-typed. In our own research, among both same-sex and heterosexual couples, partners' satisfaction decreased as reported amount of gender-role behavior increased. Additionally, being in the feminine role was less satisfying than being in the masculine role (Cardell, Finn, & Marecek, 1981). Partners in the feminine role in highly gender role-typed relationships were the least satisfied of all.

What mediates the relationship between gender-role-playing and satisfaction in couples? One possible explanation is that many individuals have come to hold an egalitarian ideology and, thus, to advocate role-free relationships. Relationships that are not consonant with such values would be less satisfying to such individuals. The ideology of egalitarianism is especially likely to be espoused by young, middle-class, well-educated individuals; such individuals are also overrepresented among study populations. Were we to study individuals with different personal backgrounds, we might find the relationship between gender roles and satisfaction to be more complex than it currently appears. Another possible explanation focuses on the constriction of behavior that gender-role-playing entails. This constriction may limit self-expression and in other ways diminish the richness of one's experience, decreasing satisfaction in the relationship.

Neither of the processes just described explains why the feminine role might be less satisfying than the masculine role. Additional factors must be examined. For example, the feminine role may be inherently less satisfying than the masculine role because it affords less autonomy and, at least as regards housework, requires the performance of more menial chores. Alternatively, the feminine role may be less satisfying because society at large values feminine attributes less highly than masculine ones. The influence of societal values on one's satisfaction with one's role may be especially pronounced in the case of men who are labelled "effeminate" because they assume feminine roles.

CONCLUSION

This paper was stimulated by recent research on the intimate relationships of gay men and lesbians. In particular, it addresses reports that gender-role-playing sometimes can be found in these relationships, though less commonly than in heterosexual relationships. We have suggested reasons why this might be the case. Also, we have speculated on various ways in which the division of roles between members of a couple might be made. Finally, we proposed various reasons why gender-role-playing might be negatively related to satisfaction. We hope that our ideas are thought-provoking and that they stimulate further inquiry.

REFERENCES

Bell, A. P. & Weinberg, M. S. *Homosexualities: A study of diversity among men and women*. New York: Simon and Schuster, 1978.

Cardell, M., Finn, S., & Marecek, J. Sex-role identity, sex-role behavior, and satisfaction in heterosexual, lesbian, and gay male couples. *Psychology of Women Quarterly*, 1981, *5*, 488-494.

Finn, S. E. & Mahowald, M. A scale for measuring cross-gender identity in transsexual populations. *Journal of Personality Assessment*, in press.

Money, J., & Erhardt, A. *Man and woman, boy and girl*. Baltimore: Johns Hopkins University Press, 1972.

Peplau, L. A., & Amaro, H. Understanding lesbian relationships. In W. Paul & J. D. Weinrich (Eds.), *Homosexuality as a social issue*. Beverly Hills, CA: Sage Press, in press.

Peplau, L. A., & Gordon, S. L. The intimate relationships of lesbians and gay men. In E. R. Allgeier & N. B. McCormick (Eds.), *Gender roles and sexual behavior: The changing boundaries*. Palo Alto, CA: Mayfield Press, 1983, pp. 226-244.

The Association of Selected "Masculine" Sex-Role Variables with Length of Relationship in Gay Male Couples

Rex Reece, PhD
Allen E. Segrist, PhD

In much of the small amount of research literature that exists today, and in popular conception as well, it is assumed that gay men are unable to establish or maintain ongoing relationships. Hoffman (1968, p. 166) has written that "the most serious problem for those who live in the gay world is the great difficulty they have in establishing stable relationships with each other." Dank (1973) wrote that these relationships are generally short-lived. The present research project was designed to begin gathering information about the differences between gay men who stay in ongoing couples and those who have separated. It is hoped that such information will be helpful to those who attempt to establish or maintain such relationships, as well as to the men and women in the helping professions who assist them in that effort.

Certain cultural conditions contribute to the difficulties faced by gay men in the continuation of their relationships. The lack of social, legal, or economic support systems such as exist for institutionalized marriages is the most obvious practical consideration. Hoffman (1968) reasoned that the social prohibition against homosexual expression prevent many individuals from becoming involved in stable relationships.

It would be useful to generalize the dynamics of relationships to many kinds of coupling, regardless of whether the two people are married or single, female or male, of the same or opposite sexes. However, it is also reasonable to expect that some relationships reflect additional or different dynamics and difficulties as a result of their particular structural variance or because the participants vary from the familiar cultural norms. For the purposes of this study it was assumed that, since gay men are biologically male and culturally conditioned as such, a significant degree of their self-esteem and sex-role identification will be tied to certain behaviors and attitudes labelled "masculine" in our culture. It was also assumed that a special group of concerns involved in gay male coupling has resulted from masculine training and socialization. This article describes the connection of degrees of so-called masculine characteristics (competition, lack of self-disclosure, and sexual promiscuity) and sexrole type with longevity in gay male relationships.

Until very recently, little descriptive research on gay couples had been reported. Some research studies (Bell & Weinberg, 1978; Chaffee, 1976; Lee, 1976; Nuehring, Fein, & Tyler, 1974; Sonenschein, 1968) have attempted to develop typologies of gay relation ships. McWhirter and Mattison (Note 1) have reported a wide ranging descriptive study of over 150 gay male couples. A few studies (Chaffee, 1976; Dailey, 1979; De Cecco & Shively, 1978; Jones & Bates, 1978; Oliver, 1976) have tried to measure the degrees of satisfaction, conflict, or intimacy in gay male coupling. Dailey's (1979) study tied some aspects of male homosexual relationships to longevity.

Westwood (1960) and Hooker (1962, 1965) have offered evidence to refute the popular assumption that gay men model their sexual and role relationships on traditional feminine-masculine dichotomies. Stringer and Grygier (1976) concluded that homosexual males may exhibit high femininity and low masculinity in some areas of their personalities but in other areas be no different from heterosexual men. Cotton (1972) suggested that there may often be a difference in sex role or some other social, cultural, or economic difference between members of a gay male couple and that this stimulates the generally accepted complementarity in heterosexual pairings. Freedman (1975), however, wrote that sex-role dichotomies are not crucially important to gay people. Westmoreland (1975) found that most of the gay male couples she studied saw themselves as equals or as involved in a complementary leader-follower relationship. Her evidence suggested that some gay men have the ability to be flexible in their sex-typed roles and are able to switch between typically masculine and typically feminine behaviors. Along with other researchers and writers, Bem, Martyna, and Watson (1976) have begun to use the concept of psychological androgyny as a way of thinking about the integration of both feminine and masculine characteristics within one individual. This conceptualization of sex role raises a question: Are androgynous gay men better able to adopt a complementary role in a relationship? If sex-role complem entarity has a positive effect on longevity in relationships, then the question is particularly relevant to the present study.

A number of studies (Broverman & Vogel, 1972; Goodenough, 1957; Kagan, 1964; Watson, 1959) have shown that men and boys are more competitive than women and girls. Research by Aller (1962), Cutler and Dyer (1965), and Katz, Goldstone, Cohen, and Stucker (1963) indicates that for wives to conform to their husbands' expectations and use more adjustive and cooperative responses is likely to contribute to role complementarity and satisfaction in heterosexual relationships. When men have been taught they must be competitive in order to fulfill their proper socio-biological roles, it seems likely that some role complementarity is prerequisite to maintaining mutually satisfying and supporting relationships between them. This in turn raises the question: Can two men who are both apt to have competitive temperaments integrate that characteristic into their ongoing intimate relationship?

Another role-characteristic that might affect the relations between two gay men is the general unwillingness of males to express their feelings openly. Balswick and Peek (1971), Broverman and Vogel (1972), Clark (1972), Fasteau (1974), and Komarovsky (1967) have reported on various aspects of male emotional inexpressiveness. Much has been written (Fromm, 1955; Halverson & Shore, 1969; Jourard, 1958, 1963) about the positive effect of self-disclosure on the formation and development of closeness and intimacy in a dyadic relationship. Jourard (1964) has argued that self-disclosure is a vital factor in the ability to maintain relationships that are satisfying and long-lasting.

The issue of sexual plurality, the term used by Lee (1976) and intended to be less derogatory than "promiscuity," is repeatedly interwoven in discussions and explorations of gay male relationships. Studies reported by Bell (1973), Bell and Weinberg (1978), Fein and Neuhring (Note 2), Schafer (1977), and Sonenschein (1968) lend support to the belief that gay men are likely to have many more sexual partners in their lifetimes than lesbians or heterosexual men and women. Dannecker and Reich (1974), McWhirter and Mattison (Note 1), and Stevens (1975) offer evidence that gay men in stable relationships frequently renounce sexual fidelity. Harry and Lovely (1979) reported that among their coupled gay male respondents sexual fidelity was inversely related to longevity. In our clinical and social observations, the present authors have found a frequent concern to be the quest for and management of an ongoing relationship combined with sexual plurality. Parental models of sexual interaction, most often assumed to be monogamous, probably contribute to the difficulty experienced when two men with past pluralistic sexual behavior attempt to establish a permanent pairing – especially when the subculture to which they belong supports sexual activity with many partners. There are, however, few data regarding the degree to which sexual plurality existed in couples that later broke up.

In light of the literature on the nature of relationships generally, on androgyny, and on specific male role expectations with respect to competition, lack of self-disclosure, and sexual plurality, it seems likely that the gay men most androgynous, cooperative, self-disclosing, and accepting of pluralistic sex would be most apt to maintain ongoing relationships. This constellation of characteristics would modify some of the typical "masculine" barriers to close male-male relationships and thereby affect the longevity of gay male coupling. These issues were investigated in the present study.

METHOD

Subjects

A purposive sample (Goode & Hatt, 1952) of 130 men (33 ongoing and 32 separated couples) who identified themselves as gay or homosexual responded sequentially to a set of self-report instruments.

Several researchers (Bass-Hass, 1968; Bell, 1973; Hooker, 1957; Morin, 1977) have discussed the conditions that make it impossible to obtain a random sample of gay people, especially when the research interest is in couples. For this study, an entry into "friendship networks" (De Cecco & Shively, 1978) was accomplished by first contacting the heads of gay religious, political, social, interest, academic, educational, and service groups in greater Los Angeles. The selection of subjects was controlled along the following dimensions: (1) race: all subjects were Caucasian; (2) citizenship: all were born in the United States; (3) age: all subjects were between 21 and 37 years old, with almost 50% falling within the 31-35 age range; (4) length of relationship: all subjects were now involved, or within the last year had been involved, in an ongoing cohabitant relationship of between three and seven years duration, with the mean length falling between four and five years; (5) obvious emotional disturbance or physical handicap: no subject had any.

These narrow ranges of age and relationship longevity were selected in order to reduce the number of factors that might influence relationship status. In particular, by limiting the study to young adulthood, it was hoped to avoid factors peculiar to adolescence, middle, or old age. Wider ranges would have increased the likelihood that time, age differences, economics, or psychological or emotional factors had influenced couple status. Since the authors' intent was to study "established" as opposed to "tentative" relationships, it was decided to choose as subjects couples who had been together for a minimum of three years. There is no literature on gay couples that shows separation trends, so the seven-year maximum was based on divorce statistics from heterosexual marriages, which indicate higher frequencies of separation at seven years (Bureau of the Census, 1976). Subjects were assigned to two groups according to the present status of the relationship: (1) ongoing; or (2) separated (no longer defining themselves as a couple) within the last year.

Instruments

Jourard's Self-Disclosure Questionnaire (Jourard & Lasakow, 1958) was used to examine the degree of self-disclosure within couples. Several forms of the JSDQ have been employed in research; the form selected for this study is adapted from that reported by Small (Jourard, 1971). It consists of 23 statements of information about the self, such as "the occasions in my life in which I was the happiest" and "my favorite forms of erotic play and sexual lovemaking." The Questionnaire asks to what degree that information is shared with others. Slight changes were made to make the questions more relevant to a male homosexual relationship: A question referring to marriage was dropped and two from another form of the JSDQ—questions regarding body image and one's reaction to a "charming, flirtatious male"—were added.

The Altruism Scale (Sawyer, 1966) was used to measure the degrees of cooperation within a couple relationship. It consists of two parts: (1) two 3 x 3 scaled matrices with various combinations of desirable Self-Other outcomes in response to specific hypothesized situations involving differences in the incomes of the two partners and in their responses to a sexual "come on" by an attractive third party, and (2) a 21-point scale directly estimating altruistic responses to a particular situation. Again, some changes in wording were made to make the Scale more applicable to gay male relationships. Lake, Miles, and Earle (1973) wrote that Sawyer's conceptualization, as well as the results of the validity and reliability studies, verified the ability of the Altruism Scale to measure degrees of cooperation. They stated that the test did not really measure altruism but is a relatively good indicator of a cooperative orientation.

The Bem Sex Role Inventory (Bem, 1974) was used to categorize subjects as either sex-typed masculine (high masculine, low feminine), sex-typed feminine (high feminine, low masculine), androgynous (high masculine, high feminine), or undifferentiated (low masculine, low feminine). The BSRI is a sex-role measure composed of 20 alternating items for each of its three scales: Masculinity, Femininity, and Social Desirability. Items consist of trait-oriented descriptive words or phrases that the respondents use to rate themselves. At the time the data were collected for this study (1978), articles by Bem (1975), Bem and Lenny (1976), Bem et al. (1976), Fitzgerald (Note 3), and Gaudreau (1977) indicated that the BSRI was essentially valid as a measure of sex roles and as a predictor of sex-typed behaviors. However, recent articles by Bem (1979), Helmreich, Spence, and Holahan (1979), Pedhazur and Tetenbaum (1979), Spence and Helmreich (1979), and Storms (1979) show that the BSRI does not predict sex-role preference but, instead, instrumental and expressive sex-linked traits. The articles also question the concept of androgyny on the ground that M-F characteristics still appear to be dichotomized in most respondents' concepts of self.

Sexual plurality was measured by asking for the number of sexual encounters with people other than the lover during the relationship.

Data were analyzed in accord with scoring methods used in earlier research, in order to compare the present findings with those of other studied populations.

Procedure

Four gay men, trained by the researcher to follow standardized procedures, systematically administered the four instruments to each of the subjects at the subjects' homes. In addition, information on sexual plurality and data on the demographic variables of occupation, income, age, education, and length of relationship, were collected. Each interviewer administered approximately 30 sets.

Ongoing couples usually responded to the questionnaires simultaneously, but it was often necessary for separated subjects to respond in different locations at different times. After an appropriate and cooperative separated subject had been located, his ex-partner was contacted. If both agreed to participate, separate appointments were scheduled. Each partner in the separated couple was requested not to discuss the experience with the other until both had responded.

RESULTS AND DISCUSSION

Over half of the subjects fell into the manager/supervisor or professional/technical occupational categories; the remainder were scattered among several other labels: artist/craftsperson, clerical, civil servant, sales, services, skilled labor, and other. A chi-square test showed no significant differences in occupations between the separated and ongoing couples (χ^2 = 14.34, df = 8) nor in the incomes of the two groups (χ^2 = 3.51, df = 3). The median annual income frequency range for both groups was $15,000 to $19,999. When the data were submitted to a *t*-test (t = .13, df = 118), no significant difference was found in the length of the relationships maintained by the two groups. The mean length of the relationship for ongoing subjects was 4.68 years; for separated subjects it was 4.72 years. Chi-square analysis did yield a significant difference between the two groups in educational levels (χ^2 = 13.22, df = 5, $p < .05$). Of the separated subjects, 60% were college graduates, as contrasted with 80% of the ongoing subjects.

It was expected that (1) there would be an association between couple status and sex-role type and that (2) ongoing couples would contain higher numbers of androgynous respondents than separated couples. Chi-square test results reported in Table 1 indicate that there were significant differences in the mean scores on the BSRI (Sample: χ^2 = 7.9, df = 3, $p < .05$; Bem: χ^2 = 15.2, df = 3, $p <$ .01). When Bem's medians were used for scoring and also when the present sample medians were used, more than twice as many men in the separated group, as compared with the ongoing group, fell into the androgynous category. The median split method of analysis was

Table 1: Number and Percent by Sex-Role Category and Couple Status, Using Both Sample Medians and Bem's Medians for Scoring

		Androgynous		Masculine Sex-Typed		Feminine Sex-typed		Undifferen-tiated	
		Sample	Bem	Sample	Bem	Sample	Bem	Sample	Bem
Ongoing	N	12	16	15	20	11	13	22	11
	%	32.4	30.2	60.0	69.0	47.8	65.0	62.9	61.1
Separated	N	25	37	10	9	12	7	13	7
	%	67.6	69.8	40.0	31.0	52.0	35.0	37.1	38.9
Total	N	37	52	25	29	23	20	35	18
	%	100.0	100.0	100.0	100.0	100.0	100.0	100.0	100.0

Sample: X^2 = 7.9, df = 3, p .05
Bem: X^2 = 15.2, df = 3, p .01

used for purposes of comparison with Bem's medians and with other research, even though it has not proved to be dependable with small samples. Table 2 shows that on scores derived by using a femininity and a masculinity score for each respondent, there was no significant difference between the ongoing and separated groups' masculinity scores when submitted to *t*-tests ($p < .146$), but that there were significant differences between the groups' femininity scores ($p < .001$).

The results contradict the expectation and question the common assumptions regarding the nature and value of gay relationships generally.[1] If Bem (1977) is correct, androgyny is associated with high self-esteem; because ongoing men were less likely to be androgynous, then it may be inferred that they have lower self-esteem. Of course, a contrasting value may intervene here. Perhaps masculine sex-typed men would score higher on self-esteem than androgynous men, since masculinity is more consistent with the expected male role and more supported in this culture. If maintaining an ongoing relationship has to do with self-esteem, and if we assume that gay men with higher masculinity scores feel better about themselves than those with lower scores, it's easier to understand the higher masculinity scores for subjects in ongoing couples. Although "self-esteem" may be quite different from "satisfaction," Bell and Weinberg's (1978) results, which indicate that "single" gay male subjects were more satisfied than their "open-coupled" subjects, suggest that being in an ongoing relationship is not always a more positive condition than being single. This point questions the expectation on the part of many single gay men that being in a couple should somehow make them happier.

It was expected that gay men in ongoing couples would be to their partner than recently separated men had been with their former partners. A *t*-test revealed no significant difference in the means of the two groups on the self-disclosure scale ($t < .90$, df = 118). Even though no significant difference was found between categories of

[1]In order to assess whether differences in their sex-type category affected the relationship of two men in a couple, a chi-square test was also conducted, but no significant difference was found ($\chi^2 = 1.17$, df = 1).

Table 2: Group Differences on Masculinity and Femininity Scores

Variable	Couple Status	N	Mean	t	df	p
Masculine	Ongoing	60	5.11	-1.46	111.3	.146
	Separated	60	5.31			
Feminine	Ongoing	60	4.80	-3.41	116.0	.001
	Separated	60	5.09			

partners, it was thought that there would perhaps be differences in the types of information disclosed. Accordingly, a factor analysis was conducted on the JSDQ and the responses given by this population. A varimax rotated factor analysis resulted in three sub-scales: positive feelings about self, worries and inadequacies, and everyday activities. No significant difference between the mean sub-scale scores emerged when a *t*-test was conducted ($t < .92$, 187, 1.93, df = 118). This did not support the expected result and was contrary to the assumption of Jourard (1964) that self-disclosure was necessary in order to maintain a relationship. Some other dynamics may be more important in a gay male population, or perhaps other aspects of self-disclosure than those measured by this form of the JSDQ may be the more important ones. Related research by Harry and Lovely (1979) indicated that intimacy did not correlate with continuity in gay male relationships. There is more to be learned about the effects of self-disclosure on gay male relationships. Perhaps such traditional positive values as being "open" about one's feelings and behavior in a relationship may not be so useful here.

It was expected that gay men in ongoing relationships would have higher cooperation scores than men who had separated. A *t*-test revealed a significant difference between the means of the two groups on the Altruism Scale ($t < 4.33$, df = 118, $p < .001$). The mean for the men in ongoing couples was .69 on a range from −1.00 to 1.00, while the mean for the separated group was .43.

Another manipulation of the data added support to the association of cooperation with longevity of a coupled relationship. Education and income levels were combined with the selected sex-role variables, and these data were submitted to a step-wise multiple regression in an attempt to identify those variables that might be the best predictors for ongoing and separated status. As shown in Table 3, scores on cooperation, androgyny (using sample medians, not Bem's medians), educational level, and income level accounted for almost one-third of the variance. Having a low score on cooperation, being androgynous (as opposed to the non-androgynous categories: masculine sex-typed, feminine sex typed, or undifferentiated), having less education, and having higher income were predictors of separated status.

These findings were further supported when the data were submitted to a discriminant function analysis, using Masculinity and Femininity as continuous scales and including the variables of cooperation, education, and income. Table 4 shows that 57.8% of the variance was explained by the discriminant function composed of these five variables. In Table 5 it can be seen that 74.2% of "grouped" cases were shown to have been correctly classified when accuracy tests were conducted using the discriminant function coefficients.

Since men in our culture are believed to be competitive, or at least more competitive than women, gay men are likely to compete

Table 3: Stepwise Multiple Regression Summary for Variables Predicting Couple Status

Variable	R^2	R Change	r	Beta
Cooperation	.137	.137	.37	-.33
Androgynous (vs. other categories)	.196	.058	.23	.19
Education	.275	.078	.21	-.27
Income	.292	.017	.16	.19

R^2 = .292

Table 4: Canonical Discriminant Function Coefficients for Variables Predicting Couple Status

Variable	Function
Cooperation	.813
Education	.744
Masculinity	-.549
Femininity	-.516
Income	-.194

Eigenvalue = .578

Table 5: Predictive Accuracy for Membership in Ongoing or Separated Groups from Discriminant Function Analysis

Actual Group	N	Predicted Group			
		Ongoing		Separated	
		N	%	N	%
Ongoing	60	44	73.3	16	26.7
Separated	60	15	25.0	45	75.0

Percentage of "Grouped" cases correctly classified: 74.2%

among themselves; this competition might be destructive to an ongoing relationship. Whether gay men are like other men on this dimension was not examined, but it was found that higher scores on the cooperation scale were more frequent among men in ongoing relationships.

The expectation that men in ongoing relationships would be likely to have had a greater number of outside sexual partners during the time of the relationship than would the recently separated men, was not fulfilled. There were no significant differences among the frequency categories when a chi-square test was conducted ($\chi^2 = 12.22$, df = 6). As shown in Table 6, after collapsing the original seven frequency ranges to monogamous and nonmonogamous categories (for purposes of frequency count, not for analysis for significant differences), very few of the couples in either group (16 of 60, or less than 14%) had been sexually monogamous. This affirms the popular belief, and supports other research findings, that gay men are not monogamous in their couple relationships. In addition, the results argue against the assumption that gay men cannot maintain relationships because they are too "promiscuous." The fact is that most of the participants in this study, separated or ongoing, did experience outside sexual contacts. It appears then, that monogamy vs. sexual plurality is not tied to relationship status. However, this finding does not minimize the importance for each couple to resolve the issue of sex outside the relationship. It is likely that gay men will continue to have mixed feelings and varying needs regarding their own and their partner's sexual plurality.

CONCLUSIONS

The results of this study suggest that relationship continuity may have something to do with degree of cooperation between the participants as well as with the sex-role type of the men involved, but that it is not likely to be a function of degrees of self-disclosure or

Table 6: Number and Percent of Monogamous and Non-monogamous Respondents by Couple Status

Sexual Plurality status	Ongoing		Separated		Total	
	N	Percent	N	Percent	N	Percent
Monogamous	9	15.0	7	11.7	16	13.3
Non-monogamous	51	85.0	53	88.3	104	86.7
Total	60	100.0	60	100.0	120	100.0

sexual plurality. Furthermore, the findings warn against possible errors in generalizing from heterosexual models of relationships to gay male relationships. Relationship dynamics and the motivations for being coupled may sometimes differ between gay male and heterosexual populations. Additional research must be undertaken to discover variables unique to this special population and to identify a cluster that accurately reflects the nature of today's gay male relationships.

There are several limitations on the interpretation of these results. First, the measuring instruments used were developed on a heterosexual assumption. Such instruments are compromised in degrees of validity and reliability when adapted for gay populations. Tests used to understand gay people need to be written specifically for the gay subculture and should be standardized and normed on gay populations. Second, the Bem Sex Role Inventory cannot be used to discover whether there is a relation between sex-type and relationship status because, as pointed out earlier, recent research has indicated that BSRI does not necessarily measure what previous investigators sought to measure. Third, it must be mentioned that all of the instruments used here are also subject to the usual self-report limitations. There is no reason to expect, for example, that recently separated couples would be able to remember or report past feelings accurately, especially considering the probable emotional state connected with separation. Finally, the fact that the sample is limited in size, that the use of friendship networks no doubt yielded a rather homogeneous sample, and that the two groups were significantly different on educational levels, also limits the generalizability of the study.

REFERENCE NOTES

1. McWhirter, D., & Mattison, A. M. *Male homosexual coupling*. Paper presented at the National Conference of the Society for the Scientific Study of Sex, Las Vegas, October, 1977.

2. Fein, S. B., & Nuehring, E. M. *Perspectives on the gender-integrated gay community: Its formal structure and social functions*. Paper presented at the meeting of the Southern Sociological Society, Atlanta, April, 1974.

3. Fitzgerald, L. F. *Sex, occupational membership, and the measurement of psychological androgyny*. Paper presented at the meeting of the American Psychological Association, Washington, D.C., 1976.

REFERENCES

Aller, F. A. Role of the self-concept in student marital adjustment. *Family Life Coordinator*, 1962, *11*, 43-45.

Balswick, J. O., & Peck, C. W. The inexpressive male: A tragedy of American soiety. *The Family Coordinator*, 1971, *20*, 363-368.

Bass-Hass, R., The lesbian dyad: Basic issues and value systems. *Journal of Sex Research*, 1968, *4*, 108-126.

Bell, A. P. Homosexualities: Their range and character. In J. K. Cole & R. Deinstbier (Eds.), *Nebraska Symposium on Motivation* (Vol. 21). Lincoln: University of Nebraska Press, 1973.

Bell, A. P. & Weinberg, M. S. *Homosexualities: A study of diversity among men and women*. New York: Simon and Schuster, 1978.

Bem, S. L. The measurement of psychological androgyny. *Journal of Consulting and Clinical Psychology*, 1974, *42*, 155-162.

Bem, S. L. Sex role adaptability: One consequence of psychological androgyny. *Journal of Personality and Social Psychology*, 1975, *31*, 634-643.

Bem, S. L. On the utility of alternative procedures for assessing psychological androgyny. *Journal of Consulting and Clinical Psychology*, 1977, *45*, 196-205.

Bem, S. L. Theory and measurement of androgyny: A reply to the Pedhazur-Tetenbaum and Locksley-Colten critiques. *Journal of Personality and Social Psychology*, 1979, *37*, 1074-1054.

Bem, S. L. & Lenny, E. Sex typing and the avoidance of cross-sex behavior. *Journal of Personality and Social Psychology*, 1976, *33*, 48-54.

Bem, S. L., Martyna, W., & Watson, C. Sex typing and androgyny: Further explorations of the expressive domain. *Journal of Personality and Social Psychology*, 1976, *34*, 1016-1023.

Broverman, I. K., & Vogel, S. R. Sex-role stereotypes: A current appraisal. *Journal of Social Issues*, 1972, *28*, 59-65.

Bureau of the Census, Superintendent of Documents. *Statistical abstract of the United States*. Washington, D.C.: U.S. Government Printing Office, 1976.

Chaffee, P. N. *Personality factors relating to stability in male homosexual relationships*. Unpublished doctoral dissertation, Boston University Graduate School, 1976.

Clark, D. Homosexual encounter in all-male groups. In L. Soloman & B. Berzon (Eds.), *New perspectives on encounter groups*. San Francisco: Jossey-Bass, 1972.

Cotton, W. L. Role playing substitutions among homosexuals. *Journal of Sex Research*, 1972, *8*, 310-323.

Cutler, B. R. & Dyer, W. G. Initial adjustment processes in young married couples. *Social Forces*, 1965, *44*, 195-201.

Dailey, D. M. Adjustment of heterosexual and homosexual couples in pairing relationships: An exploratory study. *Journal of Sex Research*, 1979, *15*, 143-157.

Dank, B. M. The homosexual. In D. Spiegal & P. Keith-Spiegal (Eds.), *Outsiders, U.S.A.: Original essays on 24 outgroups in American society*. New York: Rinehart, 1973.

Dannecker, M., & Reiche, R. *Der gewohnliche Homosexuelle*. Frankfurt: Fischer, 1974.

De Cecco, J.P., & Shively, M. G. A study of perceptions of rights and needs in interpersonal conflicts in homosexual relationships. *Journal of Homosexuality*, 1978, *3*, 205-216.

Fasteau, M. F. *The male machine*. New York: McGraw-Hill, 1974.

Freedman, M. Far from illness, homosexuals may be healthier than straights. *Psychology Today*, 1975, *8*, 30-31.

Fromm, E. *The sane society*. New York: Rinehart, 1955.

Gaudreau, P. Factor analysis of the Bem sex-role inventory. *Journal of Consulting and Clinical Psychology*, 1977, *45*, 299-302.

Goode, W. J. & Hatt, P. K. *Methods in social research*. New York: McGraw Hill, 1952.

Goodenough, E. W. Interest in persons as an aspect of sex differences in the early years. *Genetic Psychology Monographs*, 1957, *55*, 287-323.

Halverson, C. F., Jr., & Shore, R. E. Self-disclosure and interpersonal functioning. *Journal of Consulting and Clinical Psychology*, 1969, *33*, 213-217.

Harry, J., & Lovely, R. Gay marriages and communities of sexual orientation. *Alternative Lifestyles*, 1979, *2*, 177-200.

Helmreich, R. L., Spence, J. T., & Holahan, C. K. Psychological androgyny and sex role flexibility: A test of two hypotheses. *Journal of Personality and Social Psychology*, 1979, *37*, 1631-1644.

Hoffman, M. *The gay world: Male homosexuality and the social creation of evil*. New York: Basic Books, 1968.

Hooker, E. Adjustment of the male overt homosexual. *Journal of Projective Techniques*, 1957, *21*, 18-31.

Hooker, E. The homosexual community. In *Proceedings of the XIV International Congress of Applied Psychology*. Copenhagen: Nielson, 1962, *2*, 40-59.

Hooker, E. An empirical study of some relations between sexual patterns and gender identity in male homosexuals. In J. Money (Ed.), *Sex research: New developments*. New York: Holt, Rinehart and Winston, 1965, 25-52.

Jones, R. W., & Bates, J. E. Satisfaction in male homosexual couples. *Journal of Homosexuality*, 1978, *3*, 217-224.

Jourard, S. M. A study of self-disclosure. *Scientific American*, 1958, *198*, 77-82.

Jourard, S. M. *Personal Adjustment: An approach through the study of health personality*. New York: Macmillan, 1963.

Jourard, S. M. *The transparent self*. New York: Van Nostrand, 1964.

Jourard, S. M. *Self-disclosure: An experimental analysis of the transparent self.* New York: Wiley-Interscience, 1971.

Jourard, S. M., & Lasakow, P. Some factors in self-disclosure. *Journal of Abnormal and Social Psychology*, 1958, *56*, 91-98.

Kagan, J. Acquisition and significance of sex-typing and sex-role identity. In M. F. Hoffman & L. Hoffman (Eds.), *Review of child development research*. New York: Russell Sage Foundation, 1964.

Komarovsky, M. *Blue-collar marriage*. New York: Random House, 1967.

Katz, I., Goldstone, J., Cohen, M., & Stucker, S. Need satisfaction, perception and cooperative interaction in married couples. *Marriage and Family Living*, 1963, *25*, 209-214.

Lake, D. G., Miles, M. B. & Earle, R. B., Jr. *Measuring human behavior: Tools for the assessment of social functioning*. New York: Teachers College Press, 1973.

Lee, J. A. Forbidden colors of love: Patterns of gay love and gay liberation. *Journal of Homosexuality*, 1976, *1*, 401-418.

Morin, S. F. Heterosexual bias in psychological research on lesbianism and male homosexuality. *American Psychologist*, 1977, *32*, 629-637.

Nuehring, E. M., Fein, S. B., & Tyler, M. The gay college student: Perspectives for mental health professionals. *Counseling Psychologist*, 1974, *4*, 64-72.

Oliver, L. S. *Male homosexual dyads: A study of thirty couples*. Unpublished doctoral dissertation, George Washington University, 1976.

Pedhazur, E. J. & Tetenbaum, T. J. Bem sex role inventory: A theoretical and methodological critique. *Journal of Personality and Social Psychology*, 1979, *37*, 996-1016.

Sawyer, J. The altruism scale: A measure of cooperative, individualism, and competitive interpersonal orientation. *American Journal of Sociology*, 1966, *71*, 407-416.

Schafer, S. Sociosexual behavior in male and female homosexuals. *Archives of Sexual Behavior*, 1977, *6*, 355-364.

Sonenschein, D. The ethnography of male homosexual relations. *Journal of Sex Research*, 1968, *4*, 69-83.

Spence, J. T., & Helmreich, R. L. The many faces of androgyny: A reply to Locksley and Colten. *Journal of Personality and Social Psychology*, 1979, *37*, 1032-1046.

Stevens, D. J. H. *Cohabitation without marriage*. Unpublished doctoral dissertation, University of Texas, Austin, 1975.

Storms, M. D. Sex role identity and its relationships to sex role attributes and sex role stereotypes. *Journal of Personality and Social Psychology*, 1979, *37*, 1779-1789.

Stringer, P., & Grygier, T. Male homosexuality, psychiatric patient status and psychological masculinity and femininity. *Archives of Sexual Behavior*, 1976, *5*, 15-27.

Watson, R. I. *Psychology of the child*. New York: Wiley, 1959.

Westmoreland, C. *A study of long-term relationships among male homosexuals*. Unpublished doctoral dissertation, United States International University, San Diego, California, 1975.

Westwood, G. *A minority—A report on the life of the male homosexual in Great Britain*. London: Longmans, Green, 1960.

Value Orientations in the Intimate Relationships of Gay Men

Letitia Anne Peplau, PhD
Susan D. Cochran, PhD

In a recent critique of research on homosexuality, Morin (1977) urges to give greater attention to gay relationships and to the diversity of gay life-styles. This paper presents a new approach to understanding variations in gay men's intimate relationships, one which emphasizes individual differences in relationship values—in people's beliefs about what is important in intimate relationships. For example, whereas some people may consider it essential that a relationship be sexually monogamous, others may prefer sexually open relationships. This paper examines gay men's relationships values and explores links between these values and characteristics of the men's actual intimate relationships. Implicit in this approach is the assumption that individuals' values determine, in some measure, the sort of intimate relationships they seek and the nature of the relationships they experience. It should, of course, be recognized that other causal links also occur. For example, people's experiences of close relationships may change their values.

In conceptualizing relationship values, it is important to look beyond specific values, such as sexual exclusivity, in order to identify more general themes or dimensions. Family theorists (e.g., Hess & Handel, 1959; Raush, 1977) have proposed that a fundamental issue in all close relationships is the balancing of intimacy and independence. Our research explored the extent to which these two themes, referred to as *dyadic attachment* and *personal autonomy*, are reflected in the relationship values of gay men.

The dimension of dyadic attachment concerns the value placed on having an emotionally close and relatively secure love relationship. A strong desire for intimate attachment is illustrated in the following statement by a gay man explaining why he wants to be in a love relationship:

> The most important thing such a relationship would bring is the knowledge that someone loves and needs me as I would love and need him. It would be a stabilizing force in my life, and give me a sense of security. . . . (quoted in Spada, 1979, p. 198)

An emphasis on dyadic attachment can be reflected in an individual's placing importance on security and permanence in relationships, on shared time and activities with the partner, and on sexual exclusivity. Whereas some may value such qualities in a relationship, others may prefer lesser degrees of "togetherness."

The second theme, personal autonomy, concerns the boundaries that exist between individuals and their close relationships. While some individuals wish to immerse themselves entirely in a relationship to the exclusion of outside interests and activities, others prefer to maintain greater personal independence. A strong emphasis on personal autonomy is expressed in the following account by a gay man of why he prefers not to live with a lover:

> I have my own lifestyle and am sufficiently crotchety to be happy in my independence. I recognize the pleasures of living with another man from previous relationships—shared household duties, . . . having the other guy to lean on emotionally, sometimes financially, etc. However, the loss of my own freedom is too high a price to pay. (quoted in Spada, 1979, p. 200)

Personal autonomy values might include wanting to have separate interests and friendships apart from a primary relationship and preserving one's independence within a relationship by dividing finances and decision-making in an egalitarian manner. It is likely that gay men vary considerably in how much they value the maintenance of personal autonomy in the context of intimate relationships.

The primary purpose of the present study was to investigate gay men's values concerning love relationships. If the themes of attachment and autonomy are as basic as theorists have suggested, they should be applicable to gay relationships. Indeed, they may provide a useful way to describe the variation among gay men's orientations toward close relationships. Support for this possibility comes from an earlier study of lesbian relationships (Peplau, Cochran, Rook & Padesky, 1978). In that study, a sample of 127 lesbians rated the personal importance they gave to various features of relationships, including joint activities, sexual compatibility and exclusivity, self-disclosure, similarity of attitudes, permanence in the relationship, power, and having friends and interests outside the relationship. A factor analysis indicated that responses formed two independent sets of values corresponding closely to themes of attachment and autonomy. In the present study, it was predicted that gay men's responses to similar questions would also reflect dimensions of attachment and autonomy.

A second goal of the research was to examine the links between relationship values and characteristics of gay men's intimate relationships. It was expected that men's values would be related to such aspects of their love relationships as satisfaction, future expectations, sexual behavior, power, and reactions to breakups. Since the general orientation of this study was descriptive and exploratory rather than hypothesis-testing, no detailed predictions were made.

A final goal was to examine personal characteristics of gay men that might be associated with relationship values. In the earlier lesbian study clear evidence was found that relationship values were associated with general conservatism. Among lesbians, a strong emphasis on attachment was correlated with endorsement of traditional sex-role attitudes and with religiousness; a strong emphasis on autonomy was correlated with endorsement of feminist beliefs and with participation in lesbian-feminist activities. We expected that gay men would show a similar pattern, with attachment values linked to general conservatism and autonomy values associated with greater liberalism.

METHOD

Recruitment

Men were recruited for a study of "Gay Men's Relationships" by ads placed in a university newspaper and a gay community newsletter. Contacts were also made through the Los Angeles Gay Community Services Center, church-related gay groups, and associations of gay university students in southern California.

Participants spent approximately one hour completing a detailed questionnaire. Most men completed the questionnaire in a group setting, either at UCLA or at various community locations. Other men participated individually. Questionnaires were administered in 1976 by two male students who assisted in the project. All responses were completely anonymous.

Participants

The 128 men in the sample ranged in age from 18 to 65, with a median of 25 years. The majority were white (84%), with 8% Chicano, 5% Asian American, and 3% Black. Half of the sample were students in college or graduate school. The majority of men (81%) either held a bachelor's degree or were currently students. One quarter of the participants had some graduate training. Among those men who were currently employed, the monthly salary ranged from $75 to $5,000, with a median income of $800.

Participants had diverse religious backgrounds: 33% were raised as Protestants, 39% as Catholics, and 16% as Jews. Most indicated that currently they were not very religious (mean 3.7 on a 9-point scale of religiousness). Only 17% said they attended religious services weekly, and 54% said they went to religious services less than once a year.

At the time of the study, 41% of the men reported being in an ongoing "romantic/sexual relationship" with a man,[1] and the remaining respondents had previously had at least one "romantic/sexual relationship" with a man. Most reported having had several gay relationships. The median number of gay relationships was three; 21% had had six or more. The length of the men's longest gay relationship ranged from two months to 11 years, with a median of 15 months. The men's age when their first gay relationship began ranged from 12 to 38 years, with a median of 20 years.

Most of the men indicated that they had had heterosexual relationships at some point in their lives. Over 92% had "dated" a woman. Two-thirds had had sexual intercourse with a woman; among these, the median number of heterosexual partners was three. About 55% of the men said they had been in at least one "romantic/sexual relationship" with a woman, and 7% had been married. Only 14% of participants indicated that in the future they might have a "serious romantic relationship with a woman"; 67% were sure they would not become involved with a woman; the rest were uncertain.

The sample represents a fairly diverse group of self-identified gay men who have had at least one "romantic/sexual relationship" with a man. It is important to recognize, however, that our sample does not represent all gay men either in Los Angeles or elsewere; representative sampling of members of a hidden population is not possible (Morin, 1977). The men in our sample tended to be relatively young, well-educated, and middle-class. The model participant was a 25-year-old college-educated white male who worked full-time. Since the men were recruited through social organizations and student associations, rather than through gay bars or gay political groups, they may be somewhat more conservative in their life-styles than other gay men. It also seems likely that men who volunteer for research are more open about their homosexuality and more trusting

---

[1]Men in the sample were never provided with an explicit definition of the term "romantic/sexual relationship." All of the men who indicated that they were currently in such a relationship had had genital sex with their partner, and 83% indicated that they and their partner were "in love." Thus it appears that most men interpreted this phrase as referring to a relationship that involved both affection and sexual relations.

of psychologists than are other gay people. Thus, our results should not be taken as descriptive of all gay men.

The Questionnaire

Participants completed a 24-page questionnaire composed of items based in part on previous questionnaires used in studies of lesbians (Peplau et al., 1978) and of heterosexual couples (Hill, Rubin, & Peplau, 1976; Peplau, Rubin & Hill, 1977; Peplau, 1979; Rubin, Peplau, & Hill, 1981). The first part of the questionnaire concerned the respondent's background and involvement in gay activities. Questions probed attitudes toward gay relationships as well as more general beliefs about romantic relationships. The second part of the questionnaire focused on a specific "romantic/sexual relationship." For men who were currently in a relationship, questions assessed love and satisfaction, future expectations, sexual behavior, living arrangements, and the balance of power. Men who were not currently in a relationship answered similar questions about their most recent past relationship, with the addition of questions concerning their reaction to the breakup.

RESULTS

Relationship Values

The questionnaire asked men to rate on a 9-point scale the importance for them personally of 23 statements relevant to a romantic/sexual relationship. These included statements about self-disclosure, sexual compatibility and exclusivity, joint activities and finances, similarity of attitudes, permanence of the relationship, power, and interests and friends outside the relationship.

As a group, the men gave greatest importance to "Being able to talk about my most intimate feelings" (mean 8.1), "Each of us being able to have our own career" (7.8), "Sexual compatibility" (7.5), "Having a supportive group of friends as well as my romantic/sexual partner" (7.4), and "Having an egalitarian (equal-power) relationship" (7.3). Least important were "Both partners being equally involved in gay political activities" (mean 3.3), "Having similar political attitudes" (3.4), and "Being able to have sexual relations with people other than my partner" (4.0). Nonetheless, there was considerable diversity among these gay men in the importance given to particular relationship characteristics.

The central goals of the research were to examine the patterning of men's relationship values and to learn whether these values correspond to separate factors of personal autonomy and dyadic attachment. A factor analysis of the 23 items was performed, and the best fit to the data was obtained by an orthogonal three-factor solution. Table 1 presents the items loading above .40 on each factor. Results clearly support the importance of factors of dyadic attachment and personal autonomy.

The first factor reflected attachment values of having a close-knit, sexually exclusive, and relatively permanent relationship. Emphasis was given to spending as much time together as possible and to sharing various activities. Two other items about emotional expressiveness did not load on this factor: "Being able to talk about my most intimate feelings" and "Being able to laugh easily with each other." Both of these statements were endorsed strongly by all the men in our sample and did not differentiate among the three factors.

The second factor included personal autonomy values of having a life apart fron one's primary intimate relationship. Included were statements about the importance of having separate careers, interests, friends, and sexual partners outside the relationship. Within the primary relationship, emphasis was given to equal sharing in power and financial responsibilities. These later items concerning equality may seem less intrinsic to the abstract concept of autonomy but have appeared as part of this factor in both the gay men's sample and the earlier lesbian sample. In both samples individuals who valued independence outside their relationship also valued equality within their relationship. The emergence of two orthogonal factors corresponding to attachment and autonomy provides empirical support for the theoretical view (Hess & Handel, 1959; Raush, 1977) that attachment and autonomy are independent dimensions, not polar opposites.

An unexpected third factor also emerged. This factor concerned

Table 1

The Dyadic Attachment, Personal Autonomy, and Political Similarity Scales

Scale Items	Loadings
Dyadic Attachment Scale (Factor 1)	
1. Sexual fidelity in the relationship	.75
2. Living together	.73
3. Spending as much time together as possible	.70
4. Sharing as many activities with my partner as possible	.66
5. Knowing that the relationship will endure for a long time	.64
6. Being able to have sexual relations with people other than my partner	-.58
7. Knowing that my partner depends on me	.41
Personal Autonomy Scale (Factor 2)	
1. Each of us being able to have our own career	.73
2. Trying new sexual activities or techniques with my partner	.57
3. Having an egalitarian (equal-power) relationship	.47
4. Having major interests of my own outside of the relationship	.46
5. Sharing financial responsibilities equally in the relationship	.44
6. Having a supportive group of friends as well as my romantic/sexual partner	.43
7. Being able to have sexual relations with people other than my partner	.42
Political Similarity Scale (Factor 3)	
1. Both of us having similar political attitudes	.71
2. Having similar attitudes toward gay issues	.64
3. Both partners being equally involved in gay political activities	.55

Note: Based on a rotated orthogonal factor analysis of a set of 23 items. Items loading above .40 were used to define each scale.

political similarity and included all three items about the importance of having similar beliefs concerning gay issues and politics. The importance of attitudinal similarity within close relationships has long been recognized by social psychologists (e.g., Berscheid & Walster, 1978). In this study, such similarity was generally rated fairly low in importance but appeared nonetheless as a separate factor distinct from attachment and autonomy.

On the basis of the factor analysis, separate scales of Dyadic Attachment, Personal Autonomy, and Political Similarity were constructed. Each man was assigned scale scores based on the average of his responses to the items in each scale listed in Table 1. For the 128 men in our sample, there was no association between scores on the Attachment and Autonomy Scales ($r = -.01$). Men who gave great importance to attachment were equally likely to value or to devalue autonomy. There were small but statistically significant correlations between scores on the Political Similarity Scale and scores on both Autonomy ($r = .28, p < .001$) and Attachment ($r = .21, p < .008$).

Values and Men's Intimate Relationships

A major objective of this research was to investigate links between men's relationship values and characteristics of their actual relationships. To simplify the presentation of results, only data concerning the Attachment and Autonomy Scales will be reported here.[2]

At the time of the study, 41% of the men were currently in a "romantic/sexual relationship": the rest were not then in such a relationship but had been in the past. For men in ongoing relationships, analyses examined links between values and several aspects of the relationship, including love and intimacy, future expectations, sexual behavior, and power. For men who described a past relationship, analyses focused on reactions to the breakup.

Love and Intimacy. When the men were asked how long they had

---

[2]Scores on the Political Similarity Scale were significantly related to belonging to a gay political organization [$\chi^2(1) = 8.7, p < .003$], to attending a greater number of political events [$t(235) = 1.93, p < .06$], and to reporting greater personal involvement in gay political organization [$\chi^2(1) = 8.7, p < .003$], to attending a greater number of polany other measures of men's attitudes and background. No systematic relationship was found between political similarity scores and features of men's current relationships or their reactions to the breakup of a past love relationship. Consequently, discussion of this scale has been omitted from the body of the article.

known their current partner, their answers ranged from one month to 6.5 years, with a median of 16 months. About half (51%) of the men were living with their partner; the median length of cohabitation was 12 months. Men who were not living with their partner reported seeing him frequently, with a median of about three times per week. Most men described their current relationship in highly favorable terms, rating it as extremely satisfying (mean 7.3 on a 9-point scale) and extremely close (mean of 7.7 on a 9-point scale). Most men (83%) said they and their current partner were "in love"; only 9% said they were not in love and 8% were undecided.

It was expected that men who valued dyadic attachment would report more frequent and intimate interaction with their partner. This would be consistent with the attachment emphasis on spending time together and sharing activities. Strong evidence in support of this prediction was found. Men who scored high on attachment reported seeing their partner significantly more often ($r = .39$, $p < .01$), were more likely to live with their partner ($\chi^2(1) = 4.5$, $p < .03$), and more often rated their relationship as close ($r = .31$, $p < .01$), than did low-scorers. Also included in the questionnaire was Rubin's (1973) "Love Scale," an instrument assessing feelings of dependency, caring, and intimacy toward one's partner. Scores on this 9-item scale were strongly related to dyadic attachment values ($r = .51, p < .001$). These results indicate that men who valued emotionally close and relatively secure relationships were likely to report greater intimacy in their current relationship. Since these data are correlational, the direction of causality is ambiguous. It is possible that men who value attachment tend to idealize their partner and the relationship; it is also possible that attachment values are fostered by being in a close, secure relationship or by wanting to justify spending considerable time with one's partner.

No clear relation was predicted between scores on the Autonomy Scale and measures of love or intimacy. The items on the Autonomy Scale have little to do with closeness in the relationship; instead they focus on the person's having separate interests outside the relationship. As might be expected, then, scores on the Autonomy Scale were not significantly related to any measures of love, closeness, or satisfaction. Men who strongly valued personal independence were no less likely than other men to find their current relationship intimate and personally rewarding. Autonomy values were, however, related to the length of the current relationship. Men who strongly valued autonomy reported being in relationships of shorter duration ($r = .41, p < .001$). There were also nonsignificant trends for high-autonomy men to see their partners less frequently and to live apart from them. We can only speculate about the reasons for the shorter duration of relationships among men who are strong proponents of autonomy values. Men who value autonomy may find shorter term relationships more comfortable and rewarding; this would be consistent with the finding that high-autonomy men are no less satisfied than low-autonomy men with their current relationship. It is also possible that the type of relationship preferred by high-autonomy men is harder to sustain over long periods of time.

Future Expectations. The questionnaire asked men to estimate the likelihood that their current relationship would exist in the future. Most men expressed confidence that the relationship would continue, at least in the short run. About 60% of men were certain (7 on a 7-point scale) that their relationship would continue for six months, 49% were certain it would last for one year, and 28% were certain it would continue for five years. Additional questions assessed men's willingness to make major changes in their own lives in order to continue their relationship. One question asked men to imagine that their partner had decided to move to another city to pursue an attractive job or educational opportunity. How likely was it that the respondent would move with his partner? About half the men said they would definitely (25%) or probably (23%) move in order to preserve the relationship, 19% said they were uncertain what they would do, and 33% said they would probably or definitely not move. Responses to a parallel question gauging the probability that the partner would move to follow the respondent showed a similar pattern. In sum, the men exhibited considerable variation in their relative commitment to the relationship versus their own work or education.

Analyses examined whether measures of expectations and commitment were related to men's values. Since the Attachment Scale includes items concerning the importance of permanence (e.g.,

"Knowing that the relationship will endure for a long time"), it is reasonable to expect that attachment scores would be related to measures of commitment. Results indicated that men who scored high on attachment were more certain than low scorers that their relationship would continue for six months ($r = .26, p < .05$), one year ($r = .31, p < .05$), or five years ($r = .24, p < .05$). Attachment was also related to men's willingness to move to follow their partner ($\chi^2(4) = 12.1, p < .01$). Among high-attachment men, 38% said they would definitely move and only 4% were certain they would not move; among low-attachment men, the pattern was reversed, with only 11% being certain they would move and 31% sure they would not move.

In contrast, no relation was found between personal autonomy values and any measures of expectations and commitment. This may suggest that high-autonomy men value having outside interests *in addition to* an intimate relationship, not as a substitute for it. Autonomy values were not consistently associated with a willingness to sacrifice individual educational or work plans for the sake of a relationship, nor were they associated with a readiness to sacrifice a relationship for personal goals.

Sexual Behavior. The questionnaire examined three aspects of sexual behavior: sexual satisfaction and frequency, the nature of the relationship between the respondent and his partner when they first had sex, and sexual exclusivity. The men in this sample reported considerable satisfaction with the sexual aspects of their relationship (mean of 5.8 on a 7-point scale of overall sexual satisfaction). When asked how often the man and his partner had "engaged in genital sex with each other" during the past month, the mean reported frequency was two to three times per week. About 27% of the men said they had sex two to three times per week, 43% reported having sex less than twice per week, and 30% reported having sex more than three times per week. Desired sexual frequency with the current partner was relatively similar: 42% of the men wanted sex about two to three times per week, 21% preferred to have sex less often, and 37% preferred to have sex more often. Consistent with earlier data suggesting that high-attachment men tend to perceive their relationship more positively than do low-attachment men, attachment scores were positively correlated with reported sexual satisfaction ($r = .25, p < .05$) and with sexual frequency ($r = .30, p < .02$). Scores on autonomy were unrelated to sexual satisfaction or frequency.

Other questions concerned how well the respondent and his partner knew each other at the time when they first had genital sex with each other. The most common response (46%) was that the men had been friends; 27% said they had been casual acquaintances and 27% reported being strangers. Among the men in our sample, 25% said they had been "in love" with their partner at the time when they first had sex with each other. Additional analyses examined the time interval between when partners first met and when they first had genital sex. About 60% of the men reported having sex within one month after their first meeting; the remaining 40% waited up to 18 months after the first meeting.

Scores on attachment, but not on autonomy, were related to the experience of first sex within the current relationship. Men scoring above the median on attachment were more likely than low-attachment men to have been friends when they first had sex (41% versus 8%) and not to have been strangers [15% versus 29%, $\chi^2(3) = 7.4$, $p < .06$]. Attachment was also associated with a longer time interval between first meeting and first having sex with the partner ($r = .37, p < .001$).

A final set of questions concerned sexual exclusivity versus openness. Most men (73%) reported that they had had sex with someone else at least once since their current relationship began; over half (54%) had had sex outside their primary relationship during the past two months. Scores on attachment were significantly related to sexual exclusivity. Men scoring above the median on attachment were significantly less likely than low scorers to have had sex outside the relationship during the preceding two months [$\chi^2(1) = 4.1, p < .04$]. Also during that two-month interval, 30% of high attachment men had had sex with another partner, as compared to 80% of low-attachment men. Men who scored high on the Attachment Scale strongly valued closeness and exclusivity, and these values were often reflected in their sexual behavior.

Surprisingly, no relation was found between scores on the Personal Autonomy Scale and any measure of sexual behavior, exclusivity, or satisfaction. Men who strongly valued personal independence outside the relationship were no more and no less likely than men who devalued autonomy to have sexually open relationships.

The Balance of Power. The research also examined gay men's perceptions of the balance of power in their current relationships. Respondents indicated which partner "has more of a say about what you and ______ do together." Responses were made on a 5-point scale from "I have much more to say" to "(______) has much more say." A later question asked which partner should have more say in the relationship. (For details about these measures and data from a heterosexual sample, see Peplau, 1979.) Virtually all men (92%) in the sample said that ideally both partners should have "exactly equal say" in the relationship. Not all men achieved this ideal, however. Only 37% reported that their current relationship actually was "exactly equal." No association was found between the perceived balance of power and scores on either autonomy or attachment.

Reactions to Breakups. For men in the sample who were not currently in a relationship, the questionnaire examined the respondent's most recent past relationship and his reactions to the ending of that relationship. Men were asked to indicate the extent to which they had experienced various emotions (in a list taken from Hill et al., 1976) immediately after the breakup. The most common responses were feeling depressed, lonely, and empty. One might expect that men scoring high on attachment, who strongly desire an intimate and secure relationship, would react more negatively to a breakup than would men scoring lower on attachment values. The data confirmed this prediction. Scores on the Dyadic Attachment Scale were significantly correlated with the total number of negative feelings the man reported ($r = .27, p < .01$) and with the average severity of his negative feelings ($r = .25$, $p < .02$). No relation was found between scores on the Personal Autonomy Scale and reactions to breakups.

Personal Correlates of Relationship Values

Further analyses examined links between relationship values and personal characteristics of gay men, including their background, attitudes, and involvement in gay social and political activities.

Background Characteristics. In general, relationships values were not strongly associated with variations in the demographic characteristics assessed in this study. Both attachment and autonomy values cut across various social groups represented in the sample. Scores on the Attachment Scale were not significantly related to age, income, level of education, ethnic background, or parental education. Scores on the Autonomy Scale were significantly related to only two background factors. A comparison of high versus low scorers (medial split) on the Autonomy Scale indicated that men who strongly valued autonomy tended to have somewhat less educated parents [for mother, $t(121) = 2.2, p = .03$; for father, $t(120) = 1.9, p = .06$]. In addition, there was a small but significant negative correlation between autonomy and age ($r = -.21, p < .01$); younger men tended to be stronger proponents of autonomy values. This latter trend may reflect life cycle changes associated with aging or represent a cohort effect in which younger men have been exposed to newer cultural values that encourage independence and autonomy.

Attitudes. It was predicted that an emphasis on dyadic attachment would characterize men with more conservative or traditional attitudes and that an emphasis on autonomy would be strongest among more liberal men. Three types of attitudes were examined. First, on a 9-point scale, men rated the degree of their own religiousness. They also indicated how frequently they attended religious services. Although many men indicated that they were not very religious, differences in religiousness were associated with relationship values. As predicted, self-ratings of religiousness were positively correlated with attachment scores ($r = .21, p < .01$) and negatively correlated with autonomy scores ($r = -.29, p < .001$). A similar pattern was found for church attendance. Those men who attended religious services regularly were most likely to endorse attachment values and to de-emphasize autonomy values.

Second, to examine the possibility that traditional beliefs about love might affect relationship values, a 6-item Romanticism Scale (adapted from Rubin, 1969) was included. Items assessed beliefs such as that true love lasts forever or that love can overcome barriers of race, religion, and economics. High scores on this scale reflect adherence to a romantic view that "love conquers all." As expected, romanticism scores were positively correlated with attachment ($r = .24, p < .01$) and negatively correlated with autonomy ($r = -.17, p < .05$).

A final measure of attitudinal conservatism concerned men's support for the goals of the women's movement. Most men reported being highly supportive of the women's movement (mean of 7.6 on a 9-point scale); pro-feminist attitudes were not related to either attachment or autonomy scores.

Gay Social Activities. The study also investigated possible links between men's participation in the gay community and their relationship values. Other researchers (e.g., Harry & Lovely, 1979) have used a single continuum (ranging from low to high) of involvement in the gay community. In contrast, we were interested in potentially important distinctions among various forms of participation in gay life. The questionnaire contained separate sections inquiring about the respondent's participation in "gay social activities" and in "political gay activities and gay liberation."

Three kinds of gay social activities were distinguished. *Community social activities* were described as including "events or activities sponsored by gay groups, such as the Gay Community Services Center, Gay Students' Union, organizations for gay professionals, gay churches/synagogues, etc." *Private social activities* were described as including "events or activities sponsored by individuals, such as parties, dinners, going to the movies, or camping, etc. Private social activities involve friends or acquaintances—most of whom are gay." *Anonymous socializing* was described as including "activities such as going to gay bars or baths to spend time with people you do not know." For each type of social activity, respondents answered several questions concerning the frequency, extent, and nature of their participation.

Analyses indicated that attachment values were related to participation in gay social activities. Specifically, men scoring above the median on attachment had engaged in anonymous socializing significantly less often during the past year than had men scoring below the median [$t(124) = 3.7, p < .001$]. When this analysis was performed separately for men who were currently in a relationship and for those not in a relationship, a similar pattern emerged in both groups. Even if high-attachment men were not in a relationship, they were less likely to seek anonymous social contacts. This finding is consistent with the view that attachment values reflect a more conservative orientation. Attachment values were not related to participation in either community or private social activities. Finally, no significant relationships were found between scores on the Personal Autonomy Scale and any measure of gay socializing.

Gay Political Activism. A separate section of the questionnaire inquired about men's involvement in gay political activities. Respondents varied considerably in their participation in such activities. About a third (31%) of the men indicated that they currently belonged to or participated in "a gay political or gay activist group or organization." Men were also asked how often in the past year they had attended "political or gay activist events (lectures, workshops, conferences, demonstrations, etc.)." The median number of activities reported was two, with 39% of the men saying that they never attended any events and 11% saying they attended six or more events. On self-rated involvement in "gay political activities," most men reported being uninvolved (mean 2.6 on a 9-point scale), and only 7% rated themselves above 6. (Note that these percentages reflect in large measure results of our recruitment procedures and should not be taken as representative of the political activism of gay men in general.)

Consistent with the view that proponents of dyadic attachment are more conservative, high-scorers were less actively involved in both gay politics and "gay liberation." Men scoring above the median on attachment reported less frequent attendance at gay political events [$t(125) = 3.3, p < .001$] and rated themselves as less politically involved [$t(124) = 2.0, p < .04$] than did low-scorers on attachment. Scores on attachment were not, however, related to merely belonging to a gay political organization, which suggests that high attachment men may be joiners but are not active participants. Personal autonomy was not related to political gay activism.

Taken together, these results indicate that relationship values were related to men's self-reported personal characteristics. Men scoring high on the Dyadic Attachment Scale were more religious, believed more strongly in romantic conceptions of love, were less likely to socialize at gay bars or baths, and were less involved in gay political activities than were men scoring low on attachment. Men scoring high on the Personal Autonomy Scale tended to be younger, had somewhat less educated parents, and reported being less religious and less romantic.

DISCUSSION

The results of this study of gay men's intimate relationships support several general conclusions. First, the men in this sample reported that their current relationships were extremely close and personally rewarding. While this finding may not characterize the relationships of all gay men, it clearly indicates that gay men can and do establish intimate and satisfying relationships. In many respects, the descriptions gay men gave of their current love relationships were remarkably similar to those of lesbians and of heterosexual college students who have participated in similar studies. For example, gay men's reports of closeness, love and satisfaction, actual and desired sexual frequency, and the balance of power were highly similar to those of lesbians (Cochran & Peplau, Note 1) and of heterosexual dating couples (Peplau, 1979; Peplau et al., 1977; Rubin et al., 1981) who have answered similar questions about their relationships. Since the participants in these various studies differed in many respects, precise comparisons are unwarranted. Nonetheless, it seems that there may be considerable commonality in the internal dynamics of love relationships, regardless of the sexual orientation of the participants.

Where gay men appeared to differ most from the lesbians and heterosexual individuals in these studies was in their behavior outside their primary relationship. For example, when asked if they had had sex with someone other than their primary partner during the past two months, 54% of the gay men said they had, compared to only 13% of the lesbians and 14% of the college-aged dating men and women. (These general findings are quite consistent with data from gay men and lesbians reported by Schafer, 1977 and reviewed by Omark, Note 2.) Thus, it is in the general area of autonomy, and more specifically in the area of sexual exclusivity, that the largest differences between gay men's relationships and those of others have been documented to date.

Second, the patterning of gay men's relationship values clearly reflected themes of personal autonomy and dyadic attachment. The results of a factor analysis of gay men's values indicated factors corresponding to autonomy and attachment; the content of these two factors was quite similar to that found in a comparable study of lesbians (Peplau et al., 1978). It appears, therefore, that theoretical analyses of the importance of attachment and autonomy (Hess & Handel, 1959; Raush, 1977) based on studies of heterosexual relationships would also apply to homosexual relationships. Results for gay men and lesbians also support the conceptualization of attachment and autonomy as independent value dimensions rather than as mutually exclusive opposites.

Third, although separate value dimensions of attachment and autonomy were identified, only the attachment dimension was consistently related to characteristics of gay men's relationships. Men who scored high on the Dyadic Attachment scale were relatively more conservative than low-scorers in their attitudes and behavior. Compared to men who de-emphasized attachment, high-attachment men believed more strongly in romantic conceptions of love and were less likely to frequent gay bars and baths. When high-attachment men first had sex with their current partner, they were more likely to have been friends and to have known each other longer than was true for low-attachment men. Men who strongly valued attachment saw their partner more frequently, reported greater closeness and love, and expressed greater certainty that their relationship would continue in the future. High-attachment men also reported greater sexual satisfaction than did low-attachment men and were more likely to have a sexually exclusive relationship. In reflecting on past relationships, high-attachment men reported greater distress following breakups than did low-attachment men. Thus it appears that variations in attachment values were related in a consistent and meaningful way to features of men's actual love relationships.

In contrast, few links were found between autonomy values and features of men's intimate relationships. High-autonomy men reported being in relationships of shorter duration than low-autonomy men, but scores on autonomy were not significantly related to men's frequency of seeing their partner, future expectations, sexual behavior, or reactions to breakups. These results stand in sharp contrast to those from the earlier study of lesbian relationships (Peplau et al., 1978). Among lesbians, personal autonomy values were significantly related to spending less time with the partner, being less willing to maintain the relationship at the expense of work or education, and being more likely to have a sexually open relationship. We can only speculate about the reasons for the limited association of autonomy values with features of gay men's relationships.

A possible explanation is that, due to sex-role differences in socialization, variations in autonomy values are less relevant to the relationship experiences of gay men than to those of lesbians. In this culture, men have traditionally been taught to divide their energies and commitment between a primary relationship (typically a family) and a career (Angrist & Almquist, 1975; Horner, 1970). Men may think of their love relationship as quite separate from the rest of their lives spent at work and with friends. Also, men may learn to separate sexual behavior from love and emotional intimacy (Gagnon & Simon, 1973; Schafer, 1977; Omark, Note 2)—a tendency that may be reinforced by norms within the gay men's community (Harry, 1977; Warren, 1974). Thus, all gay men, regardless of individual differences in autonomy values, may learn the basic idea that they should maintain an independent life and identity apart from a primary intimate relationship. If men implicitly assume that a high degree of personal autonomy is to be expected in intimate relationships, then minor variations in autonomy values may have little impact.

In contrast, women have traditionally been taught to devote themselves to a primary relationship, often to the exclusion of a career or major outside interests. Thus, women more often experience difficulty in reconciling personal goals concerning work or education with love relationships (Angrist & Almquist, 1975; Horner, 1970). Because women also learn to integrate emotional intimacy and sexual expression, love is traditionally an important prerequisite for sex (Gagnon & Simon, 1973; Omark, Note 2). As a consequence, variations in women's endorsement of autonomy values, including the importance of independent interests and the acceptance of sex outside a primary love relationship, may have considerable impact on women's actual love relationships.

Providing an adequate understanding of the nature and diversity of intimate relationships experienced by gay men and women should be a high priority for social science researchers. Our research provides one approach to this important enterprise. Further research on attachment and autonomy, including studies of heterosexual relationships, is needed to clarify the reasons for the sex differences observed in comparing gay men and lesbians. The preceding interpretation suggests that because of sex differences in integrating intimate relationships and outside activities, individual variations in autonomy values may be relatively unimportant in understanding gay men's relationships. However, the alternative possibility, that the autonomy dimension has been poorly operationalized for men and that the lack of consistent findings in our data reflects a methodological or conceptual problem, should not be overlooked.

REFERENCE NOTES

1. Cochran, S. D., & Peplau, L. A. *The interplay of autonomy and attachment in love relationships: A comparison of men and women*. Paper presented at the annual meeting of the Western Psychologic, April 1979.

2. Omark, R. C. *On the sexual scripts of gay males and lesbians*. Unpublished manuscript, Central Michigan University, 1978.

REFERENCES

Angrist, S. S. & Almquist, E. M. *Careers and contingencies*. New York: Dunellen, 1975.

Berscheid, E., & Walster, E. H. *Interpersonal attraction* (2nd ed.). Menlo Park, CA: Addison-Wesley, 1978.

Gagnon, J., & Simon, W. *Sexual conduct*. Chicago: Aldine, 1973.

Harry, J. Marriage among gay males: The separation of intimacy and sex. In S. G. McNall (Ed.), *The sociological perspective* (4th ed.). Boston: Little, Brown, 1977.

Harry, J. & Lovely, R. Gay marriages and communities of sexual orientation. *Alternative Lifestyles*, 1979, *2*(2), 177-200.

Hess, R. D., & Handel, G. *Family worlds: A psychosocial approach to family life*. Chicago: The University of Chicago Press, 1959.

Hill, C. T., Rubin, Z., & Peplau, L. A. Breakups before marriage: The end of 103 affairs. *Journal of Social Issues*, 1976, *32*(1), 147-168.

Horner, M. S. Femininity and successful achievement: A basic inconsistency. In J. M. Bardwick, E. Douvan, M. S. Horner, & D. Gutmann, *Feminine personality and conflict*. Belmont, CA: Brooks/Cole, 1970.

Morin, S. F. Heterosexual bias in psychological research on lesbianism and male homosexuality. *American Psychologist*, 1977, *32*, 629-637.

Peplau, L. A. Power in dating relationships. In J. Freeman (Ed.), *Women: A feminist perspective* (2nd ed.). Palo Alto, CA: Mayfield, 1979.

Peplau, L. A., Cochran, S., Rook, K., & Padesky, C. Loving women: Attachment and autonomy in lesbian relationships. *Journal of Social Issues*, 1978, *34*(3), 7-27.

Peplau, L. A. Rubin, Z., & Hill, C. T. Sexual intimacy in dating couples. *Journal of Social Issues*, 1977, *33*(2), 86-109.

Raush, H. L. Orientations to close relationships. In G. Levinger & H. Raush (Eds.), *Close relationships: Perspectives on the meaning of intimacy*. Amherst, MA: University of Massachusetts Press, 1977.

Rubin, Z. *The social psychology of romantic love*. (Doctoral dissertation, University of Michigan, 1969.) (University Microfilms No. 70-4179.)

Rubin, Z. *Liking and loving: An invitation to social psychology*. New York: Holt, Rinehart & Winston, 1973.

Rubin, Z., Peplau, L. A., & Hill, C. T. Loving and leaving: Sex differences in romantic attachments. *Sex roles*, 1981, *7*, 821-835.

Schafer, S. Sociosexual behavior in male and female homosexuals: A study of sex differences. *Archives of Sexual Behavior*, 1977, *6*(5), 355-364.

Spada, J. *The Spada report*. New York: Signet, 1979.

Warren, C. A. B. *Identity and community in the gay world*. New York: Wiley, 1974.

Relationship Quality of Gay Men in Closed or Open Relationships

Lawrence A. Kurdek, PhD
J. Patrick Schmitt, PhD
Wright State University

The focus of this study was on the relationship quality of gay couples who agreed that their relationship was sexually exclusive ("closed") or not sexually exclusive ("open"). Controversy currently exists over the role that sexual openness plays in gay male relationships. Some view openness as indicative of problems in the relationship, whereas others see it as facilitating the development of long-term relationships (Harry, 1984; Peplau, 1982). This controversy may, in part, be attributed to difficulties in conceptualizing the exclusivity/openness continuum. Thus, partners can describe their relationships along this continuum in terms of current behavior, the history of cumulative behavior in the relationship, norms regarding acceptable behavior, or the match between actual behavior and accepted norms (Blasband & Peplau, in press). For two reasons, we studied exclusivity/openness in terms of actual behavior. First, both the scientific (e.g., Blumstein & Schwartz, 1983; McWhirter & Mattison, 1984) and popular (e.g., Kleinberg, 1984; Meredith, 1984) literatures have indicated that openness is inevitable among coupled gays. Second, openness has received renewed interest because of speculative links between multiple sex partners and Acquired Immunity Deficiency Syndrome (AIDS) and resulting efforts to guide gay males toward "safe sex" practices.

Previous comparisons between gay men in closed or open relationships are not extensive. McWhirter and Mattison (1984) studied 156 couples from the San Diego area and claimed that *all* of the couples together more than five years had open relationships. They further indicated that openness enhanced couple longevity. Harry (1984) reported similar findings for a Chicago sample of 774 men involved in a relationship. Bell and Weinberg (1978) compared 67 closed couples and 120 open couples from San Francisco along a variety of sexual, social, and psychological dimensions. Compared to men in open relationships, men in closed relationships attributed more importance to their partner, were more politically liberal, reported themselves as being happier now than they were five years ago, and reported higher self-acceptance. Conversely, men in open relationships were more likely to have been married, had more gay friends, were more depressed, and were more tense. Peplau (1981) described a study of 40 male couples who had been together three years or longer. No differences were found between partners in closed and open relationships on intimacy, satisfaction, security, and commitment. Finally, Blasband and Peplau (in press) report that 23 sexually open couples and 17 sexually closed couples did not differ in relationship satisfaction and commitment.

The authors who conclude that nonmonogamy facilitates couple longevity (Harry, 1984; McWhirter & Mattison, 1984) recruited geographically restricted urban samples. Given the scope of this conclusion, the first purpose of this study was to assess whether partners in an open relationship lived together longer than partners in a closed relationship in a sample that was more geographically diverse than those used in previous studies.

The second purpose of this study was to assess differences between partners in closed and open relationships on dimensions of psychological adjustment. Although Bell and Weinberg (1978) did report greater psychological adjustment among closed couples, their assessment of psychological adjustment involved self-report items whose psychometric properties were not addressed directly. We compared partners in closed and open relationships on the Symptom Checklist 90, a measure with well established reliability and validity (Derogatis, 1977). In addition to a Global Severity Index used as a measure of general psychological adjustment, we also used the specific scale scores which assessed Somatization, Obsession-Compulsion, Interpersonal Sensitivity, Depression, Anxiety, Hostility, Phobic Anxiety, Paranoid Ideation, and Psychoticism.

The third purpose of this study was to examine differences in reported relationship quality between partners in closed and open relationships. Peplau (1981) and Blasband and Peplau (in press) reported no differences in relationship quality for men in closed and open relationships, but their assessment of relationship quality was not extensive. Given the multi-dimensional character of the relationship quality construct (Lewis & Spanier, 1979), we assessed different dimensions of relationship quality by means of four measures. Rubin's (1970) Love scale taps affiliative and dependent need, predisposition to help, and exclusiveness and absorption. Rubin's Liking scale, on the other hand, taps favorable evaluation and respect for one's partner as well as perceived similarity between partner and self. Spanier's (1976) Dyadic Adjustment Scale yields four scores: Dyadic Consensus, reflecting the extent of agreement on matters of importance to dyadic functioning; Affective Expression, assessing satisfaction with demonstrated affection and sexual relations; Dyadic Satisfaction, measuring the lack of tension in the relationship; and Dyadic Cohesion, tapping the amount of activity shared by both partners. Finally, the Marital Satisfaction Scale (Roach, Frazier, & Bowden, 1981) is a uni-dimensional scale assessing the favorability of attitude toward one's relationship. In the absence of relevant data regarding multiple dimensions of relationship quality in closed and open couples, we made no predictions regarding differential levels of relationship quality.

The fourth purpose of this study was to identify and to compare the correlates of relationship quality in closed and in open gay couples. In previous studies not distinguishing between these two types of relationships, relationship quality in gays has been found to be related to cooperation, shared decision making, an androgynous sex role self-concept, appreciation for the partner, and lack of conflict (Harry, 1984; Jones & Bates, 1978; Reece & Segrist, 1981). Based largely on studies of relationship quality in heterosexual couples, we selected the following variables as potential predictors of high relationship quality among gay couples: relationship benefits and costs, specifically, a large number of Attractions to the relationship, a large number of Barriers to leaving the relationship, and few Alternatives to the relationship (Lloyd, Cate, & Henton, 1984; Rusbult, 1980, 1983); relationship beliefs, specifically, low endorsements of the views that Disagreement is Destructive to the Relationship, Mindreading is Expected, Partners Cannot Change, and Sexual Perfection (Eidelson & Epstein, 1982; Ellis & Harper, 1975); a Masculine sex role self-concept, encompassing agency and instrumentality, a Feminine sex role self-concept, encompassing nurturance and expressiveness, and an androgynous sex-role self-concept, incorporating both high Masculinity and high Femininity (Antill, 1983; Baucom & Aiken, 1984); a high value on Dyadic Attachment, a low value on Personal Autonomy (Peplau & Cochran, 1981) and a strong Interpersonal Orientation (Swap & Rubin, 1983); Shared Decision Making (Blumstein & Schwartz, 1983; Peplau, 1983); Social Support from Friends and Family (Bloom, Asher, & White, 1978; Caplan, 1983; Kelley, 1983; Whitaker & Garbarino, 1983); and General Psychological Adjustment (Bell & Weinberg, 1978; Bloom et al., 1978).

The final issue addressed in this study was the degree of similarity between partners in closed and open relationships on demographic characteristics, relationship quality, and the correlates of relationship quality listed above. Partners in heterosexual relationships have been found to be similar to each other on both intrapersonal and interpersonal personality dimensions (Buss, 1984; Lesnick-Oberstein & Cohen, 1984), and these similarities have been thought to facilitate interpartner communication, understanding, and empathy. We explored whether gay partners in the two relationships of interest would show comparable degrees of similarity to each other.

In sum, the purposes of this study were: (a) to compare gay males in closed or open relationships on time living together, psychological adjustment, and relationship quality: (b) to compare the correlates of relationship quality for closed and open couples; and (c) to compare the similarity between partners in closed and open relationships on demographic and relationship-oriented variables.

METHOD

Subjects

Participants were 98 men in closed relationships and 34 men in open relationships. Partners in each of the 66 couples lived together, and both partners in each relationship independently agreed on the open/closed status of the relationship. Participants were recruited through our own personal contacts and through responses to a description of the study published in three gay periodicals (*The Advocate, Bodyworks* and *Guide Magazine*).

Measures and Procedure

Each couple was mailed a pair of identical questionnaires. In order to ensure honest responses, data were collected anonymously, partners were directed not to discuss their responses until after the forms had been completed and returned, and partners were asked to respond honestly. Completed forms were returned to us in two separate postage-free envelopes.

Demographic and Background Information

Participants provided information regarding: Age; Income, represented by 12 intervals ranging from < $5,000 to > $50,000; Education, represented by 8 intervals ranging from less than seventh grade to a graduate doctoral degree; Job Prestige, represented by the 10 Hollingshead (1977) occupational groupings ranging from Unemployed to Executive, Owner of a Large Business, or Major Professional; and Sexual Orientation, represented by the 7-point Kinsey scale which ranged from Exclusively Heterosexual to Exclusively Homosexual. In addition, partners indicated how many months they had been living together, and noted whether they had been married, divorced, divorced more than once, or had ever lived with another partner. Finally, partners were asked to choose which of two descriptions based on Bell and Weinberg (1978) better characterized their relationship: (a) We are closely bound to each other. We look to each other rather than to outsiders for interpersonal and sexual satisfaction. We spend most of our leisure time together, or (b) While attached to each other, we have an "open" relationship. We receive interpersonal and sexual satisfaction not only from each other but from others outside of the relationship as well.

Measures of Relationship Quality

For all measures, original references to "marriage" or "spouse" were changed to "relationship" and "partner," respectively. Cronbach's alpha was used to assess the internal consistency of all summed composite scores. The mean alpha across all composite scores was .75.

Affiliative/dependent need. Rubin's (1970) 13-item Love scale assessed affiliative and dependent need, predisposition to help, and exclusiveness and absorption.

Respect/perceived similarity. Rubin's (1970) 13-item Liking scale assessed favorable evaluation of the partner, as well as the perception that the partner was similar to oneself.

Favorable attitude toward the relationship. A general favorable attitude toward the relationship was assessed by the Marital Satisfaction Scale (Roach et al., 1981). Subjects indicated their degree of agreement with each of 48 items.

Extent of agreement, satisfaction with affection and sex, low tension and shared activity. Spanier's (1976) 32-item Dyadic Adjustment Scale measured Dyadic Consensus, agreement between partners on important issues (13 items); Affectional Expression, satisfaction with levels of demonstrated affection and sexual relations (4 items); Dyadic Satisfaction, degree of tension in the relationship (10 items); and Dyadic Cohesion, amount of activity shared by partners (5 items).

Correlates of Relationship Quality

Attractions, barriers, and alternatives. Attractions to the relationship, barriers to leaving the relationship, and alternatives to the relationship were assessed by a 30-item scale we constructed for this study. There were 10 items each for the Attractions (e.g., "My relationship with my partner is rewarding."), Barriers (e.g., "Many things would prevent me from leaving my partner even if I were unhappy."), and Alternatives (e.g., "In general, alternatives to being in a relationship with my partner are not very appealing.") scales.

Relationship beliefs. The Relationship Beliefs Inventory (Eidelson & Epstein, 1982) required subjects to indicate how strongly they feel each of 32 items is true or is false for them. Eight items were included for each of four subscales: Disagreement is Destructive (e.g., "I cannot tolerate it when my partner disagrees with me."); Mindreading is Expected (e.g., "I do not expect my partner to sense all of my moods."); Partners Cannot Change (e.g., "My partner does not seem capable of behaving other than he does now."); and Sexual Perfection (e.g., "I get upset if I think I have not completely satisfied my partner sexually.").

Sex-role self-concept. Masculinity, Femininity, and Androgyny scores were derived from the Bem Sex Role Inventory (Bem, 1974), which required subjects to indicate the extent to which each of 20 Masculine, 20 Feminine, and 20 Neutral adjectives describes them. Men above the median of both the Masculinity and Femininity scores were classified as Androgynous; all others were classified as nonandrogynous.

Dyadic attachment/Personal autonomy. Dyadic attachment and personal autonomy were assessed by Peplau and Cochran's (1981) survey of relationship values. Subjects indicated how important each of 13 items was to their relationship. Seven items assessed Dyadic Attachment (e.g., "Spending as much time together"), and six assessed Personal Autonomy (e.g., "Having major interests of my own outside of the relationship").

Interpersonal orientation. The Interpersonal Orientation Scale (Swap & Rubin, 1983) required subjects to indicate the extent of their agreement with each of 29 items that assessed an interest in interpersonal relationships (e.g., "The more people reveal about themselves, the more inclined I feel to reveal things about myself.").

Shared decision making. This scale was partly based on the Decision Making Scale devised by Gray-Little (1982). This measure required subjects to indicate for each of 27 items whether final decisions regarding the item was generally Always Made by My Partner, Usually Made by My Partner, Made By Both of Us Together, Usually Made by Myself, or Always Made by Myself. The score derived reflected the number of items in which decisions were Made by Both of Us Together.

Social support. The Perceived Social Support Scale (Procidano & Heller, 1983) required subjects to assess the degree of support experienced from friends and family members. The Friends scale and the Family scale each have 20 items (e.g., "My friends give me the moral support I need." and "My family enjoys hearing about what I think.").

Psychological adjustment. Specific psychological adjustment was assessed by the nine subscales (Somatization, Obsession-Compulsion, Interpersonal Sensitivity, Depression, Anxiety, Hostility, Phobic Anxiety, Paranoid Ideation, and Psychoticism) of the Symptom Checklist 90 (Derogatis, 1977). For each of 90 items, subjects indicated how much discomfort the item had caused during the past seven days. General psychological maladjustment was assessed by the Global Severity Index, which measures an overall level or depth of disorder.

RESULTS

Comparability of Couple Types

Partners in closed or open relationships were compared on nine demographic characteristics (Age, Income, Education, Job Prestige, Proportion Ever Married, Proportion Divorced, Proportion Divorced More Than Once, Proportion Having Lived With Previous Partner, and Sexual Orientation). A one-way (Type of Relationship) multivariate analysis of variance indicated that men in the two groups were equivalent on these characteristics (F (Pillai's) $(9,122) = 1.81, p > .05$). Mean scores for this entire sample were as follows: Age 33.92 years, Income 5.89, Education 5.92, Job Prestige 6.97, Proportion Never Married .78, Proportion Divorced .12, Proportion Divorced More Than Once .01, Proportion Having Lived With A Previous Partner .36, and Sexual Orientation 6.75. (See

Method section above for clarification of score values.) The geographical representation of couples in both groups was diverse yet comparable, with the majority residing in the Midwest. The percentage of couples residing in the Midwest, West, East, and Southwest for the closed couples was 63%, 19%, 8%, and 8%, respectively. Percentages for the open couples were 44%, 25%, 25%, and 6%, respectively. This sample is clearly not random and does not represent all coupled gays.

Differences Between Partners in Closed and Open Relationships on Months Living Together

A one-way (Type of Couple) analysis of variance indicated that partners in open relationships lived together significantly more months than did partners in closed relationships (Ms = 79.12 and 42.24, repectively) ($F(1,130) = 14.49, p < .0001$). The range for months living together for partners in closed and in open relationships was 4 to 151 months and 6 to 305 months, respectively. The percentage of closed and open couples living together for more than five years was 20% and 47%, respectively.

Differences Between Partners in Closed and Open Relationships on Psychological Adjustment

A one-way (Type of Couple) multivariate analysis of variance using the nine subscores (Somatization, Obsession-Compulsion, Interpersonal Sensitivity, Depression, Anxiety, Hostility, Phobic Anxiety, Paranoid Ideation, and Psychoticism) from the Symptom Checklist as dependent variables revealed no difference between partners in the two types of relationships (F(Pillai's) $(9,122) = 0.18, p > .05$). Furthermore, a one-way (Type of Couple) analysis of variance of the Global Severity score was also nonsignificant ($F(1,130) = 0.75, p > .05$).

Differences Between Partners in Closed and Open Relationships on Relationship Quality

The seven relationship quality scores were submitted to a oneway (Type of Couple) multivariate analysis of variance using Months

Living Together as a covariate. The effect was significant (F(Pillai's) (7,123) = 2.98, $p < .01$). Subsequent one-way (Type of Couples) uni-variate analyses of variance indicated that this multivariate effect was attributed to differences on Affiliative/Dependent Need, Favorable Attitude Toward the Relationship, and Low Tension ($F(1,129)$ ranging from 4.87 to 9.16, $p < .05$). Respectively, the means for closed and open couples were 97.24 vs. 91.74; 205.17 vs. 198.17; and 40.27 vs. 38.29. In all cases, partners in closed relationships had higher scores than partners in open relationships.

Correlates of Relationship Quality for Partners in Closed and Open Relationships

Pearson correlations were computed between the 7 relationship quality scores and the 17 predictors of interest. However, given the large number of variables involved in these correlational analyses, a more compact picture of the predictors of relationship quality for partners in closed and open relationships would be obtained by a stepwise multiple regression. Because of the relatively few number of open couples, we maximized the reliability of this analysis by creating a composite relationship quality score by summing the standardized z scores of each of the 7 relationship quality scores. The moderate internal consistency of this composite score (Cronbach's alpha = .72) justified this procedure.

The Pearson correlations between this composite Relationship Quality score and each of the 17 predictors are presented by type of couple in Table 1. Looking at these correlations, one can see that a similar pattern of correlations was obtained for each type of couple. High Relationship Quality was related to many Attractions, many Barriers, few Alternatives, few Disagreement is Destructive beliefs, few Partners Cannot Change beliefs, high Dyadic Attachment, high Shared Decision Making, and low Psychological Maladjustment. One difference of note is that high Masculinity was related to Relationship Quality in open couples but not in closed couples.

A stepwise multiple regression indicated that a subset of the pool of 17 potential predictors was significantly related to Relationship Quality (multiple R = .81 and .84, respectively, $p < .01$). The

Table 1

Correlations and Beta Weights Between Predictors of Relationship Quality and Composite Relationship Quality Score by Type of Couple

	Type of Couple			
	Closed (n = 98)		Open (n = 34)	
Predictor	r	beta	r	beta
COSTS/BENEFITS				
Attractions	.59**	.45**	.55**	.36**
Barriers	.18*		.28*	
Alternatives	-.36**	-.15*	-.32*	
BELIEFS				
Disagreement	-.39**	-.27**	-.40**	-.27**
Mind Reading	.00			-.09
Sexual Perfection	-.13		-.17	
RELATIONSHIP VALUES				
Dyadic Attachment	.38**	.27**	.49**	.39**
Personal Autonomy	-.09	-.18*	.02	
SOCIAL SUPPORT				
Friends	.09		.08	
Family	.04		.18	
SEX ROLE SELF CONCEPT				
Masculinity	.02	.12	.30*	
Femininity	.15		.11	
Androgyny	.01		-.03	
INTERPERSONAL ORIENTATION	.16		-.08	
SHARED DECISION MAKING	.40**	.28**	.41**	
MALADJUSTMENT	-.26*		-.43**	-.21*

* $p < .05$. ** $p < .01$.

standardized beta weights presented in Table 1 give an idea of which particular predictors contributed the most information in explaining Relationship Quality for each couple type. For both couple types, Relationship Quality was significantly predicted by many Attractions, few Disagreement is Destructive beliefs, and high Dyadic Attachment. In addition, few Alternatives, low Personal Autonomy, high Masculinity, and high Shared Decision Making were significant predictors for only closed couples, while few Partner Cannot Change beliefs and low Psychological Maladjustment were significant predictors for only open couples.

Intracouple Correlations

In order to assess the relation between partners' scores, partners were randomly assigned to Partner 1 or Partner 2 positions. The Pearson correlations between partners' demographic scores indicated that partners in both closed and open relationships were similar only on Age (rs = .37 and .58, respectively, $p < .05$ here and below). Pearson correlations were also computed between partners' relationship-oriented scores. Partners in closed and open relationships were similar to each other in their appraisal of a Favorable Attitude Toward the Relationship (rs = .39 and .64, respectively); Extent of Agreement (rs = .50 and .47, respectively); Satisfaction with Affection and Sex (rs = .56 and .47, respectively): and Low Tension (rs = .46 and .73, respectively). Partners in closed and open relationships were also similar to each other in their Partners Cannot Change belief scores (rs = .32 and .48, respectively) and their Dyadic Attachment scores (rs = .45 and .47 respectively). Only partners in closed relationships were similar to each other on Personal Autonomy ($r = .28$), Shared Decision Making ($r = .47$), and General Psychological Maladjustment ($r = .48$). Only partners in open relationships were similar to each other in their evaluations of Attractions to and Barriers to the relationship (rs = .49 and .71, respectively) and Interpersonal Orientation ($r = .52$). Of particular note, these partners also tended to have *opposite* Femininity scores ($r = .45$).

DISCUSSION

Because our sample was small and nonrepresentative, our findings need to be viewed with caution. Some of our findings are consistent with previous research on relationship quality, whereas others are not.

Differences Between Partners in Closed and Open Relationships

Consistent with the findings of McWhirter and Mattison (1984) and Harry (1984), we found that partners in open relationships lived together longer than did partners in closed relationships. Because we have no information regarding the history of our subjects' relationships, we do not know if open couples made a transition from exclusiveness to openness as limerance decreased. Blasband and Peplau (in press), however, note that only 20% of their 40 couples indicated that their relationship evolved from exclusivity to openness. In addition, because we found that 20% of our couples in closed relationships had been together longer than 5 years, openness does not appear to be an inevitable outcome in the development of long term gay relationships. Context effects, however, may influence the occurrence of openness or exclusivity. Settings where gays are numerous and visible may lead to couples' valuing openness, whereas settings in which gays are more hidden may lead to couples' prizing and protecting exclusivity.

Unlike Bell and Weinberg (1978), we did not find any differences between men in closed and open relationships on either general or specific psychological adjustment. As noted earlier, Bell and Weinberg's sample was from San Francisco, and the psychometric integrity of their assessments of psychological adjustment is difficult to evaluate on the basis of information presented. With both a geographically varied sample and a psychometrically sound measure of psychological adjustment, we found no evidence that psychological adjustment is related to type of coupling.

Statistically controlling for differences between couple types in the length of time living together, we found that partners in closed relationships reported higher relationship quality than did partners in open relationships. In particular, partners in closed relationships reported a stronger Affiliative/Dependent need, a more Favorable Attitude Toward the Relationship, and less Tension in the relationship than did partners in open relationships. Our finding that the two types of couples did not differ in Respect/Perceived Similarity, Agreement, Satisfaction with Affection and Sex, and Shared Activities is consistent with Harry's (1984), Peplau's (1981), and Blasband and Peplau's (in press) finding that partners in open and closed gay relationships were equivalent in intimacy, security, satisfaction, and commitment. Because we found differences on some dimensions of relationship quality and not on others, future studies of relationship quality would do well to incorporate multi-dimensional assessments of relationship quality (*cf.* Sternberg & Grajek, 1984). We speculate that the significant differences we did obtain regarding the relationship quality of men in closed and open relationships indicate that personality characteristics such as affiliation and dependency may enhance the maintenance of monogamous relationships, that favorable attitudes toward the relationship may enhance the mutual attraction between monogamous partners, and that lower tension in closed relationships may reflect, in part, the absence of conflict regarding sexual contacts outside of the relationship.

Correlates of Relationship Quality

Our selection of potential correlates of relationship quality was primarily based on studies of heterosexual couples. Generally, our findings based on partners in closed and open gay relationships are congruent with these studies in that we found that global relationship quality was related to many perceived Attractions to the relationship, many Barriers to leaving the relationship, and few Alternatives to the relationship (Lloyd, Cate, & Henton, 1984; Rusbult, 1980, 1983); the absence of dysfunctional relationship beliefs, particularly regarding the destructiveness of disagreement and the unchangeability of partners (Eidelson & Epstein, 1982); a high value on Dyadic Attachment (Peplau & Cochran, 1981); Shared Decision Making (Blumstein & Schwartz, 1983; Peplau, 1983); and low Psychological Maladjustment (Bloom et al., 1978). The correlational nature of these data, of course, preclude any inferences of a causal nature.

We found little evidence that relationship quality in gay couples was related to Personal Autonomy, Social Support, and Sex Role Self-Concept. However, these are areas in which homosexual relationships are distinct from heterosexual relationships. As Blumstein and Schwartz (1983) note, the lack of institutionalized marriages for homosexuals both removes significant barriers to leaving the relationship, e.g., legal, financial, and social restrictions, and precludes the facile development of social support networks. Further, gay relationships in particular are distinct from heterosexual relationships in that they are frequently based on expectations of equality, reciprocity, and autonomy (Blumstein & Schwartz, 1983; McWhirter & Mattison, 1984).

Intracouple Correlations

As with heterosexual couples (e.g., Buss, 1984; Lesnick-Ober stein & Cohen, 1981), we found that partners in gay couples tended to be similar to each other in Age. We also found that these partners were similar in ratings of Relationship quality, beliefs regarding Partner Changeability, and Dyadic Attachment. However, we also found that partner similarity varied by type of couple. Only for closed couples were partners' Affiliation/Dependency, Shared Activity, Personal Autonomy, and Shared Decision Making scores related. This finding could reflect that partners in closed relationships agree on the importance of intimate dyadic interaction. We also found that partners in closed relationships tended to have similar levels of Psychological Adjustment, but we have no ready interpre tation of this finding.

Only for partners in open relationships were Attractions, Barriers, and Interpersonal Orientation scores related. While few attractions to the relationship and persuasive alternatives to the relationship have often been viewed as reasons for the dissolution of gay relationships (Blumstein & Schwartz, 1983; McWhirter & Mattison, 1984), it may be that gay couples together for long periods of time, like our open couples, may themselves develop mutually recognized barriers to leaving the relationship. These may include sexual variety, shared interpersonal relationships, reciprocal trust, shared property, shared material possessions, joint financial resources, and the symbolism of serving as models of a relationship that has endured (McWhirter & Mattison, 1984). We also found that Femininity scores were inversely related for partners in open relationships. This does not mean that partners in these relationships adopt complementary masculine/feminine roles. Rather, it means that one partner in an open relationship tends to be nurturant, expressive, and yielding while his partner does not. Because we have little information regarding the possible transition of male couples along the dimension of exclusivity/openness, it would be instructive if future studies related Femininity to the decision making dynamics involved in that transition.

REFERENCES

Antill, J. K. (1983). Sex role complementarity versus similarity in married couples. *Journal of Personality and Social Psychology, 45*, 145-155.

Baucom, D. H. & Aiken, P. A. (1984). Sex role identity, marital satisfaction, and response to behavioral marital therapy. *Journal of Consulting and Clinical Psychology, 52*, 438-444.

Bell, A. P., & Weinberg, M. S. (1978). *Homosexualities: A study of diversity among men and women*. New York: Simon & Schuster.

Bem, S. L. (1974). The measurement of psychological androgyny. *Journal of Consulting and Clinical Psychology, 47*, 155-162.

Blasband, D., & Peplau, L. A. (in press). Sexual exclusivity versus openness in gay male couples. *Archives of Sexual Behavior*.

Bloom, B. L., Asher, S. J. & White, S. W. (1978). Marital disruption as a stressor. *Psychological Bulletin, 85*, 867-894.

Blumstein, P., & Schwartz, P. (1983). *American couples*. New York: William Morrow.

Buss, D. M. (1984). Toward a psychology of person-environment (PE) correlation. *Journal of Personality and Social Psychology, 47*, 361-377.

Caplan, G. (1983). The family as a support system. In H. I. McCubbin, A. E. Cauble, & J. M. Patterson (Eds.), *Family stress, coping, and social support* (pp. 200-220). Springfield, IL: Charles C. Thomas.

Derogatis, L. R. (1977). *SCL-90: Administration, scoring, and procedures manual–for the revised version*. Johns Hopkins University School of Medicine, Baltimore, MD.

Eidelson, R. J. & Epstein, N. (1982). Cognition and relationship maladjustment: Development of a measure of dysfunctional relationship beliefs. *Journal of Consulting and Clinical Psychology, 50*, 715-720.

Ellis, A., & Harper, R. A. (1975). *A new guide to rational living*. Englewood Cliffs, NJ: Prentice-Hall.

Gray-Little, B. (1982). Marital quality and power processes among black couples. *Journal of Marriage and the Family*, *44*, 633-646.

Harry, J. (1984). *Gay Couples*. New York: Praeger.

Hollingshead, A. B. (1977). *Four factor index of social status*. Unpublished manuscript, Yale University, New Haven,

Jones, R. W., & Bates, J. E. (1978). Satisfaction in male homosexual couples. *Journal of Homosexuality*, *3*, 217-225.

Kelley, H. H. (1983). Epilogue: An essential science. In H. H. Kelley, E. Berscheid, A. Christensen, J. H. Harvey, T. L. Huston, G. Levinger, E. McClintock. L.A. Peplau, & D. R. Peterson (Eds.), *Close relationships* (pp. 586-589). San Francisco: W. H. Freeman.

Lesnick-Oberstein, M., & Cohen L. (1984). Cognitive style, sensation seeking, and assortative mating. *Journal of Personality and Social Psychology*, *46*, 112-117.

Levinger, G. (1979). A social psychological perspective on marital dissolution. In G. Levinger & O. C. Moles (Eds.), *Divorce and separation* (pp. 37-60). New York: Basic Books.

Levinger, G. (1983). Development and change. In H. H. Kelley, E. Berscheid, A. Christensen, J. H. Harvey, T. L. Huston, G. Levinger, E. McClintock, L. A. Peplau, & D. R. Peterson (Eds.), *Close relationships*(pp. 315-359). San Francisco: W. H. Freeman.

Lewis, R. A., & Spanier, G. B. (1979). Theorizing about the quality and stability of marriage. In W. R. Burr, R. Hill, F. I. Nye, & I. L. Reiss (Eds.), *Contemporary theories about the family* (Vol. 1, pp. 268-294). New York: Academic Press.

Lloyd, S. A. Cate, R. M., & Henton, J. M. (1984). Predicting premarital relationship stability. *Journal of Marriage and the Family*, *46*, 71-76.

McWhirter, D. P., & Mattison, A. M. (1984). *The male couple: How relationships develop*. Englewood Cliffs, NJ: Prentice Hall.

Meredith, N. (1984, January). The gay dilemma. *Psychology Today*, pp. 56-62.

Peplau, L. A. (1981, March). Whnt in relationships. *Psychology Today*, pp. 28-38.

Peplau, L. A. (1982). Research on homosexual couples: An overview. *Journal of Homosexuality*, *8*(2) 3-8.

Peplau, L. A. (1983). Roles and gender. In H. H. Kelley, E. Berscheid, A. Christensen, J. H. Harvery, T. L. Huston, G. Levinger, E. McClintock, L.A. Peplau, & D. R. Peterson (Eds.), *Close relationships* (pp. 220-269). San Francisco: W. H. Freeman.

Peplau, L. A., & Cochran, S. D. (1981). Value orientations in the intimate relationships of gay men. *Journal of Homosexuality*, *6*(3) 1-19.

Procidano, M. E., & Heller, K. (1983). Measures of perceived social support from friends and from family: Three validation studies. *American Journal of Community Psychology*, *11*, 1-24.

Reece, R., & Segrist, A. E. (1981). The association of selected "masculine" sex-role variables with length of relationship in gay males. *Journal of Homosexuality*, 7(1) 33-48.

Roach, A. J., Frazier, L. P., & Bowden, S. R. (1981). The marital satisfaction scale: Development of a measure for intervention research. *Journal of Marriage and the Family*, *40*, 537-546.

Rubin, Z. (1970). Measurement of romantic love. *Journal of Personality and Social Psychology*, *16*, 265-273.

Rusbult, C. E. (1980). Commitment and satisfaction in romantic associations: A test of the investment model. *Journal of Experimental Social Psychology*, *16*, 172-186.

Rusbult, C. E. (1983). A longitudinal test of the investment model: The development (and deterioration) of satisfaction and commitment in heterosexual involvements. *Journal of Personality and Social Psychology*, *45*, 104-117.

Spanier, G. B. (1979). Measuring dyadic adjustment: New scales for assessing the quality of marriage and similar dyads. *Journal of Marriage and the Family*, *38*, 15-28.

Sternberg, R. J., & Grajek, S. (1984). The nature of love. *Journal of Personality and Social Psychology*, *47*, 312-329.

Swap, W. C., & Rubin, Z. (1983). Measurement of interpersonal orientation. *Journal of Personality and Social Psychology*, *44*, 208-219.

Whitaker, J. K., & Garbarino, J. (1983). *Social support networks*. New York: Aldine.

V. HOW TO SOLVE PROBLEMS IN GAY RELATIONSHIPS

Within the intricate web of both partners' needs, desires, and expectations, as described in the introduction to this volume, problems inevitably arise in a gay relationship. One key to its lasting is the ability of partners to recognize and face problems and the willingness to invest the ingenuity and make the sacrifices necessary for their resolution. The articles in this section offer some guidance in these matters.

The study by Randall Jones and John Bates provides a benchmark for assessing the quality of gay relationships. They compared partners who were highly satisfied with their coupledom with those who were only moderately so. Their major findings pertain to how satisfaction with relationships is related to how much the relationship conforms to or departs from the marriage model and to the presence or absence of support from a gay community.

Returning to the article by McWhirter and Mattison (i.e., the second part), we find how each stage in their developmental model for gay relationships can pose its own problems. In the "blending" stage, for example, the slightest effort by one partner to put some psychological distance between him and his partner can raise the spectre of a doomed relationship. Once romantic idealism is confronted by the reality of dealing with an imperfect human being, as it presumably does in stage two, the scene is set for many disagree ments. Other possible sources of difficulty are mentioned—the fact that the lovers are at different stages in the sequence or the pervasive homophobia that surrounds gay relationships and may be internalized by the partners. McWhirter and Mattison suggest how therapy can help resolve such problems in gay relationships.

The expectation that gay men share equally the power and benefits of their intimate relationships was alluded to in the earlier discussion of age-egalitarianism. It is a product of the gay liberation movement which has detoxified homosexuality and endorsed sexual and emotional intimacy between men. Our raw psychological needs, however, tend to be voracious and imperious, brooking little delay in complete gratification. Democracy, on the other hand, sometimes requires the forestalling of gratification and rests on the basic respect of democratic rights, others' as well as our own. Michael Shively and I were therefore interested in how conflicts in gay relationships were resolved when the psychological needs of one partner clashed with those of the other. A democratic resolution of such conflicts would honor the rights of both parties in the attempt to satisfy, to some extent, the needs of both. Such conflict resolution would take the form of negotiation rather than unilateral action. The article addresses the question of whether negotiation occurred in gay relationships and, if so, did it work?

There are relationships that are doomed from the start. They are often erected on the fathomless guilt of one party and the unshakeable conviction of the other about his ultimate invincibility and, when things inevitably don't measure up, his innocent victimization and exploitation. Such relationships are not intended to bring happiness. Instead, they provide endless occasions for atonement by the "guilty" party and a ready target of hostile resentment for the "injured" party. These needs may run so deeply and are sometimes so repressed that such a relationship can drag on for years or until one or the other party is destroyed. Scott Whitney describes this awful dynamic as it occurs in the relationships of alcoholics and their non-drinking partners, who are addicted to guilt as deeply as their partners are to drinking. Although this article does not tell you how to solve the problems that occur in a "good" relationship, it can help you recognize a "bad" one and to find the courage and means to end it.

Satisfaction in Male Homosexual Couples

Randall W. Jones
John E. Bates, PhD
Indiana University

A number of homosexual men have expressed concerns to us regarding their long-term love relationships. However, we were able to find little systematically collected information on gay couples that would help us in our counseling efforts. The present study represents a beginning attempt to acquire such information.

Although it seems likely that many homosexuals have little desire for a long-term, intimate relationship, many others indicate that they would ideally like to share their lives with a partner (Saghir & Robins, 1973; Williams & Weinberg, 1974). Such a relationship is seen as solving many of the problems they encounter (Cory, 1951; Hoffman, 1968). Williams and Weinberg (1974) found that gay male couples, compared with gay singles, were less worried about public intolerance of their sexual behavior, had more self-esteem, and were less lonely, guilty, or depressed. Despite these apparent advantages, homosexual male relationships are generally regarded as short-lived and infrequent, compared with the number of gay men living alone (Dank, 1973). There may be two explanations for this situation: (a) lack of institutional pressures promoting homosexual unions comparable to those promoting heterosexual unions, and (b) influences of elements of gay subculture and personal identity of homosexuals themselves which oppose or weaken long-term homosexual pair-bonding (Weinberg, 1972). Nevertheless, Stevens (Note 1) argues that gay liberation, by lessening social sanctions and increasing gay pride, is lowering relationship costs and increasing rewards enough that more and more homosexual couples will live together in long-term relationships in future years.

If professionals wish to be of help to gay men desiring stable love relationships, one logical place to begin is an improved understanding of such relationships that do exist despite the pressures against them. Sonnenschein (1968) described members of gay couples as sharing similar interests, just as one would find in heterosexual couples, but not adhering to the heterosexual stereotype of active versus passive role differentiation. Sonnenschein also reported that the homosexual couples saw common gay activities, such as going to gay bars and baths, as threats to the relationship and that they were less involved than singles in such activities. Further information, particularly about the factors that might contribute to stability, seems necessary.

The present study is an effort to explore one possible factor in stability: satisfaction in the relationship.

METHOD

Preliminary Procedures

Fourteen male homosexual couples, ranging from 20 to 50 years of age, were interviewed and given a preliminary questionnaire by one of the authors. All couples were obtained in a small, midwest college town. Each couple met the criteria of identifying itself as a couple and stating that the relationship had been the primary one (i.e., closest friendship and main or exclusive sexual outlet) for each partner for at least 5 months prior to the study. Subjects were recruited through acquaintances of the researchers and advertising in a gay newspaper and a nongay local paper. Data from one additional couple were excluded because they broke up prior to the end of the study. Questions for the couples were initially derived from the literature on marital satisfaction and the gay subculture. The preliminary procedure resulted in a questionnaire with 50 open-ended questions concerning the functioning of a gay couple. The open-ended format was selected because of the early stage of the research. This questionnaire will be referred to as the Gay Relationship Questionnaire.

Relationship Questionnaire

Forty-five items of the Gay Relationship Questionnaire were grouped a priori into 16 areas of possible relevance to couple stability. These areas and their contributing items are described in Table 1. The items were rated according to presumed contributions to satisfaction and stability, on the basis of marital research, homosexual research, and our own knowledge of the gay subculture. The responses were scored for each individual and added for the couple. For example, on the item concerning number of friends knowing the person's sexual orientation (part of the individual social support scale), one member of the couple, who has three or more friends who know, would receive the maximum rating of 3; the other member, who has no friends who know, would be rated 1; and the couple would receive a score of 4. Five items (e.g., where the lovers met) were not included in scales because of a lack of clear relevance to couple stability.

Satisfaction Measure

As a criterion measure, the items of the Marital Relationship Inventory (MRI – Burgess & Locke, 1968) were slightly modified to describe a homosexual relationship. The modified questionnaire is referred to as the Couples Relationship Inventory (CRI). The CRI was scored in the same manner as the MRI, and for lack of better norms, the norms of the MRI were used to describe the level of satisfaction of the couple. Scores from two partners were averaged to create one CRI score for each couple.

Subjects

Twenty-eight couples meeting the same criteria as the preliminary sample were recruited through acquaintances and gay organizations. There were 118 questionnaire packets sent out with postage-free return envelopes, the majority in urban areas. The 21% rate is low, but seems reasonable considering the indirect method of recruitment, the lack of strong incentive for completing the questionnaire, the need for cooperation from both partners, and the lengthi-

TABLE 1

Items in the Scales of the Gay Relationship Questionnaire

Scale	Item
1. Background similarity	a. Similarity in age b. Similarity in religion c. Similarity in urban vs. rural childhood d. Similarity in level of education e. Similarity in current occupation
2. Length of prior acquaintance	
3. Length of relationship	
4. Symbols of the relationship	a. Anniversary date b. Special places, etc. (e.g., "our song")
5. Individual social support	a. Number of "true" friends b. Number of friends who know sexual preference c. Parental knowledge of sexual preference d. Sibling knowledge of sexual preference
6. Couple social support	a. Number of friends aware of relationship with lover b. Parental awareness of relationship with lover c. Number of people knowing lover and self as couple d. Number of friends held as couple
7. Social independence	a. Number of friends of self and not of lover b. Activities not shared with lover c. Degree of sexual fidelity d. If "open relationship," frequency of outside contacts
8. Acceptance of homosexuality	a. Homosexuality considered normal b. Have not talked to counselor or psychologist about sexuality c. Participation in gay liberation activities
9. Common interests	a. Number of recreation activities as couple b. Sexual activities as couple with another people
10. Commitment (live together)	
11. Role differentiation in household tasks	
12. Affection	a. Degree of affection display in straight public b. Degree of affection display in gay public c. Degree of affection in private d. Frequency of sex with lover
13. Appreciation	a. Positive aspects of relationship and lover b. Appreciation of sex with lover c. Positive changes in life-style
14. Lack of conflict	a. Lack of negative aspects to relationship b. Infrequency of fights and arguments c. Lack of conflict-producing problems
15. Communication	a. If not strict fidelity, shared agreement regarding this b. How equally arguments are resolved
16. Stability factors	a. Positiveness of overall appraisal of relationship b. Things that make relationship special c. Positiveness of feelings about love relationship in general d. Lack of thoughts of breaking off relationship e. Future plans as couple (e.g., building house) f. Number of prior lovers g. Number of factors keeping couple together

ness and highly personal nature of the questionnaire. The 56 subjects ranged in age from 18 to 50; ages were relatively evenly distributed over the range, with a mean of 31.1 years.

RESULTS AND DISCUSSION

On the basis of their CRI satisfaction scores, couples were divided into two groups; 12 couples who were adequately satisfied and functioning (average score of 86 to 102), and 16 couples who were very satisfied and effectively functioning (103-117). Then a discriminant analysis was performed with the Gay Relationship Questionnaire variables as discriminator variables. For the sake of reducing the number of dependent variables in an analysis with a relatively small number of subjects, Variable 3 (length of love relationship) was eliminated from this analysis on the basis of high correlations with other variables. Variables 9, 10, and 11 (common interests, commitment, and role differentiation) were previously eliminated because of lack of variance—all couples scored high. Variables 5 and 6 (individual social support and couple social support) were combined for this analysis because of a high correlation.

The discriminant analysis showed that the Gay Relationship Questionnaire variables could be combined to differentiate the adequately and well-functioning couples. Both direct and stepwise methods yielded the same solution. The discriminant function approached significance, Wilk's lambda = .405, $\chi^2 = 19.45$, $df = 11$, $p < .06$. Ninety-three percent of the couples were correctly classified by the function. The standardized discriminant function coefficients for each discriminator variable are displayed in Table 2, along with the means and F tests of the differences between the means. The correlations among the variables are shown in Table 3.

As can be seen from the discriminant coefficients in Table 2, Variables 4, 13, and 14 (symbols of the relationship, and lack of conflict) were the most heavily weighted in differentiating the two kinds of couples. The importance of appreciation and lack of conflict is not surprising, since these bear conceptual resemblance to the satisfaction and functioning items of the CRI. The negative weight for symbols of the relationship is surprising, especially

TABLE 2

Means, F Values, and Standardized Discriminant Function Coefficients

Variable	Adequate CRI	High CRI	F^a	Discriminant Coefficient
1. Background similarity	16.92	17.13	.05	-.36
2. Length of prior acquaintance	3.08	5.75	1.08	-.58
4. Symbols of the relationship	4.33	4.25	.18	-1.02
6. Couple and individual social support	18.96	17.81	1.12	.16
7. Social independence	17.83	17.31	.08	-.52
8. Acceptance of homosexuality	13.50	13.19	.31	-.42
12. Affection	18.33	18.00	.16	-.34
13. Appreciation	16.17	17.50	5.14*	1.10
14. Lack of conflict	9.17	12.38	7.73**	1.02
15. Communication	10.00	9.81	.05	-.61
16. Stability factors	31.33	34.38	4.68*	.68

[a] $df = 1, 26$.
*$p < .05$.
**$p < .01$.

given the very small mean difference between the groups. We had expected that relationship symbols would be positively associated with a more satisfying relationship. However, the negative weight seems likely to be a result of low relationship to the criterion and moderate, positive relationship to one of the variables having a high correlation with the criterion, that is, variable 16 (stability factors).

It seemed possible that the degree of similarity or difference in a couple's satisfaction as measured by the CRI would relate to the other measures. However, in fact, the size of discrepancy between the two members' CRI scores did not correlate strongly with other variables. The highest correlations were $-.36$ ($p < .05$), $-.31$ ($p < .10$), and $-.26$ ($p < .10$) between the discrepancy index and variables 5, 6, and 7, respectively (individual social support, couple social support, and social independence).

The picture that emerges from the analyses is that homosexual male couples who describe their relationship as highly successful in conventional heterosexual terms on a true-false inventory also do so

TABLE 3

Correlations among Gay Relationship Questionnaire Variables

Variable	1	2	3	4	5	6	7	8	12	13	14	15	16	17
1. Background similarity	--	00	-14	-04	05	15	-22	-00	25[a]	08	21	-06	02	19
2. Length of prior acquaintance		--	26[a]	-30[a]	-22	-23	-07	23	-20	10	48[d]	17	30[a]	32
3. Length of love relationship			--	-15	-06	15	12	-18	-60[e]	-10	01	-12	-20	-17
4. Symbols of the relationship				--	07	01	-23	02	05	54[d]	-01	-10	06	09
5. Individual social support					--	76[e]	33[b]	47[d]	31[a]	04	-09	28	15	-27[a]
6. Couple social support						--	26[a]	36[b]	26[a]	-16	-03	09	05	-24
7. Social independence							--	-08	-03	-02	05	54[d]	30[a]	-18
8. Acceptance of homosexuality								--	36[b]	-01	17	-15	16	01
12. Affection									--	03	08	-11	16	-08
13. Appreciation										--	13	14	47[d]	46[c]
14. Lack of conflict											--	06	45[c]	57[e]
15. Communication												--	62[e]	09
16. Stability factors													--	55[a]
17. CRI score														--

Note. n = 28. Decimals are omitted from the table. [a]$p < .10$. [b]$p < .05$. [c]$p < .01$. [d]$p < .005$. [e]$p < .001$.

on an open-ended instrument. Relative to male couples who describe their relationship as moderately successful, highly successful couples report greater appreciation of the partner and the couple as a unit, less conflict, and more feelings that could contribute to stability, such as positive feelings about love relationships and future plans as a couple. Factors that we thought might be particularly relevant to gay couples – social support or lack or support, independence or dependence, and acceptance or rejection of homosexual identity – did not show strong relationships with success.

However, the present study cannot be seen as a definitive description of aspects of success in gay couples. For one thing, the criterion measure, the Couples Relationship Inventory, is not fully validated as a measure of success. The present study provides some concurrent validation, but we cannot be sure that we have assessed all of the variables that might be associated with success and unique to gay relationships. We had hoped the study would yield predictive validity information. However, the most we can report is that of the 21 couples we were able to contact again 3 to 12 months after completion of the questionnaire, all described their relationships as unchanged or even improved. This may suggest some predictive validation for the measures of the study, since the sample members had all originally described their relationships in positive terms. It also points up, however, the narrow range of couple success in the sample, which further attenuates our conclusions.

The main value of the study is the foundation it provides for further work. It suggests that it is reasonable to describe the successfulness of gay relationships in ways that are similar to those used to describe straight relationships. Future studies might seek out couples who entered into relationships with the same hopes as those in our sample, but who now range from poorly to well satisfied. If the satisfaction measure proves concurrently and predictively valid, further studies in the example of marital research might be conducted to see what behavioral qualities of interpersonal interaction are associated with different levels of satisfaction. Such work would provide a clear focus for gay counseling efforts.

In summary, the present study represents an early attempt at measuring satisfaction in homosexual male couples. The Couples Relationship Inventory, a slight modification of the Marital Relationship Inventory, was used to divide gay couples into adequately and well-satisfied groups. These two groups were most importantly differentiated by responses to concurrent, open-ended questions regarding appreciation of the partner and the couple as a unit, amount of conflict, and feelings indicative of desire for stability in the relationship. Further validation of the satisfaction measure and research into the interaction styles associated with levels of satisfaction are recommended as subsequent steps in efforts to aid gay relationships.

REFERENCE NOTE

1. Stevens, D. *Alternatives to the family*. Paper presented at the meeting of the Southwestern Sociological Association, Texas, April 1976.

REFERENCES

Burgess, E., & Locke, H. *The Family*. New York: American Book Co., 1968.

Cory, D. W. *The homosexual in America*. New York: Greenberg, 1951.

Dank, B. M. The homosexual. In D. Spiegel & P. Keith-Spiegel (Eds.), *Outsiders U.S.A.: Original essays on 24 outgroups in American society*. New York: Rinehart, 1973.

Hoffman, M. *The gay world: Male homosexuality and the social creation of evil*. New York: Basic Books, 1968.

Saghir, M. T., & Robins, E. *Male and female homosexuality*. Baltimore: Williams & Wilkins, 1973.

Sonnenschein, D. The ethnography of male homosexual relationships. *Journal of Sex Research*, 1968, *4*, 69-83.

Weinberg, G. *Society and the healthy homosexual*. Garden City, N.Y.: Doubleday, 1972.

Williams, C., & Weinberg, M. *Male homosexuals: Their problems and adaptations*. New York: Oxford, 1974.

Psychotherapy for Gay Male Couples

David P. McWhirter, MD
Andrew M. Mattison, MSW, PhD
University of California, San Diego, CA

THE ASSESSMENT

Most therapists agree that the accurate assessment or diagnosis of the problem is critical to the process of treatment. As we began working with gay male couples, the paradigms used for assessment were all based on opposite-sex partnerships. The inaccuracies introduced into our diagnoses by the use of values and assumptions found among heterosexual couples accounted for many early failures. Just two examples of differences from heterosexual couples are: (1) Among many gay men the expectation of sexual exclusivity diminishes rapidly after the first year; and (2) many maintain strict separation of money and possessions during the early years of their relationship. Couples and therapists can even share old myths, such as that all male relationships are short-term or that gay men assume butch/fem roles within their partnerships. (The evaluation of the anti-homosexual attitudes, discussed later in this paper, is also essential to a full clinical assessment.)

Assessment can be accomplished by a team composed of two males, by a female and male therapist, or by a single therapist of either sex. Experience with all these combinations inclines us toward a single therapist, since studies in our clinic show the outcomes are about the same and a single therapist costs less. The assessment usually requires several sessions: an initial session with the couple together, followed by individual sessions for collecting background and developmental histories. During the assessment we look for answers to four questions: (1) the nature of the presenting problems as perceived by both partners; (2) the quality and the stage of the couple's relationship; (3) a diagnosis of the personality of each individual, i.e., how each characteristically deals with anxiety, fear, anger, etc.; (4) an evaluation of any extenuating circumstances, e.g., medical or health issues, differences in ages, or other factors outside the couple itself. The following example illustrates the use of these assessment guidelines.

Jim is a 37-year old business executive and Tom is a 36-year old accountant. They have been together just over 8 years. Jim is more assertive and outgoing. He belongs to business organizations and is active in public affairs, while Tom is more retiring, content to focus all his energy on the relationship and their home. In the 6 months prior to seeking therapy, Tom has been almost completely withdrawn from Jim, talking only when spoken to, staying home, having trouble sleeping, etc. Jim has two children (boys aged 9 and 11) from a prior marriage; they spend two weekends each month with Jim and Tom. The couple disagrees about childrearing—Tom is lenient, Jim is firm. There has been a marked decline in their sexual contact in the past year. Tom is interested in trying to meet new friends, but Jim is afraid that Tom will find a new lover if that happens. Jim has frequent brief sexual encounters with others, which Tom knows about. Tom gets jealous but does not interfere.

1. With this couple, the nature of the problem is different for each partner. Although both come to therapy with considerable unhappiness, each has a different laundry list of complaints. Tom wants more freedom within the relationship; he feels that Jim is too dominant and overpowering. Tom also complains bitterly about the inadequacy of their sexual activity and is angry about Jim's outside contacts. Jim complains about Tom's passivity, withdrawal, and general lack of enthusiasm. Jim is also fearful of Tom's desire for greater freedom.
2. Although this couple has been together 8 years and, according to theory, should be in Stage Four, there appears to be considerable developmental discrepancy between the two men. Tom is struggling to individualize—a process common to Stage

Three—while Jim has already individualized but is not encouraging Tom to do the same. Tom's continued dependence on Jim is a problem for these men.
3. Tom is quite depressed. He uses avoidance, denial, and withdrawal as personality defenses. Jim is more assertive and demanding; he utilizes rationalization and intellectualization. He is also unaware of the degree of Tom's depression.
4. The couple has the additional pressure of Jim's children.

As this case clearly illustrates, some problems gay couples encounter can be completely separate from the stages of their relationships, and others can be stage-related.

STAGE-RELATED PROBLEMS

Each of the stages has a unique set of problems. What follows is not intended to be a complete list of such problems, but rather some examples of common stage-related difficulties.

Couples in Stage One tend to believe that the love and togetherness of blending and high limerence are the critical indicators of their relationship; they see the least rupture in this togetherness as heralding the end of the relationship. When each partner begins to feel less intense, or when there is a mutual diminution of feeling, men withdraw from each other. This is the most common cause for gay men to end their relationship before the end of the first year. An accompanying problem is the fear of intimacy generated by the intensity of the blending. This fear, which can be as difficult as the loss of feelings of limerence, may also be manifested in the individual's resistance to the process of blending.

The most common problems in Stage Two arise from differences between the partners, in contrast to the problems caused by similarities in Stage One. High passion declines and no longer shields partners from their annoyances with each other. Familiarity brings the diversity in their values and tastes to the surface and sets the stage for disagreement. The partners begin to notice each other's failures and shortcomings. This stage also sees the onset of outside sexual interests and a resulting increase in jealous possessiveness.

The problems in Stage Three are provoked by the beginning of individualization and the consequent fears of loss. Misunderstandings arise from the partners' newly felt needs to be separate, specifically their increasing need for outside sexual activity. The risk-taking involved at this stage tends to generate new anger and anxiety.

As a consequence of the activity taking place outside the relationship, Stage Four is a time of considerable distancing from each other. This distancing generates fears of loss but is also partially responsible for cementing the dyad; for despite the distancing, there is a consolidation in the couple's efforts together. "Stage discrepancy," which will be discussed below, occurs most frequently in Stage Four.

In addition to problems related to the length of time in the relationship (10 to 20 years), couples in Stage Five have the burden of concerns accompanying the process of aging. Routine and monotony can become the enemy in Stage Five. The tendency to become more fixed or rigid in personality characteristics while struggling to change each other can also plague men who have been together over 10 years.

Couples in Stage Six often continue to have the problems seen in Stage Five, but with the increase in age and the attainment of goals there is restlessness, sometimes withdrawal and feelings of aimlessness. Some, but not all, gay couples change partners at this point. Men in this stage grew up as homosexual men prior to the 1960s. Being products of a more repressive era, their beliefs and feelings may reflect anti-homosexual attitudes. Although at the present time they appear to be stage-related, these problems may not be found among gay men in the future.

STAGE DISCREPANCY

More often than not, couples do not progress through the stages simultaneously. If there is a wide difference, problems arise which we have identified as "stage discrepancies." It is very common to find couples together 7 or 8 years with one partner in an individualized, comfortable position (Stage Four) and the other still dependent and clinging (Stage Two or Three). In clinical practice, regardless of the presenting problems, we find over half the couples seen in our Institute are laboring with some degree of stage discrepancy. Couples experience considerable relief when this concept is explained to them, just as the man with chest pain is relieved when the physician tells him it is only muscle strain – and not a heart attack.

When couples understand the concept of stage discrepancy they realize that their problems are not flaws in themselves or their partnerships but correctable, developmental differences in the growth of the relationships. Although all discrepancies may not lend themselves to rapid adjustment, the understanding derived from the cognitive framework of stage discrepancy makes the affective problems easier to handle and to treat (After all, when a man with chest pain knows the exercise will not injure him, running need no longer be anxiety-provoking.)

NON-STAGE RELATED PROBLEMS

Aside from all the difficulties found when two separate personalities combine to form a primary relationship, there are problems unique to the experience of gay persons in relationships. (Some apply both to gay men and lesbians, but in this paper we are limiting the observations to gay men.)

Anti-Homosexual Attitudes

The pervasiveness of anti-homosexual attitudes touches every person but affects gay people profoundly. These attitudes include: (1) ignorance, (2) prejudice, (3) oppression, and (4) homophobia. All together, or in some combination, are overtly or covertly present in every gay male couple we have ever seen. Many men have been able to understand and minimize their influence, but most have not completely recognized the depth of their own homophobia or the degree of their own self-oppression. A careful assessment and differentiation among the four attitudes is important as the couple's therapy begins.

Of these four anti-homosexual attitudes, homophobia is the most insidious and difficult to identify and treat. A diagnosis of homophobia is confirmed by ruling out the other anti-homosexual attitudes. Ignorance is changed by knowledge. We use extensive reading of books and articles, the viewing of video tapes, attendance at lectures, and other sources of accurate information to dispel the partners' lack of knowledge. It requires more than knowledge to change prejudice: There must be some accompanying impactful positive emotional experience, such as can occur with a group. Oppression, especially self-oppression, may take the form of unwitting assumptions about the negative attitudes of others toward homosexual persons. Homophobia is recognized by its persistence in the face of knowledge and the reduction of prejudice. The continued presence of low self-esteem and lack of self-acceptance, resistance to coming out, and the continued rejection of some aspects of homosexuality are evidence of homophobia's virulence. The clinician must be alert and evaluate the extensive hidden manifestations of these anti-homosexual attitudes.

Levels of Openness

Another issue peculiar to gay relationships is the degree to which couples are open about their sexual orientation. This openness has been called being "out of the closet." The degree to which individuals and couples are out to friends (gay and non-gay), family, employers, colleagues, etc., can be a focus for problems. It is very important to consider the coming-out process when evaluating gay couples.

Role Models

Gay couples lack role models for their relationships. Since each partner is the product of a heterosexual relationship, gay couples tend to share the expectations and rule of opposite-sex couples. As mentioned above, examples of heterosexual expectations include equating fidelity with sexual exclusivity; expecting one partner to assume the "feminine" and the other the "masculine" role; and one partner anticipating being taken care of by the other, much as the wife expects to be taken care of by the husband. Men who build their relationships on rules or expectations like these often find themselves in distress.

Even among gay couples who do not follow the heterosexual models, there is some vague uneasiness about how they function as a couple, as well as curiosity as to how other gay couples deal with their everyday lives, finances, outside relationships, family, sex, etc.

Communications

For most heterosexual couples seeking therapy, lack of communication is a major problem. Although gay men do encounter communication difficulties, especially at later stages in their relationship, in fact gay men have a tendency to over-communicate with each other. At times they process their feelings and behaviors "to the death," causing relationship fatigue and distress.

Other Causes

Socio-economics, family backgrounds, levels of education, religions, differences in values, previous relationships, illness, financial setbacks, individual emotional problems, sexual dysfunctions, and jealousy are examples of other sources of conflict between gay men that are not related to stages. These issues are also unrelated to sexual orientation.

Regardless of the causes, couples seeking therapy manifest their distress in a limited number of ways, including anger and hostility, withdrawal and depression, increased anxiety, fear, or some other form of unhappiness. Identification of the problem and its probable causes, achieved through adequate assessment, is the key to the choice of therapy and its ultimate effectiveness in improving the quality of life for those seeking assistance.

CHOICE OF THERAPY

In addition to evaluating the problem and its roots, the therapist should ask the couple about their needs and expectations. The therapeutic approach must be tailored to the individual couple. (1) For those with stage-related problems, a short-term counseling approach that may include explanations, reading, and a few group sessions with other couples in similar circumstances, can send them on their way with renewed confidence. (2) If the assessment exposes depression, anxiety, or fear in one partner or the other, a move toward individual, dynamically oriented therapy is indicated and recommended. In instances where individual therapy is recommended for one partner only, we continue to see the couple together at intervals, to include the other partner in the treatment process. (3) Some couples have stage discrepancies based on personality characteristics of a partner. These couples require a marital-therapy approach with emphasis on their interactional dynamics. Marital therapy is also useful for couples with conflicts unrelated to sexual orientation or the stages of their relationship: for example, jealousy or differences in values and expectations. Gay male couples share with their heterosexual counterparts the flotsam and jetsam of everyday problems. (4) For couples with sexual dysfunctions, the choice of sex therapy may be specific or adjunctive to marital therapy, depending upon the results of assessment (McWhirter & Mattison, 1978; 1980). (5) Crisis intervention for couples in acute distress requires more rapid assessment with very directive short-term (two or three sessions) treatment focused on the specific causes of the crisis. (6) Group therapy for couples can be particularly effective when socialization, problem-solving, and sharpening of communication skills are major therapeutic goals. (7) Assessment may indicate no need for psychotherapy per se but rather a need for education and information accompanied by socialization with other gay men and women. The use of social, academic, and recreational groups and clubs for gay people is a valuable tool here.

THE THERAPIST

Writing on the psychotherapy of gay couples tends to imply that there is a specific therapy for gay men. We do not believe there is. A therapist might be trained in Gestalt, behavioral modification, psychoanalysis, bioenergetics, etc., and be very able to provide effective and useful treatment for gay couples. Regardless of the specific approach, however, there are certain attitudes and levels of knowledge the therapist must possess in order to be minimally competent on the job. We believe that therapists need to know about their own anti-homosexual attitudes, especially their own homophobia and how it affects them and their clients. Therapists must also see gay relationships as viable and desirable life-styles in general, if not necessarily for each and every couple seeking help. Therapists who believe that homosexuality represents a distinct psychopathological condition in itself are encouraged to refer gay couples to colleagues who do not share that belief.

Most gay men will be able to appraise the level of a therapist's knowledge about homosexuality and gay life-styles in a very short time. A therapist's honest admission to a lack of knowledge enhances that therapist's value to gay clients. At the very least, however, therapists do need to know the resources that are available to gay persons in the form of books, films, periodicals, organizations, etc. They need to know that there are differences between gay and heterosexual couples and ought to be open-minded enough to recognize the effects of these differences.

CONCLUSION

Since so little has been written on the subject of therapy with gay male couples, we must continue to rely on those in therapy to teach us more about themselves and their relationships. It appears that gay male couples have learned lessons about coupling that may be useful to heterosexual couples in untraditional relationships. In particular, the concept of developmental stages has extensive therapeutic ramifications. Although couples therapy with gay men is just now moving toward full-fledged legitimacy in the therapeutic community, it has much to contribute to the body of knowledge.

NOTE

1. In *Love and Limerence* (1979), Dorothy Tennov introduces the word "limerence" to describe the state of falling in love or being romantically in love. Tennov describes the basic components of limerence, which include: (1) intrusive

thinking about the desired person (who is the limerent object); (2) acute longing for reciprocation of feelings and thoughts; (3) buoyancy (a feeling of walking on air) when reciprocation seems evident; (4) a general intensity of feelings that leaves other concerns in the background; and (5) emphasizing the other's positive attributes and avoiding the negative (or rendering them, at least emotionally, into positive attributes). Tennov includes sexual attraction as an essential component of limerence, but admits exceptions. Sexual attraction alone, however, is not enough to denote true limerence.

REFERENCES

Coleman, E. Developmental stages of the coming out process. *Journal of Homosexuality*, 1981/1982, 7(2/3).
Malyon, A. K. Psychotherapeutic implications of internalized homophobia in gay men. *Journal of Homosexuality*, 1981/1982, 7(2/3).
McWhirter, D. P., & Mattison, A. M. The treatment of sexual dysfunction in gay male couples. *Journal of Sex and Marital Therapy*, 1978, *4*, 213-218.
McWhirter, D. P., & Mattison, A. M. Treatment of sexual dysfunction in homosexual male couples. In S. R. Leiblum & L. A. Pervin (Eds.), *Principles and practices of sex therapy*. New York: The Guildford Press, 1980.
Spock, B. *Baby and child care*. New York: Simon and Schuster, 1945.
Tennov, D. *Love and limerence*. New York: Stein and Day, 1979.

A Study of Perceptions of Rights and Needs in Interpersonal Conflicts in Homosexual Relationships

John P. De Cecco, PhD
Michael G. Shively, MA

The purpose of this pilot study was to examine the interpersonal conflicts of homosexual men with other men, and of homosexual women with other women. It was part of a larger study, conducted in 1974, to determine how the patterns of rights and needs of individuals differed for interpersonal and institutional conflicts. The institutional component of this pilot study was funded in 1975.

In this pilot study, *conflicts* were defined as specific incidents that occurred between particular parties, at particular times and places, that aroused anger which moved one or both parties to action.

RESEARCH QUESTIONS

Five research questions were posed. Three of these were based on earlier conflict research (De Cecco & Richards, 1974). They rested on two assumptions: (a) that constructive conflict resolutions are essential to the development of relationships, and (b) that conflicts can clarify individual goals, values, and rights (Coser, 1956; Deutsch, 1973).

These three questions were also based on a theory of civil liberties that distinguished four democratic rights: participation in decision making, equality, dissent, and due process (De Cecco & Richards, 1974). *Participation in decision making* is the right of each party to make and implement decisions and rules that govern the relationship. *Equality* is the right of each party to the same opportunities in the relationship. *Dissent* is the right to disagree, criticize, and protest. *Due process* is the right to hear and answer charges of wrongdoing before punishment is considered or imposed.

The first research question asked (a) which democratic rights homosexual men and women most frequently perceived as issues in their conflicts and (b) how their perceptions compared with those of trained coders.

The second question asked to what extent conflict was resolved by constructive resolutions. Constructive resolutions were conceived as negotiations in which both parties to the conflict fully participated. Negotiation is a way to protect democratic rights of each party to the conflict. A three-step model of negotiation based on previous research (De Cecco & Richards, 1974) was used: (a) a statement of issues by both sides made with direct verbal expression of anger; (b) agreement by both sides on a common statement of issues; and (c) bargaining by both sides, with each side gaining and making concessions.

The third research question asked to what extent parties to conflicts were able to decenter—specifically, to see issues from both sides (Piaget, 1969). Decentering is the cognitive ability of each party to see the conflict from the other's as well as his own point of view. It is an important ability for negotiation.

The last two questions were based on clinical data on conflicts in homosexual relationships (Bieber, Dain, Dince, Drellich, Grand, Gundlach, Kremer, Rifkin, Wilbur, & Bieber, 1962; Ovesey, 1963).

The fourth research question asked (a) which psychological needs were perceived most frequently as issues by the respondents in their conflicts and (b) how their perceptions compared with those of trained coders.

Three needs were identified as psychological issues in the conflicts. These needs were power, dependency, and competition. They were defined as follows: *Power* is the need of one person to control the decisions and actions of another person. *Dependency* is the need of one person to submit to the decisions and actions of another person. *Competition* is the need of one person to attract more attention or gain more favor than another person.

Sexuality was included as a fourth psychological need. The purpose of this inclusion was to clarify the extent to which sexual needs were issues in conflicts between homosexuals. *Sexuality* was defined as the need of one person to make sexual contact with another person.

The fifth research question asked (a) whether homosexual men and women viewed the consideration of democratic rights or psychological needs as more important in resolving conflicts and (b) how their perceptions compared with those of trained coders.

Human beings have needs as well as rights. Each need represents a potential source of conflict with each right. Sometimes parties to conflicts are more conscious of their rights; other times they are more conscious of their needs.

METHODOLOGY

Sample

The sample consisted of 125 homosexual men and women (72.8% men and 27.2% women). About 90% of the subjects were from the San Francisco Bay Area. The remainder were from New York City, Detroit, Los Angeles, and Saint Louis. Subjects ranged in age from 18 to 55, with the mean age falling between 26 and 30. The majority of subjects had at least some college education, and most were white-collar workers, college students, or professionals.

The vast majority of subjects (82%) called themselves homosexual, and the remainder called themselves bisexual. Of the men, 19.7% were bisexual; of the women, 11.7% were bisexual. The majority of the subjects spent most of their leisure time with other homosexuals and most of their work time with heterosexuals.

We interviewed subjects as they were available through friendship networks and public meeting places of homosexuals. It is not possible to obtain random samples of the homosexual population, since most homosexual men and women are not publicly identified or identifiable (Bell, 1973). For the population of homosexual men and women in the San Francisco Bay Area, this sample was probably biased in the following ways: (a) subjects probably had higher than average amounts of education; (b) they were largely from the middle and upper middle classes; (c) they tended to be more open about their homosexuality to friends and family than most homosexuals; and (d) they were more willing than most homosexuals to talk about intimate experiences.

Interviewers

The interviewers were volunteers. They were three trained psychologists, three students majoring in psychology, and one student majoring in political science. Five interviewers were men, and two were women. The interviewers and respondents were the same biological sex.

Interviewers participated in the construction and pilot testing of the interview form. They also coded the data for summary and analysis.

Interview Form

To obtain the necessary data a modified interview-questionnaire form developed in previous research was used (De Cecco & Richards, 1974; Richards & De Cecco, 1975). The form had three sections. The first section asked for demographic information. In the second section respondents described conflict incidents in which at least one of the parties involved was homosexual. They were asked (a) when and where the conflict happened, (b) who was involved, (c) what actually occurred, (d) how the conflict was handled, and (e) what alternative ways for handling it they could think of. In the third section the respondents were asked to assign ranks to the specific needs and rights.

Interviewers recorded verbatim descriptions of conflict incidents. The following is an example of a conflict description:

> The incident happened several years ago at a rock concert. It involved my lover and I. (We are no longer lovers.) He was a disc jockey at a radio station which played rock music so he

> often had tickets to attend most live productions. On this particular evening there were many young "kids" around, screaming, etc., while the show was going on. I said to my lover in the middle of the show that this (the unruly audience) is the reason I don't like rock concerts. Most of the people act like wild animals. That's one of the reasons I like live classical concerts. The audience knows how to treat the performer and each other with some human respect. I had expressed this attitude before. It often made him angry, although he never argued with me about it but instead just ignored me. This time, though, in a very angry tone of voice he said, "I am going backstage." He stormed off without saying how long he would be or where I should meet him. We had this same conflict over and over. It was never resolved. We eventually broke up and haven't seen each other since. I'm sure that this difference in musical taste and related problems played a large part in our breaking up.

Once the conflict was recorded, respondents were given a list of psychological needs with the definition for each need. Using this list, respondents were asked to do the following: (a) assign ranks of 1 and 2 to the needs of the first party that were most central to the conflict; (b) assign ranks in a similar fashion to the needs of the second party; and (c) give reasons for assigning a particular need a rank of 1.

After ranking the needs, respondents were given a list of democratic rights with the definition for each right. Using this list, respondents were asked to do the following: (a) assign ranks of 1 and 2 to the rights of either party they believed were violated in the conflict, and (b) give reasons for assigning a particular right a rank of 1.

Finally, they were asked to choose which set of issues they believed parties should spend most of their time discussing in working for a practical conflict resolution. They could choose (a) psychological needs, (b) democratic rights, (c) both, or (d) not sure. They were then asked to give a reason for their choice.

Coding of Data

The first research question dealt with the extent to which respondents perceived democratic rights and which rights they most frequently perceived as conflict issues. To answer this question, coders ranked the four democratic rights as they perceived them applying to each conflict. The coders' rankings were considered to be the expert judgments. We then compared coder and respondent rankings of democratic rights.

The second question dealt with the use of negotiation to resolve conflicts. Using the negotiation model, the conflicts were coded "yes" or "no" for each step. Negotiation could consist of one, two, or three steps of the model.

The third question dealt with decentering. The respondent was considered to decenter if her or his rankings for the opposing party's needs agreed with the rankings of the coders.

The fourth question dealt with psychological needs. Coders ranked the four psychological needs as they perceived them applying to each conflict. Coders' rankings were considered to be the expert judgments. Then coder and respondent rankings of psychological needs were compared.

The fifth research question dealt with the relative importance of psychological needs as compared with democratic rights in resolving the conflict. The choices of respondents and coders were compared.

In the conflict over the rock concert described above, the respondent saw only his democratic right of dissent violated and only his lover's right of due process violated. The coders saw both parties' rights of decision making and due process as violated. As for psychological needs, the respondent saw only power as his own unsatisfied need and gave no response for the needs of his lover. The coders saw both parties' needs of power and dependency as unsatisfied. The respondent saw democratic rights as more important issues than psychological needs. The coders saw rights and needs as equally important issues.

To establish coding reliability two members of the research team read each conflict and ranked and coded the data. The reliability coefficient was .75.

RESULTS

For all the research questions there were no significant differences for gender, age, and educational level.

The first research question dealt with perceptions of respondents and coders of democratic rights involved in conflicts. Table 1 shows results for the respondents. Using the first rankings, respondents saw decision making as the right most frequently violated. Using the second ranking, respondents saw dissent as the right most frequently violated. The no-response rate increased by 10% from the first to the second ranking. The greatest difference (14%) between the first and second rankings was for equality. Using the combined ranks, decision making was seen as an issue more often (22.8%) than any other right. There appears to be little difference for each right and for the no-response category.

Table 2 compares the combined rankings of both respondents and coders. There was a highly significant difference between respondent and coder choices. The no-response category was included as one possible choice. Decision making was the democratic right most frequently (38.8%) ranked by the coders. There was a 16% difference in the frequency with which coders and respondents chose decision making. Whereas there was 22% no-response for respondents, there was only 8.4% no-response for coders. The percentage no-response for coders was all for the second rank. Whereas

TABLE 1

Respondents' Rankings of Democratic Rights

	Rank of 1		Rank of 2		Total 1 & 2	
Democratic Right	*f*	%	*f*	%	*f*	%
Decision making	31	24.8	26	20.8	57	22.8
Dissent	24	19.2	29	23.2	53	21.2
Due process	20	16.0	25	20.0	45	18.0
Equality	29	23.2	11	8.8	40	16.0
No response	21	16.8	34	27.2	55	22.0
Total	125	100.0	125	100.0	250	100.0

TABLE 2

Combined Rankings of Democratic Rights

	Respondents (1st & 2nd Ranks)		Coders (1st & 2nd Ranks)	
Democratic Right	*f*	%	*f*	%
Decision making	57	22.8	97	38.8
Dissent	53	21.2	36	14.4
Due process	45	18.0	38	15.2
Equality	40	16.0	58	23.2
No response	55	22.0	21	8.4
Total	250	100.0	250	100.0

Note. $X^2 = 32.7$, $df = 4$, $p > .001$.

dissent was chosen least frequently by coders, equality was chosen least frequently by respondents.

The second research question was concerned with the extent to which conflict was resolved by negotiation. Table 3 shows the results for each step of the model. Step 1, expressing anger and stating issues, is divided into two parts. Only about 10% of the respondents reported conflicts in which even part of Step 1 was taken. Only one respondent described parties taking all the steps of negotiation.

The third question pertained to decentering. Table 4 shows how respondents and coders perceived the psychological needs of the second parties in conflicts. Using the first rankings of respondent s and coders, there was agreement between them that power needs were the most frequent issues. The coders, however, saw power needs about 20% more frequently.

Using the second rankings of respondents and coders, there was little agreement on dependency needs. Coders saw dependency needs twice as often as did the respondents. The respondents seemed to divide between those who saw dependency needs and those who saw competition needs.

Using the combined rankings, respondents saw sexuality as an issue twice as often as did the coders.

The fourth question dealt with respondents' perceptions of the psychological needs of the parties to the conflict. Table 5 shows the respondents' perceptions of the first parties' needs. Respondents perceived power needs in 41% of the first parties. Competition needs (29%) and dependency needs (30%) were their most frequent second choices. Sexuality was perceived as a psychological issue in only 6% of the conflicts.

TABLE 3

Use of Negotiation to Resolve Conflict

Negotiation Model	Negotiation *f*	Negotiation %	No Negotiation %
Step 1--Verbally expressing anger	13	10.4	89.6
Stating issues	5	4.0	96.0
Step 2--Agreeing on issues	2	1.6	98.4
Step 3--Bargaining	1	0.8	99.2

TABLE 4

Respondents' and Coders' Rankings for the Second Parties' Psychological Needs

Psychological Need	Respondents 1st Rank *f*	%	2nd Rank *f*	%	Total *f*	%	Coders 1st Rank *f*	%	2nd Rank *f*	%	Total *f*	%
Competition	16	12.8	44	35.2	60	24.0	12	9.6	30	24.0	42	16.8
Dependency	28	22.4	30	24.0	58	23.2	18	14.4	70	56.0	88	35.2
Power	66	52.8	23	18.4	89	35.6	89	71.2	18	14.4	107·	42.8
Sexuality	13	10.4	15	12.0	28	11.2	6	4.8	6	4.8	12	4.8
No response	2	1.6	13	10.4	15	6.0	0	0.0	1	0.8	1	0.4
Total	125	100.0	125	100.0	250	100.0	125	100.0	125	100.0	250	100.0

TABLE 5

Respondents' Perceptions of First Parties' Psychological Needs

Psychological Need	Rank of 1		Rank of 2		Total 1 & 2	
	f	%	*f*	%	*f*	%
Competition	19	15.2	36	28.8	55	22.0
Dependency	34	27.2	37	29.6	71	28.4
Power	51	40.8	23	18.4	74	29.6
Sexuality	17	13.6	18	14.4	35	14.0
No response	4	3.2	11	8.8	15	6.0
Total	125	100.0	125	100.0	250	100.0

Table 6 compares the combined rankings of respondents and coders for the needs of the first parties. There appears to be more agreement in respondent and coder perceptions of psychological needs than of democratic rights. The no-response rate was 6% for needs as compared with 22% for rights. Both respondents and coders saw power and dependency needs as the most frequently occurring issues. Coders, however, saw power and dependency as issues considerably more frequently than did respondents. Respondents saw competition and sexuality needs as issues more often than did coders.

The fifth research question pertained to perceptions of the relative importance of psychological needs and democratic rights in resolving conflicts. Table 7 shows the results. Respondents and coders saw psychological needs more than democratic rights as the major focus for resolving conflicts. Respondents and coders chose psychological needs and democratic rights with about the same frequency.

DISCUSSION

In this section we will provide possible explanations of the results for the five research questions.

The first research question dealt in part with respondents' perceptions of issues of democratic rights in their interpersonal conflicts. The reason for almost equal frequency of choice of the democratic rights may be the respondents' general lack of understanding of

TABLE 6

Combined Respondents' and Coders' Ranking of the First Parties' Psychological Needs

	Respondents (1st & 2nd Ranks)		Coders (1st & 2nd Ranks)	
Psychological Need	*f*	%	*f*	%
Competition	55	22.0	45	18.0
Dependency	71	28.4	89	35.6
Power	74	29.6	100	40.0
Sexuality	35	14.0	16	6.4
No response	15	6.0	0	0.0
Total	250	100.0	250	100.0

Note. $X^2 = 28.96$, $df = 4$, $p > .001$.

TABLE 7

Choices of Needs and Rights as Conflict Resolution Issues

	Respondents		Coders	
Issue	*f*	%	*f*	%
Psychological needs only	73	58.4	69	55.2
Democratic rights only	9	7.2	12	9.6
Both needs and rights	29	23.2	42	33.6
Not sure	6	4.8	1	0.8
No response	8	6.4	1	0.8
Total	125	100.0	125	100.0

Note. $X^2 = 7.4$, $df = 3$, p .10. The no-response frequencies were not included in obtaining this chi-square value.

these rights. This interpretation is supported by the high number of respondents who made no choices at all. Interviewers noted that respondents were often reluctant to apply these concepts to their conflicts.

The first question also dealt with respondent and coder agreement on issues of democratic rights. The lack of agreement between respondents and coders supports the interpretation that respondents were not clear about which rights were violated in their interpersonal conflicts. We know that coders had less difficulty than respondents did in recognizing the rights involved in conflicts. Since coders understood the rights, it appears that rights can be applied to interpersonal conflict.

We had expected more issues of equality because of the gay liberation movement. It may be that equality is seen by respondents as an issue in institutional conflict but not in interpersonal conflict.

The second question dealt with the use of negotiation. Why was there almost no negotiation of conflict? One reason may be that parties were more conscious of their own needs than of the other parties' rights. Since the protection of rights and the fulfillment of needs are a potential source of conflict, constructive resolutions must address both rights and needs. Negotiation is a way to meet needs and protect rights. Since parties were not directly confronting each other over specific issues (Step 1 of the model), they were unable to agree to issues (Step 2), and they were unable to make concessions (Step 3). Most parties appeared to avoid direct confrontation. By avoiding negotiation, conflicts developed into serious breaks in relationships.

The third question dealt with decentering. Respondents appear to perceive power needs more often than other needs of the second parties. We know that they saw their own power needs more frequently than their other needs. This self-perception may account for their seeing the second parties' power needs.

Since they did not as readily see their own dependency needs, they may have had difficulty seeing the dependency needs of the second parties. That they somewhat more readily saw competition than dependency needs may be explained by viewing competition as an extension of power.

That dependency is part of a power-dependency interaction is supported by the finding that the coders saw both of these needs occurring more frequently than the others.

The fourth research question dealt in part with respondents' perceptions of the first parties' psychological needs as conflict issues. Why was power the need most frequently perceived? This finding is more striking if we consider competition an extension of power. The combined frequencies for power and competition made up over 50% of the first parties' rankings. Since power and competition are associated with masculinity, and since masculinity is culturally more highly valued than femininity (Broverman, Clarkson, Rosenkrants, & Vogal, 1970), parties may be able to accept power needs more readily than dependency needs. Since dependency is culturally associated with femininity, homosexual men and women may defend themselves against femininity by refusing to see dependency needs.

The fourth research question also dealt with respondent and coder agreement on psychological needs. The coder rankings support the interpretation that respondents were not seeing dependency needs. Sexuality, using both respondent and coder rankings, is apparently less of an issue in homosexual relationships than has been commonly believed (Bell, 1973). Sexuality may not be an overriding need in all homosexual relationships.

The last question dealt with the perception of the relative importance of psychological needs and democratic rights as conflict issues to be resolved. Why were needs seen as issues more often than right? Why, for example, were respondents able to see power needs as an issue but less frequently see the right to participate in decision making as an issue? If parties are unaware of the political aspects of their relationships, as we concluded above, they may concentrate exclusively on the psychological aspects of their conflicts. The fact that coders also saw more psychological needs as issues than democratic rights may be the result of respondent tendency to address only psychological issues.

Respondents, however, appear to be concentrating on their power needs and refusing to see their dependency needs. Not seeing their dependency needs may be related to not being aware of democratic rights. Parties to conflicts would possibly see democratic rights more clearly if they saw both power and dependency in both parties. When individuals can accept *both* power and dependency needs, they may better understand the need to use negotiation. Negotiation, as we have stated, is the way to satisfy both parties' needs and protect both parties' rights.

CONCLUSION

Using a newly developed interview method that allowed respondents the opportunity to analyze conflict incidents they recalled and described, an exploratory study of conflicts of same-sex couples was conducted. A partial analysis of data has been described. Future analyses will show the differences in perceptions of female as compared with male couples and the extent to which homosexual couples adhere to or depart from social sex-role stereotypes in the resolution of conflicts.

REFERENCES

Bell, A. Homosexualities: Their range and character. In *Nebraska Symposium on Motivation*. Lincoln: University of Nebraska Press, 1973, *21*, 1-26.

Bieber, I., Dain, H., Dince, P., Drellich, M., Grand, H., Gundlach, R., Kremer, M., Rifkin, A., Wilbur, C., & Bieber, T. *Homosexuality: A psychoanalytic study of male homosexuals*. New York: Basic Books, 1962.

Broverman, D., Clarkson, F., Rosenkrants, P. S., & Vogal, S. R. Sex role stereotypes and clinical judgments of mental health. *Journal of Clinical and Consulting Psychology*, 1970, *34*, 1-7.

Coser, L. *The functions of social conflict*. Chicago: Free Press, 1956.

De Cecco, J. P., & Figliulo, M. C. Methodology for studying discrimination based on sexual orientation and social sex-role stereotypes. *Journal of Homosexuality*, 1978, *3*(3), 235-241.

De Cecco, J., & Richards, A. *Growing pains: Uses of school conflict*. New York: Aberdeen Press, 1974.

Deutsch, M. *Resolution of conflict*. New Haven: Yale University Press, 1973.

Figliulo, M. C., Shively, M. G., & McEnroe, F. The relationship of departures in social sex-role to the abridgment of civil liberties. *Journal of Homosexuality*, 1978, *3*(3), 249-255.

Liljestrand, P., Petersen, R. P., & Zellers, R. The relationship of assumption and knowledge of the homosexual orientation to the abridgment of civil liberties. *Journal of Homosexuality*, 1978, *3*(3), 243-247.

Ovesey, L. The homosexual conflict: An adaptational analysis. In H. Ruitenbeek (Ed.), *The problem of homosexuality in modern society*. New York: Dutton Press, 1963.

Piaget, J. *Science of education and psychology of the child*. New York: Viking Press, 1969.

Richards, A., & De Cecco, J. A study of student perceptions of civic education. *Journal of Social Issues*, Fall 1975, *31*(2), 111-122.

Shively, M. G., Rudolph, J. R., & De Cecco, J. P. The identification of the social sex-role stereotypes. *Journal of Homosexuality*, 1978, *3*(3), 225-233.

The Ties That Bind: Strategies for Counseling the Gay Male Co-Alcoholic

Scott Whitney
San Francisco, CA

Little enough specialized clinical work is being done with gay male alcoholics and still less is known about working with their alcoholic lovers. The field of alcoholism treatment has seen an assimilation in the last 10 years of the ideas developed by family therapy practitioners and the folk wisdom of Alcoholics Anonymous which, through its support of Al-Anon family groups, has emphasized the needs of those in relationships with the alcoholic. But what, precisely, constitutes the "family group" for the gay male alcoholic, and what unique aspects of gay relationships should treatment personnel be aware of when attempting to facilitate recovery from alcoholism?

DEFINING CO-ALCOHOLISM

Basically, the co-alcoholic is a person in the alcoholic's life who intervenes in such a way as to prevent the alcoholic from facing the consequences of his actions. This rescuing behavior involves the gradual assumption, sometimes over the course of years, of responsibility for finances, social life, and vocational matters. The co-alcoholic is always the person at the front door negotiating with reality while the alcoholic is allowed to continue his toxic abdication of responsibility. Once this pattern is in place, of course, it creates a deeply ingrained *folie à deux* in which the co-alcoholic begins to share such alcoholic symptoms as denial, low self-esteem, depression, social isolation, and high anxiety states.

If treatment personnel are to adopt a whole-system intervention when working with the gay male alcoholic, they must begin to look very closely at the social support system that has maintained the addiction. Implicit in the alcoholic's recovery is the fact that his social support system will be disrupted and that systems of this sort have a way of trying to restore their own equilibrium, sometimes at the expense of the alcoholic's sobriety.

In mainstream culture, the co-alcoholic role is usually maintained by a husband or wife. With gay male alcoholics, a wider range of social roles is involved which requires close scrutiny before attempting intervention. If the alcoholic is in a coupled relationship, the lover is the most likely candidate for the co-alcoholic role. When the client is single, however, any number of people in his life might be serving this function. Since adopting a whole-system approach, our agency has discovered that the co-alcoholic role can be filled by an ex-wife, clergyman, employer, roommate, sibling, mother, father, co-worker, or (not at all uncommon) a therapist. The following is a short example of a non-lover co-alcoholic relationship:

> A 37-year old gay male alcoholic presented himself for treatment. After some discussion, it was unclear to the counselor why the man had not been fired from his job because of his numerous binges and institutional detoxifications that had involved much time away from work. Further exploration revealed that the man's employer was a closeted homosexual who maintained a wife, family, and a straight social identity. Our client was important to this man as both a drinking buddy and as a contact in the gay subculture. The employer was thus willing to make any allowances needed, including monetary, to keep our client close to him. It became obvious that intervention in this self-regulating system would be necessary to facilitate our client's progress in recovery.

COMMON CO-ALCOHOLIC ISSUES

From a longitudinal point of view, we have discovered that many gay male co-alcoholics have an alcoholic parent. This means that they have learned early in life the intricacies of rescuing, denial, and guilt. For some, it seems to be necessary for their own self-esteem to have an alcoholic in their lives. Even those co-alcoholics who have not experienced alcoholism in their family backgrounds admit, after some time in treatment, that they became involved with the alcoholic at a time in their lives when they were at some transition point and felt depressed, helpless, or disoriented. In some cases a kind of bipolar oscillation has occurred in which the alcoholic, at an earlier stage of addiction, played parent to the co-alcoholic as child.

If the co-alcoholic re-establishes himself as autonomous, then the alcoholism of the other partner begins to worsen. Conversely, this pattern accounts for the frequently noted phenomenon of the alcoholic's lover exhibiting symptoms when the alcoholic begins the recovery process. This makes "family" intervention imperative if the relationship is to stabilize during recovery.

Sometimes there are hidden sexual agendas in these relationships. The co-alcoholic partner may be older or overweight or may in some way feel less attractive than the alcoholic. When this is the case, there is a great fear on the part of the co-alcoholic that if the alcoholic sobers up, he will see his partner in a new light and seek someone else. In other cases, the two partners disagree on preferred sexual activity, and it is only when the alcoholic is drunk that he permits, for instance, anal intercourse. Alcoholics in the initial stages of recovery many times experience impotence, and this can also be a source of strain on the relationship. When any of the above dynamics is present, there is a vested interest on the part of the co-alcoholic in the continuation of the alcoholics' drinking behavior. Dealing with these issues requires that the counselor be comfortable with discussing homosexuality and have the skills necessary to create a safe environment for the disclosure of crucial issues.

In our experience, the majority of gay male co-alcoholic tends to be high-achieving, workaholic, Type-A personalities who have few sources of support and who lead highly compartmentalized lives. They manifest many symptoms including insomnia, anxiety attacks, overeating, ulcers, headaches, depression, and sexual dysfunction. In terms of interpersonal relations, they tend toward a generalized shell-shock syndrome which seems to be the result of long exposure to the unpredictable and arbitrary reactions of the alcoholic partner. They have learned to adapt to an ever-changing interpersonal environment which requires them constantly to change both the process and the content of communication depending on the shifting state of mind of the alcoholic. Co-alcoholics learn to communicate in one way when the alcoholic is sober, in another when he is drunk, and in still another when he is hung-over. Some have described this as a feeling of "walking on eggs" around the alcoholic. This shell shock continues even after the alcoholic has achieved abstinence. A primary goal in treating the co-alcoholic is retraining him to give direct, consistent messages regardless of the changing moods of the alcoholic.

STRATEGIES FOR TREATMENT

The counselor must first be aware that co-alcoholics are very difficult to bring into treatment and that progress is slow and difficult to evaluate. The co-alcoholic fears three things most of all about entering treatment. The first is that he will be blamed for the alcoholic's condition. Indeed, most co-alcoholics have already blamed themselves and fear further accusations of failure. The second fear is that the goal of treatment will be to disengage them from their relationship. Many recognize that there are few logical reasons for them to have remained with the alcoholic and have even received feedback from friends regarding the futility of maintaining the relationship. The question "Why do you stay with him?" is fraught with implications of personal inadequacy on the part of the co-alcoholic. If the co-alcoholic is also a drinker or uses other drugs, he will additionally fear a third possibility: that he will be confronted with his own addictive patterns. Even if the counselor suspects addiction in the co-alcoholic, the usual guidelines of confrontation and breaking down of denial must be set aside, at least temporarily, in order to get him into treatment. When more rapport has been established, this issue can be approached in a non-threatening manner, and (as is many times the case) the co-alcoholic can be guided into treatment for his own addictions.

Sometimes the initial contact with the treatment agency is made by the co-alcoholic. When this is the case, the counselor should use the opportunity to provide as much information as possible concerning treatment for the alcoholic as well as information on co-alcoholism and Al-Anon. One phone call may be the only opportunity for intervention.

When the alcoholic is the first to be seen by the agency, we have been successful in getting the lover to attend an initial interview by telling the alcoholic that the agency requires his partner to come in for at least one appointment to share information on the disease of alcoholism and to see how he can help in the recovery process. Suggesting that there are things to learn about helping the alcoholic hooks into the co-alcoholic's ever-present need to be of assistance to his partner and facilitates the likelihood of his making an appointment. Confidentiality is a major issue, and it must be emphasized to both parties that their disclosures will be protected from outside sources and from each other.

GAY CO-ALCOHOLICS IN THERAPY GROUPS

Ideally, the initial contact is followed by several individual sessions which serve to prepare the client for entrance into a co-alcoholic group. While recovery from co-addiction is usually considered a two- to four-year process, talking in terms of such a prolonged time-frame can be discouraging. We usually approach this issue by requesting that the client try coming to a meeting (not a therapy group) once a week for a month. A commitment can usually be negotiated on this basis with the hope that, once involved, the newcomer will form ties with other group members and remain in the group much longer.

Groups should be kept small (no more than six participants), and an atmosphere that is informational, open, and nonconfrontive must be maintained. For many clients, this is their first chance to socialize with other gay men, and in this way the group becomes a first step out of the social isolation so common among gay co-alcoholics.

A natural tendency, at least initially, is for members of such groups to spend a great deal of time blaming their partners. This tendency can be gently extinguished by the facilitator's focusing on the issues group members must face for themselves. Clients should be encouraged to exchange phone numbers and to socialize outside the group. This gives them the chance to develop social skills that will enhance self-esteem and facilitate the likelihood of their developing support for themselves outside of their toxic relationships.

Because of the kinds of symptoms manifested by co-alcoholics, we have found that educating them on concepts of stress and stress management seems to be very beneficial for symptom amelioration. Additionally, doing relaxation, meditation, and fantasy exercises with the group creates an atmosphere in which they can relax enough to begin to play. For most of them, the element of play has been absent from their lives for years.

At the beginning of treatment, many co-alcoholic clients are pessimistic about relationships in general and about gay life in particular. As involvement in the group continues, many find themselves achieving a positive gay identity, perhaps for the first time.

Because they live in what is still considered by society a deviant subculture, it has become easy for co-alcoholics to adopt the role of victim. Their involvement with a practicing alcoholic has reinforced this role and encouraged the idea that they must protect their weaker partner. Before entering treatment, they feel themselves not only separated from mainstream society but also cut off from the potential support of their subculture. Gay friends outside the relationship have been discarded because of embarrassment and shame over the alcoholic's behavior. Working in a small group format is a powerful means of overcoming the victim identity and reconnecting clients to the genuine potential for support which exists within the gay community.

CONCLUSION

Treatment personnel must look closely at the social system supporting the addictions of their gay male clients. It is important that those who serve in a co-alcoholic role within that system be contacted and, if possible, brought into treatment.

Working in small group formats that emphasize alcohol education, stress management, communication skills, and increased socialization within the gay community has proved effective in an outpatient setting. Clients should be encouraged to involve themselves in Al-Anon both as a means of deepening their knowledge of coaddiction and as a means of strengthening their own support system.

Index